ACTION RESEARCH

Dialogues on Work and Innovation

The book series *Dialogues on Work and Innovation* presents empirically based studies as well as theoretical discussions on the practice of organizational renewal.
Its publications reflect the increasingly urgent need for the development of new forms of work organization. In today's interdependent world, workplace reform and organizational effectiveness are no longer solely the concern of individual organizations; the local and the global have become closely interconnected.
Dialogues on Work and Innovation mirrors the fact that enterprise development and societal development cannot be kept separate. Furthermore, the Series focuses on the dialogue between theory and practice, and thus on the mutuality of knowledge and action, of research and development. The *Dialogues* stress the critical significance of joint reflexivity in action-oriented research and the necessity for participatory processes in organizational change.

Editors

Hans van Beinum, *Halmstad University* (Editor-in-Chief)
Richard Ennals, *Kingston University*
Werner Fricke, *Friedrich Ebert Stiftung, Bonn*
Øyvind Pålshaugen, *Work Research Institute, Oslo*

Editorial Board

Volume 8

Davydd J. Greenwood (ed.)

*Action Research: From practice to writing
in an international action research development program*

Action Research

From practice to writing in an international
action research development program

Edited by

DAVYDD J. GREENWOOD

JOHN BENJAMINS PUBLISHING COMPANY
AMSTERDAM/PHILADELPHIA

The paper used in this publication meets the minimum requirements of American National Standard for Information Sciences — Permanence of Paper for Printed Library Materials, ANSI Z39.48–1984.

Library of Congress Cataloging-in-Publication Data

Action research : from practice to writing in an international action research development program / edited by Davydd J. Greenwood.
    p.   cm. -- (Dialogues on work and innovation, ISSN 1384-6671 ; v. 8)
  Includes bibliographical references.
    1. Action research. I. Greenwood. Davydd J. II. Series.
HM48.A36   1999
300'.72--DC21   98-55950
ISBN 90 272 1778 5 (Eur.) / 1 55619 832 9 (US) (Pb: alk. paper)   CIP

John Benjamins Publishing Co. · P.O.Box 75577 · 1070 AN Amsterdam · The Netherlands
John Benjamins North America · P.O.Box 27519 · Philadelphia PA 19118–0519 · USA

Contents

Preface

Davydd J. Greenwood

The Scandinavian Action Research Development Program or ACRES (Action Research in Scandinavia) was in many ways an unusual initiative. Supported by Swedish and Norwegian agencies bilaterally, it involved action researchers from Norway, Sweden, Finland, Holland, Great Britain, and the United States. The aim was to enhance the research practices of experienced action researchers by emphasizing writing as a key to enhancing research quality. The program engaged action researchers in a variety of learning partnerships and networks, some of which are still continuing.

ACRES was also characterized by internal tensions and conflicts, both intellectual and organizational, that made the process somewhat taxing for all the participants, including the staff. These tensions are the very stuff of which the field of action research is made.

How, then, to be true to such a multifaceted process? As the editor of the resulting manuscript, I have not found this easy and I want to be straightforward about the decisions that resulted in this volume. Through a process that the participants and staff set up together, the seven case chapters in part II of the book were chosen for inclusion out of a larger number of manuscripts the participants produced. For those chapters, my job has been primarily that of an editor and commentator. One of my qualifications to serve as editor of the book is simply that I am the only native speaker of English on the staff. I was also responsible for the initial design of the writing component of the program.

The six chapters making up part I, ACRES and Action Research, are a different matter. The first five were written by members of the staff and represent their views on ACRES and on action research. One staff member, Kjell S. Johannessen, did not contribute a chapter, though he was free to do so. Chapter 6 is a contribution from several participants on the effect of the writing focus on their experience in ACRES.

In working on chapters 1 through 5, I exercised a great deal of editorial freedom. Together, Hans van Beinum and Morten Levin co-administered the ACRES program for the rest of us. I have thus placed their two general essays first. Van Beinum's introductory chapter sets the stage for ACRES and contextualizes many of the concerns that led to ACRES having the form that it did. Levin's chapter briefly lays out the main varieties of action research and traces the very different intellectual and practical itineraries by which the members of the staff came into the process.

Following these introductory chapters are a chapter by Claude Faucheux and one by René van der Vlist. In both cases, I used a heavy editorial hand. I substantially revised and shortened Faucheux's essay by trying to focus sharply on the way it provides a creative and thoughtful narration on the development of action research in philosophy and throughout the history of science. I believe this essay will be extremely valuable to many readers because it provides the kind of historical/analytical background that is so often missing in writing about action research.

Van der Vlist's contribution, a very long essay on ACRES as a social process, presented an entirely different kind of challenge. I heavily edited the English but left its length intact. This is one of the most unusual essays I have ever encountered. It painstakingly and without compassion for anyone, including himself, characterizes the aims and failings of the staff in trying to make the ACRES process work. We had many difficult moments together and were often divided on issues of theory, method, and personal style.

Such struggles are usually hidden from view in the final product of the sort that a book represents, but I have elected not to do that. In my view, and in my experience teaching action research, our entirely too sanitized accounts of action research processes make those new to the field feel completely incompetent. When they experience uncertainty, conflict, and even become enraged with the process of trying to work through action research, they often come to feel that they are uniquely at fault, uniquely unqualified to conduct such activities. While I am in no way promoting conflict for its own sake, when a diverse group of practitioners with different experiences, theories, and personal styles form a team, some conflict is inevitable. That we suffered from conflict is not surprising, that we survived it together is important, and that the resulting book is now complete is a rewarding outcome. Conflict and action research are not at opposite ends of some polarity. When we work hard on issues of fundamental importance to us personally, some degree of conflict is bound to occur. Enabling the process to survive the conflict is the key.

Van der Vlist's ethnographic specificity and almost brutal honesty about what we did and did not do is therefore a unique document in the history of action research. Publishing it in this form embodies my conviction that such perspectives should form part of reporting on action research if we want our successors to learn from more of the relevant dimensions of our experience.

This does not mean, however, that all the staff agree about van der Vlist's views, for they do not. Inevitably each of us sees the issues somewhat differently.

The chapter on writing is the only one of its kind I am aware of. ACRES broke new ground in making writing a centerpiece of action research training.

The notion of reflective practice through writing is widely accepted but rarely practiced. Here the staff was united in affirming the significance of the writing element. Much more needs to be said about writing in action research, but at least this is a start. It is followed by reports from the participants for whom the writing was an assigned dimension of their tasks. In writing their responses, they had the draft version of my own chapter on writing to work from and to use as a point of orientation. They also provided much useful feedback to me about my own chapter.

Thus, from beginning to end, ACRES has been an unusual project. Multinational, multiperspectival, writing centered, and case study focused, it provides a rare sense of the state of action research practice in Europe at the present time and a feeling for the voices of the younger generation of practitioners who are emerging on the action research scene.

I am grateful to my colleagues on the staff for their support of the writing enterprise, including their support of my editorial efforts in this final phase of the project. Katherine Gottschalk of the Writing Program at Cornell University was most generous with exceptionally useful advice and sources when Davydd Greenwood was planning the teaching approach to the ACRES workshops. Even when I had brought the manuscript to this point, it was still an immense and unwieldy set of chapters. Shaping the manuscript into its present version and improving the writing throughout is the work of a superb editor, Erica Fox, whom I thank on our collective behalf for her excellent work.

PART 1

Chapter 1

On the Design of the ACRES Program

Hans van Beinum

The idea of organizing the Scandinavian-based Action Research Development Program (ACRES) originated in Sweden as a direct result of experiences in Sweden and Norway with action research focused on workplace reform. The various concepts and assumptions underlying the design of ACRES must therefore be understood in the context of the history of these developments. In this chapter, I will lay out the characteristics of workplace reform in Scandinavia and the connection of the ACRES program to these efforts, some of the epistemological and methodological underpinnings of our approach to action research, and finally the overall design of the program.

Workplace reform in Scandinavia:
The following are some of the characteristics of workplace reform in Scandinavia (Gustavsen 1985, 1992):
- It consists of programmatic approaches, that is, broad-based initiatives on the macro-level involving the various social groups in the economic system and consisting of a number of projects.
- It was and frequently still is an expression of a political agenda.
- It is conceived and carried out in a societal context.
- In addition to organizational effectiveness, a main point of reference is democracy in the workplace.
- It has political legitimacy as a result of national legislation on health and safety in the workplace that has given a prominent place to the organization of work.[1]

Historically, workplace reform in Scandinavia can be divided into roughly three phases. The first phase was marked by the emergence of the Industrial Democracy Program in the 1960s, a collaborative effort between the Tavistock Institute of Human Relations in London and the Work Research Institute in Norway. Several experiments were conducted, each in a single organization, with a focus on the development of autonomous groups in the context of a sociotechnical redesign of the organization of work. Diffusion was a major goal of the program and was seen as a process of replication (on the assumption that a "good example" will be followed). The expectation was that this process would take place by means of the active utilization of links, ties, and networks between managers, trade unionists, and others with influence over developments in the workplace (Emery and Thorsrud 1976; Gustavsen 1985; Herbst 1976). In this first phase, there was a conceptual separation between change and diffusion.

In the second phase, starting in the 1970s, the emphasis shifted from the design of the organization of production (the sociotechnical system) to direct discussion of workplace issues. In a sense, this was a "figure-ground" reversal with workplace issues coming to the fore and the sociotechnical system moving into the background. This conceptual and strategic change resulted from experience with the so-called job design workshops (Engelstad and Ödegaard 1979) organized as a joint effort between actual members of the workforce and researchers. Groups of enterprises, each with a project group composed of union representatives, members of management, and workers participated in these workshops, the idea being to present knowledge and experiences from the experiments by means of lectures and seminars and thus to influence the initiation of new projects. But the workshops generated few viable projects.

Realizing this, the organizers of the projects began to downplay the importance of transferring knowledge from the experiments and to emphasize the issues and problems the participants themselves brought with them to the sessions (Engelstad and Ödegaard 1979; Gustavsen 1996). Because of that shift in direction, the rate of successful projects increased considerably. By recognizing and mobilizing the abilities of the participants to formulate problems and issues themselves and to use each others' experiences as a major vehicle in the process of change, the ability to communicate was brought to the fore. The role of research changed dramatically from "designing production systems" to "designing discussions" (Engelstad and Odegaard 1979; Gustavsen 1996). It began to become clear that in action research, the separation of knowledge generation and knowledge application does not work.

During the third phase, which began to emerge in the 1980s, the emphasis has been on the concept of the development organization (Gustavsen 1996). The notion here is that action research is primarily a communicative process in which the emphasis is on dialogue is further elaborated, both empirically and conceptually. The focus shifts to all the actual and potential communicative conditions and apparatuses, such as conferences, workshops, project groups, workplace meetings, and many other elements, needed to enable an enterprise to change — that is, to manage the process of going through a change cycle successfully. The functions to be taken care of by the development organization include defining the goals and other parts of the frame of reference for the development process, strategically steering the process, mapping out the problems, creating action plans, and so forth. Put another way, with the recognition that communication is the core element in action research, workplace reform in Scandinavia has taken a "communicative turn" (Gustavsen 1996).

The Swedish national program "Leadership, Organization and Codetermination" (LOM) played a key role in the development of Scandinavian workplace reform and has become a Scandinavian as well as an international landmark in action research. Since some of the experiences of the LOM program relate directly to the initiative to design ACRES, a brief discussion of LOM is appropriate and necessary.

The LOM program was based on a theory of communication — that is, the idea that there is a close interactive relationship between the act of speech and an operative action — expressed operationally as "democratic dialogue." Democratic dialogue became the LOM's conceptual as well as operational point of departure (Gustavsen 1992). LOM lasted for five years (1985–1990) and tried to merge change and diffusion by defining a cluster of organizations as the unit of change. In this way, it sought to stimulate a process of inter-organizational cooperation and learning (Gustavsen 1992, 1996).

LOM can be described in terms of three interdependent but nevertheless distinct levels of significance: the conceptual level, the organizational level, and the local operational level. On the conceptual level, LOM stands out because it was the first and only program in Scandinavia to explain itself in terms of a theory of science. It is an illustration of the linguistic turn in social science and the rejection of foundationalism. LOM considered the relationship between theory and practice, between epistemic subject (researcher) and empirical object (the researched) to be a dialogical one. Language was treated not only as representative and referential but also, and even more so, as a tool; it was seen to have a formative and a "shaping" function.

In recognizing the fundamental relationship between learning, language, and action, the LOM program punctuated a shift away from the design of a theory of workplace reform to an intellectual position that focused on the process of developing the linguistic resources management and workers can use to approach their problems. LOM was able to formulate a coherent approach that could accommodate the interpenetration of knowledge and action, the jointness and mutuality that is the crux of action research.

The organizational level also had several distinct features. The first such feature was that LOM was conceived and organized in a tripartite structure with the researchers were actively involved in workplace development together with management and workers. The researcher was neither a tool to be mobilized when necessary nor placed in the role of an expert leader showing the way but was defined as an equal partner working with the other participants on the basis of joint involvement and shared responsibility. This tripartite structure was characteristic of LOM with respect to developments on both the macro and micro level.

The second significant feature of LOM was the scope of the program, which included 150 organizations and 60 researchers, as well as a permanent coordinating secretariat playing a support role. In combination with attempts to bring the clusters of participating organizations together into broader networks, the critical mass achieved in this structure provided the basis for socially significant vertical and horizontal linkages to be made.

The operational level was characterized by its emphasis on the communicative element in the theory and practice of democracy, that is, the concept of democratic dialogue, a historically given social construction that sets out the basic conditions for open and participatory communication (Gustavsen 1992, 1996). Fundamental societal values were mobilized in a local context. The notion of democratic dialogue was operationalized by means of four action parameters: (1) the clustering of enterprises, (2) the use of a certain type of start-up conference to initiate the process of change both within and between enterprises, (3) broad-based and deep-slice projects that spanned the main levels and areas of the enterprise, and (4) the building of broad networks.

On the local level, the researchers were concerned primarily with facilitating the start-up conferences and the various follow-up activities. As equal partners with management and the unions, not only did the researchers facilitate the objectives of the LOM program and the development of linguistic resources (*i.e.*, helping to create the conditions for democratic dialogue), but, by definition, they also became part of the dialogue. Thus, the researchers were confronted on a personal and experiential level with the complexities of the relationship between learning, language, and action — that is, with being a researcher in an action research setting (van Beinum 1993; Naschold *et al.* 1993; and Gustavsen 1993).

The impact of LOM on the design of ACRES:

In that the LOM program was the first really large-scale action research program in Scandinavia, it was not surprising that many of the researchers involved were uncertain about how to handle the challenges of a relationship based on joint involvement and shared responsibility and were puzzled by the interdependency of knowledge and action in the development of organizations. It became clear that there was a strong need among the researchers for intellectual as well as social and psychological support. When the formal LOM program ended in 1990 and its structural and institutional support was discontinued, the idea came up in discussion among the LOM researchers to organize a learning program on action research that would meet these needs for further, ongoing support.

It was agreed that the principles of the LOM approach and its underlying assumptions should be used as guidelines in the development of such a program; its objectives would be to provide concrete support for action researchers in general as well as tailor-made learning opportunities for individual researchers.

Originally, three distinct interlocking and mutually reinforcing modules were envisaged. The core module would consist of a group of researchers who would meet four or five times a year for two days in a workshop setting, mobilizing and using their individual and collective experiences as their learning material to establish a realistic basis for reflecting on action research and for learning with and from each other. The second module would consist of one or two workshops in which participants would focus specifically on the dynamics of the dialogue, mapping out some features of their personal experiences and the implicit theoretical assumptions used. The third and final module would consist of one or two writing workshops in which researchers would be given assistance with any difficulties they might have in organizing their experiences in a "representational" manner and in which they would learn about writing a case report based on action research.

Because of logistical difficulties, the limited availability of staff, and financial problems, a decision was made to design four comprehensive two-day workshops to be held over one year. Also, the Swedish LOM researchers wanted the program to be linked to programs in Norway and to include an even wider cross-section of international participants.

When the LOM researchers presented their ideas to their Norwegian colleagues, they were very fortunate to find an enthusiastic partner in Morten Levin of the Norwegian University of Science and Technology in Trondheim,[2] and in 1991 it became possible to announce that the Scandinavian-based International Action Research Development Program would be a joint venture between the Swedish Center for Working Life and the university in Trondheim.

Formulation of the objectives and structure of ACRES was preceded by and based on reflection on the various aspects and elements of the LOM program, as well as on a review of experiences with action research in general, on the design of two summer schools focused on organizational redesign held in Holland in the 1970s, and on the field of management education. To state the outcome simply: the assumptions underlying the design of ACRES were based on (1) views about the nature of action research and (2) about conditions for learning.

Having said this, however, it is necessary to point out that the use of words like *design, action research*, and *learning* is somewhat problematic. Words and language are not only representational and referential, but also, and foremost, they have a formative function — they are tools to be used in dealing with reality (Gustavsen 1992, 1996). Their meaning is in the action, as "words in their speaking" (Shotter 1993a). The word is a two-sided act. V. N. Volosinov expresses the idea as follows: "[The word] is determined equally by whose word it is and for whom it is meant...It is precisely the product of the reciprocal relationship between speaker and listener, addresser and addressee. Each and every word expresses the 'one' in relation to the 'other' " (1973: 86).

In trying to explain the "design" of ACRES, I am confronted with the same difficulty all action researchers face when trying to use written text to depict the living, dialogical relationship between research and development. In written rhetoric, words unavoidably are understood by the reader as being referential, that is, as representing an unequivocal and true reality, when what we are trying to describe is a process that is formative, interactive, and unfinished. Therefore, there is some truth in the statement that it is impossible to write about action research in such a way that one can do it justice and really make clear what it is all about to the reader unacquainted with the field. To the contrary, one usually succeeds in confirming the notion that action research is neither research nor scientific.

The difficulty is that when one uses such words as *design, action research*, and *learning*, one is using words that are ambiguous and seem to suffer from lack of proper definition and clarification; however, their ambiguity is precisely the reason they are so powerful and useful as tools in dialogue, in a process of joint action, in which one is making choices and is engaged in creating meaning and constructing social reality. It is this dual nature of language — the referential and the formative, and particularly the latter — that one has to keep in mind when reading about ACRES.

Although the distinction between action research and learning is basically a false one (at best, it represents different frames of reference for reflecting on the same phenomenon), it was nevertheless used for analytical purposes, to clarify our thinking about the different aspects and elements of the ACRES program.

The term *design* also could be seen as something of a misnomer. *Designing* action research — designing a process that is, by definition, unfolding and creative — may seem like an oxymoron. In reality, it is more of a tautology. The notion of design as used here must be understood and has been used in an open manner, more like the notion of minimum critical specification as introduced by Phil Herbst, as the starting conditions for a process that is self-designing. "Design," therefore, refers not to a predetermined product or a specific method but to the very process of building and making (as well as discovering). Action research is *designing*. The design of ACRES occurs in the act of carrying out the program itself.

To talk about and reflect on the design in this manner, that is, about something that still has to happen, is similar to talking about an action research project. One cannot and should not go further than trying to identify, on an ongoing basis, the starting conditions and minimum critical specifications while engaging in a continuous shift of the horizon.

What Is Action Research?

Action research, as a practical way of dealing with organizational problems by means of mobilizing and involving social science in a specific manner, started to emerge in the 1940's with the work of the Tavistock Group in the British Army and with the experiments and ideas of Kurt Lewin in USA (Trist and Murray 1990, Lewin 1948). In Europe, after the war and driven by the need for economic, industrial and political reconstruction, the development of organizations and the democratization of work became one of the primary points of focus for the social sciences, and as such also the domain in which the practice and 'theory' of action research further developed.[3]

Action research was and still is to some extent a radical perspective both in the context of the traditional empiricist epistemological position in social science and with regard to the questions it raises about the meaning of participation and democracy in enterprise development. Consequently, it can be discussed from a variety of points of view and with regard to different social settings.

In this chapter my primary focus will not be on the various theoretical aspects of action research but on some of the critical questions one faces as a researcher when one engages in the *practice* of action research. I wish to point out though, that this distinction is more a matter of emphasis and of choosing a point of departure rather than of reference to different categories or perspectives, because when engaged in action one is inevitably faced with the various assumptions, theoretical and otherwise, underlying the action.

Action research refers to a specific way of understanding and managing the relationship between theory and practice, between the researcher and the re-searched, i.e. the 'other', or, if one wants to use a more traditional terminology, between epistemic subject and empirical object. That relationship should be understood as one of dialogue. Thus, when one engages in action research, one is engaged in a dialogue, although a very special one.

To summarize, briefly and roughly: in action research one recognizes the empirical object as subject; hence the relationship between researcher and 're-searched' (the other) is seen as an intersubjective, interactive relationship charac-terized by joint action, joint involvement and shared responsibility.

> Both researcher and researched are social actors; they are purposeful, capable and knowledgeable beings – capable in the sense that the agent 'could have acted otherwise', and knowledgeable with regard to all those things the members of a society know about that society. They are both the product and the producer of history. Recognizing the empirical object first and foremost as subject has ethical as well as epistemological implications (van Beinum *et al.* 1996).

It does away with the idea that method and object of study are separate and independent. Epistemology is not any longer reduced to a method. Although this is by now a common position in the theory of science, it is still (surprisingly or perhaps not so surprisingly) a matter of hot debate in the social sciences. Action research therefore still represents a radical perspective; and indeed, it has far reaching epistemological implications (not to mention the political/institutional ones effecting the world of academe) which we are still trying to fully comprehend.

In action research the question presented, the object of study is jointly addressed by the researcher and the researched. The objective of action research is not just to describe or understand or to explain social reality. Action research goes much further; it wants to improve a situation. In action research the researcher is confronted with a problem or a question of the other which is of such a nature that it requires research (new knowledge). Action research is a process in which the researcher is not solving a problem for the other but *with* the other. The learning is in the joint action, a process of joint learning, which, if successful, will at the same time and in the same act make a contribution to clarifying the "question", or solving the problem, as well as generate knowledge, that is, in the first instance local, contextual and historical knowledge. Action research is characterized by this mutuality in which the knowledge is in the action. This is in fact its basic epistemological feature.

As I mentioned earlier, by taking the relational aspect and thus the linguisticality of the human condition as point of departure, the relationship between theory and practice, between researcher and researched becomes one of dialogue. We are concerned with joint interpretation rather than external causal explanation. In short, in action research one does not use a pre-Einstein view of physics as model for the social sciences.[4]

Action research viewed as a thematic proposition: By definition, all social relationships are about something. Similarly, in action research the relationship between the researcher and the researched, the 'other', such as a group, an organization or other social system, is always about something. In the case of action research, that something is, in the first instance, something that bothers the other, such as a problem or question. In other words, action research is basically a social relationship, albeit a special one, and therefore is characterized like all social relationships by the fact that it has fundamental *triadic* characteristics. Social relationships involve triadic relations on different levels and of different kinds ranging from the very abstract to the very concrete.

To be more concrete, Researcher (A) and the other, the 'researched' (B), are jointly involved in addressing an issue (X). Action Research constitutes a so-called ABX system[5] consisting of these three interdependent elements in which each element can only be defined by its relationship with the other two. Furthermore, each action research setting is unique, it is contextual and historical; in every ABX there is a different A, a different B and a different X.

Because in action research one is involved in a relationship, one encounters the whole gamut of the human feelings: love, hate, fear, conflict, confusion, projections, defenses against anxiety, intra- and interpersonal processes, group dynamic features, organizational cultures, values, norms, the relationship between structure and process, etc., etc. In other words, one experiences, off and on, all the modalities of daily reality, However, although each X varies and each

ABX is different, there are certain general characteristics that come regularly to the fore in this unfolding process in which the researcher and others are jointly engaged.

For the purpose of this discussion, I therefore wish to draw attention to certain features which are of particular relevance for the practice of action research: the meaning of dialogue, the question which is being addressed and the context, the wider social setting from which the question has been distilled, the kind of psycho-dynamics one can become involved in, as well as ethical questions one has to take into account. (See Figure 1.)

These features, modalities of daily reality, are highly interdependent. One cannot have a dialogue without a content, which is being discussed in view of a particular context. Also, psychodynamic processes are inevitably part of any human encounter, and addressing a problem always requires dealing with ethical questions as well. All these aspects interpenetrate each other. One cannot discuss one without taking the others into consideration.

Action research thus is a situationally determined, many sided, multi-dimensional, multi-"triadic enterprise" which cannot be understood or characterized by means of a simple definition.

When discussing action research, we should remember, as Charles Taylor (1985) reminds us, that the use of theory as self definition has to be borne in mind when we come to explain, when we practice, social science. If we would define action research in a traditional manner, we have to draw boundaries, thereby deciding what to include and what to exclude. And, as I will discuss later, this would negate the nature of action research. Furthermore, in view of the inter-subjective relationship involved, we would draw boundaries with regard to our own learning. We would bring our own development to a stop and thereby would make it impossible to engage in action research. In other words, one consequence of this position is that *the last thing one should do in action research is to define action research.*

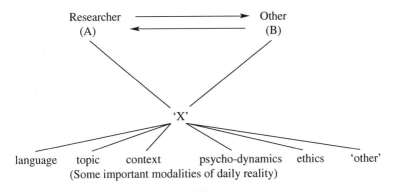

Figure 1. The ABX triadic features of action research

In place of a definition, I will provide some thematic propositions, a number of linked statements about action research in which I articulate and stress some of the key questions and issues one encounters when engaging, as a researcher, in this kind of process.

Some questions one encounters in the jointness of action research

The use of language: First of all, as is common to all human relationships, A and B are involved in a linguistic relationship. Being able to use language is the primary characteristics of the human condition. Consequently, the various social, psychological, cultural and other elements of the action research relationship are experienced, expressed and worked through in the communicative sphere. They are articulated in language and dealt with through the way in which language is being understood and used. To use a simple but fundamental distinction, language is not only referential, representing reality, but it is first and foremost a tool. It is formative, it has a shaping function, and it creates meaning. It is through language and by means of dialogue that the researcher and the researched are managing their relationship in the sense of joint action and thus are able to engage in discovery as well as in making. They traverse an epigenetic landscape.[6]

Collaboration is obviously a necessary condition, however, it is not a sufficient condition. Collaboration, in the general sense of doing something together, also happens, for instance, in laboratory experiments, in prisons or in traditional consulting, and therefore cannot be a defining principle of action research. Collaboration is relevant but alone it is insufficient to make a process action research.[7] The essence and thus the meaning of action research is situated in the quality of the relationship, that is, the quality of the dialogue between researcher and other. It lies in the joint and mutual responsibility, in being partners in conducting a dialogue in search of a 'solution'. The dialogue thus is the locus of action research. It is the social space where, in the first instance, the action takes place, where the knowledge is generated and where the relationship between theory and practice is managed.[8]

Ethics: In the dialogical setting of action research, the researcher should be oriented in the first place to *the other*. In the context of this joint action, the researcher cannot, however, avoid taking a personal stance based on his or her own value orientations. This raises questions not only to do with professional responsibility but also with one's responsibility as a human agent. There is therefore a strong and complex ethical dimension in action research that plays a role on various levels and in different contexts. First of all, any relationship with another person is, in the first instance, essentially an ethical relationship: being *for* the other (*'être-pour-l'autre'*) before one can be *with* the other.[9] In addition to the interpersonal relationship, the researcher has to make a decision whether or not he or she is comfortable with the values implied in the process of change, *i.e.* the action that is being developed. On the organizational level, there is the question of political and cultural legitimacy; whether the focus of the action and the approach taken are consonant or not with the values and culture of the organization as a whole and/or with those of the wider environment. In short, the participants in action research are confronted with the close relationship between meaning and morality in various contexts. In order to emphasize the importance of the ethical dimension and in particular to draw attention to the fundamental implication in action research of taking the question of the other as point of departure, I will use some of the statements and positions of Emanual Lévinas as 'aids' to express my views and concerns.

Lévinas points to the primacy of the other (which is his basic position) and thereby articulates the meaning and implications of the fact that in action research the other (with his or her question) is the point of departure. Furthermore we learn from Levinas that the otherness of the other can never be fully understood. The ethical philosophy of Lévinas is very complex and his writings ("Totality and Infinity", and "Otherwise than Being or Beyond Essence" 1991a and b editions by Kluwer) are often exceedingly difficult to penetrate. The reason that I nevertheless will try to make a modest use of Lévinas here is because he is one of the few, perhaps the only, philosopher who points to the far-reaching idea that Western philosophy has consistently practiced a suppression of the Other. We reduce the Other to the Same, with devastating consequences (social, psychological, intellectual, cultural, etc.). The two major mistakes we can make in action research are: (a) that we reduce the Other to the Same, that is, that we take ourselves as point of departure, and (b) that we cannot accept that we never can fully understand: the otherness of the other.

Lévina's point about Western philosophy is astonishingly simple, but it will have major philosophic consequences: philosophy, he suggests, has been characterized by its failure to think of the Other as Other. The history of philosophy has been like the story of Ulysses who 'through all his wanderings only returns to his native island'. Lévinas prefers the story of Abraham: 'To the myth of Ulysses returning to Ithaca, we would like to oppose the story of Abraham leaving his country for ever to go to a still unknown land and forbidding his servant to take even his son back to this point of departure'. Philosophy has always sought to return to familiar ground (Being, Truth, the Same). Lévina's endeavor is to take it elsewhere, to make it susceptible to an encounter with what it has always suppressed.

The problem of the Other has been misposed: rather than seeking knowledge of it (thus reducing its otherness), we should accept that we do not, cannot and should not know the Other." (Davis, 1996:33).

> The difficulty in describing the encounter with alterity lies in the constant danger of transforming the Other, however unwittingly or unwillingly, into a reflection or projection of the Same. If the Other becomes an object of knowledge or experience (my knowledge, my experience), then immediately its alterity has been overwhelmed." (Davis 1996: 45).

So far, this account of Lévina's ethics has concentrated solely on the encounter between self and Other. Since the universalization of this relationship has been ruled out, it is as yet unexplained how the validity of broader issues such as justice or social equality may be established. "He attempts to respond to this problem by introducing the notion of *le tiers* (the third party), which functions as the key to social justice." In this way, Levinas tries to make clear that there exists: "¼ a relationship outside my relationship with the neighbour [that is, the Other, HvB]" (Davis, 1996: 82). Another neighbour, a neighbour of the neighbour. In other words, according to Lévinas, in action research, when engaging jointly, with the Other with regard to the problem of the Other, we at the same time relate to society. We cannot relate to the Other without relating to the neighbour of the Other!

Role and action: Receptivity to the other thus is a methodological necessity in action research as well as an ethical position. Through 'role taking' the researcher tries to understand (*verstehen*) the other participant(s) as well as possible. One has to come close but keep distance at the same time. This requires considerable maturity from the researcher, as an understanding from 'within' means that in order to understand the other, the researcher has to mobilize his or her 'inner' life experience in an appropriate manner.

A first pre-requisite is that the researcher has considerable self-knowledge, a capacity to learn about him or herself, a strong orientation towards learning to learn. The corollary is that not every social scientist, irrespective of formal academic qualifications, is suitable for action research in terms of her or his personality characteristics, which is an issue that has hardly received any attention until now. One walks on a narrow path. One can easily 'do' too much and cause dependency, or, on the other hand, one can fail to give the other the opportunity to learn from one's experience.

A crucial feature of the dialogue is that it is concerned with a "space in between": a spatio-temporal area which is in between the researcher and the other and which has to be filled in. From this point of view, communication is not like sending that which is in my mind (between my ears *[sic]!*) to the mind of another. John Shotter refers to communication as "joint action":

> "It designates a...category of activities... lying in a zone of uncertainty somewhere in between the other two spheres of interest that have occupied our attention in the past. It lies neither wholly in the category of human action... nor in that of natural events...but shares features of both. It is its very lack of specificity, its lack of any predetermined final form, and *thus its openness to being specified or determined by those involved in it* (my italics HvB) that is the central defining feature of joint action" (Shotter, 1993b, p.4).

In other words, joint action occurs in the dialogue with others. Again, a (joint) sensitivity with regard to the distinction in the use of words, in terms of them being used in a referential or formative manner, is of the utmost importance in order to develop the necessary understanding for the critical moments in a dialogue.

The encounter between researcher and other, the joint action, usually begins with the presentation of a problem, the posing of a question, the raising of an issue which quickly leads to a process in which the originally presented problem becomes part of and is absorbed by a process of four evolving perspectives which emerge and are being clarified and given significance during the process of joint action.

They form a central frame of reference for the necessary ongoing joint reflexivity and can be named as follows:

- the *focus of the research* and its objectives, the question which has to be addressed,
- the *nature of the contextual setting* of the focus (why the focus is the focus). It refers to the wider social setting, the way of understanding the reality from which the research question has been distilled, and is a crucial perspective in the development of the action research process
- the *approach* taken, the kind of action which is considered necessary to reach the objectives,
- the *assumptions* (theoretical and otherwise) underlying the above perspectives, that is, the understanding of the context, the relevance of the focus and the appropriateness of the approach

However, we should not over-schematize this as these four elements are very interdependent, they form a shifting pattern of interrelationships, a dynamic profile of changing understandings which needs regular re-framing due to the, by definition, unfolding nature of action research. What looks like the key question, turns out to be an issue of secondary importance after a while; contexts, after some joint exploration, appear to be based on a wrong appreciation of social reality, and so on. This is a process which is strongly affected by the nature and the quality of the "joint action" in which the formative use of language plays its decisive role. These shifts, when they occur, require the participants (researcher and others) to *realign* the relationship between question, context, action and assumptions, as a result of which the participants are faced with puzzling situations which are actually quite typical for the action research process.

It is not uncommon that it is in the process of change that the objective aimed at becomes more clearly structured and definable and the characteristics of what was the initial situation become more clearly defined. One is trying to deal with a situation in which neither initial nor outcome states can be specified in operational terms.

On the interpersonal level researcher and other may find themselves on different 'situational' levels. On the organizational level, the interplay of local and global, the interactions between questions, changing contexts, local approaches and varying assumptions, raises the meaning of social practices to a higher level of complexity, that Harry Kunneman defines as interplexity (Kunneman, 1997, p.182). The question is not so much that we are faced with a more complex composed set of factors and influences within the same ontological space, but with an internally heterogeneous composition of interfering 'logics' which is not determined or accommodated by one cognitive or normative principle and which consists of a number of partially conflicting logics (Kunneman, 1997).[10]

We are rapidly moving into a 'reality' where the unit of development in organization development is no longer the organization. Consequently we have to rethink some of our understanding of workplace reform and organizational design. When the socio-technical system extends far beyond the boundaries of the local enterprise, as it often does, or when the notion of organizational choice has to be re-conceptualized in a global context, the researcher and his or her partners are then faced with complexities that can put considerable strain on the 'jointness' of the action research relationship.

Containment: In action research in particular, the researcher needs a capacity to cope with psycho-dynamic phenomena. The ability to "contain" is only one of those phenomena, but an important one because its meaning is highly relevant for action research. It refers to the fact that, in any human interaction, projections take place. In complex processes of change, people can experience strong feelings (anxieties) which are then projected onto others. These projections can often take the form of aggression and accusations. In action research, it is of great importance for the researcher to be aware of this mechanism and to have the ability to receive and hold the projections of the other without absorbing them or acting them out. This enables the researcher to mediate these projections back to the other in a more digestible form and to do so at an appropriate moment. These are important skills that will enable the researcher to clarify relationships in situations of stress and strain.

Learning: Action research is, by definition, a process of joint learning. To talk about action research *and* learning is not very meaningful. On the other hand, there appear to be different kinds of learning. For instance, learning *about* something (ourselves, mathematics or birds), learning *how to* (drive a car, read or cook), or learning *with and from* another person, and foremost, interpersonal learning. *Learning refers to a change in behavior (understanding, attitudes, skills, etc.) as a result of becoming aware of the meaning of an experience.* Learning *about*, *how to*, and *with* can all be described in those terms.

It is becoming clear that the way in which learning has been phrased (above) is much too simple. It raises questions to do with values and power, with differences and choice. Meaning is not built up through descriptions of an external reality. We did not come to know reality from a perceiving it *as it is*, but from making choices and as a result of the differences formed in daily practice.

We create social reality by the way we use it. We are not just mirrors, passively reflecting a situation we find ourselves in. We are writers not just readers, we are actors acting with other actors, a coefficient of the truth on one side, while on the other we register the truth which we help to create. We traverse an *epigenetic landscape*. A landscape we discover as well as create.

Learning is a two step affair. In the first instance, learning takes place in the context of the immediate experience. One engages in a process of reflexive awareness which, in a sense, is characteristic of all human action. To be a human being is to know, virtually all of the time, in terms of some description or another, both what one is doing and why one is doing it. That knowing is however a *doing*. All experience is learning to some extent, as there is always some awareness, the question is *what does one do with that awareness*, what does one make of it? The kind (perhaps we should say: quality) of one's reflexive awareness determines the significance of the experience. The next step is what does one do with that awareness, or to put it differently, what does one do with that first immediate doing? The meaning of learning lies ultimately in the use of learning. All learning is a learning *about* learning and is potentially a learning *to* learn, a learning *from* learning.

The use of 'objects' (the teddy bear): In that connection, I would like to draw attention to an important and very useful, and in my opinion even essential, distinction made by Winnicott (1971) about the way we make use of "objects" [11]in order to manage a transition, a distinction which is very relevant for the practice of action research. He distinguishes between using an "object" (which can be anything: a material object, a person, a situation, an animal, music, etc.) as a *transitional object* or using it as a *comforter*. It is a distinction originally used to describe and explain a critical phase in the early stages of development of the infant, *i.e.* the way a boy or a girl uses the first possession (such as the proverbial teddy bear) in order to negotiate the "transitional" or intermediate phase between primary narcissism and object relations, the ability to recognize and accept reality. The transitional object (or transitional space) refers to an intermediate area of experience to which inner reality and external life both contribute. It is an intermediate state... between "primary creative activity and projection of what has already been introjected",... between "primary awareness of indebtedness and the acknowledgement of indebtedness",... between "apperception and perception" .... "It is an area that is not challenged, because no claim is made on its behalf except that it shall exist as a resting-place for the individual engaged in the perceptual human task of keeping inner and outer reality separate yet interrelated."[11] It has the paradoxical quality of being 'me' and 'not-me' at the same time.

It has a spatial/temporal meaning in the sense that it is in between the present and the future, whilst accommodating both simultaneously; it separates areas whilst they are being merged.

The use of transitional objects or space is a normal part of psychic growth and development and it occurs also in organizations. It is an area of *illusion* which in adult life is inherent not only in such creative activities as in producing art, but in all situations of significant personal learning and organizational development.[12] To be cast, as a researcher, in the role of transitional object usually means that one finds oneself involved in a process that is not easy.

Like the teddy bear, one is "loved", "stamped upon", "slept with" and "thrown around". To be "used" in that way and to make allowance for that use, in order to facilitate the learning and working through of another person, group or organization, can create a very complex situation which will make big emotional and intellectual demands. Quite often the researcher is used in such a manner. The ability to recognize and manage these processes is an important component in the competence of the researcher involved in action research.

The notion of "comforter" is the opposite of transitional object, it refers to the use of an object which can best be described in terms of "not used as a transitional object." That is, the object is not used in order to facilitate change, the subject does not have a relationship with the object that is of importance or significance in the sense that it facilitates a break in a dependency the subject may have on ideas (theories!), people, or any specific form of awareness. The object only provides comfort. There is no disturbance.

There is no experience of discontinuity. It is a relationship of non-learning. It is not uncommon, as we all know, that educational settings or consulting practices are not used (or allowed to be used) as transitional objects but only as comforters, they are events characterized by what I would call "safe learning". They are characterized by a "comfortable" relationship between "teacher" and "pupil", organization and researcher (or consultant).

It is interesting to note that the significance of the transitional object, a "safe" transitional space, as a critical condition for processes of learning of any existential significance and for managing important transitions in one's life, is beginning to be recognized and developed further conceptually and theoretically in social science.[13]

A final remark: Action research is part of a larger development which is reflected in the fact that a growing number of epistemological positions in social science nowadays are based on the notion that all human experience is mediated — through socialization and, in particular, through language. It is through language, which is intrinsically public, that we have the means to reflect and to be aware of self as well as of others. It goes beyond saying that learning and language are very closely connected. Learning as well as the manner in which one makes use of learning takes place through the use of language. To ask the question about the nature of learning or the nature of language for that matter, does not make sense. It depends on what they are being used for. Learning and language can serve many purposes. Similarly, the meaning of action research is determined by its objectives and the ethical considerations underlying it. This brings us back to what it is all about, which may well be, as Toulmin has suggested, a matter of phronesis (Toulmin, 1996a and b). The wisdom to act in the right way, to learn to make correct judgments and the right choices. And what that is, or should be, in each specific situation depends on a lot of factors. This raises the question of the role and competence of the researcher. The discussion up till now has drawn attention to some of the important skills a researcher should possess and we could go on listing them and spelling out the dynamics of action research in a more elaborate manner. However, the key question the researcher is faced with, when it comes down to the wire, all the time is: *'What to do?*

What to do is a function of many things, but the key ingredients of knowing what to do are: (a) experience, (b) the contents of one's 'toolkit', and (c) timing.

To know *what* to do and to know *when* to do it: One needs a 'toolkit' full of all kinds of "things": narratives, theories, social and psychological skills, methods, (such as: participative design, search conference, Wittgenstein's social poetics, and many more), metaphors, a capacity to be silent, etc., etc. As one engages in action research, one starts to build such a toolkit in conjunction with developing one's experience.

One of the first things one learns is that there is no relationship between the way a problem has structured itself and presents and the logic of a discipline. One has to 'move' (figuratively speaking) from within the field. One of the classical mistakes one can make is to come too quickly with the right interpretation. One has to fight one's tendency to reduce the Other to the Same, to reduce the situation to one's theory. To struggle with the notion and the practice that ethics comes before epistemology. To be a partner, to learn to feel comfortable with a relationship which is asymmetrical in a double sense, to take the other as point of departure without denying one's identity, one's sense of self. One moves from practice to practice, and perhaps from practice to 'theory'. In action research one starts in the middle and one ends in the middle. One moves in an epigenetic landscape with a shifting horizon as in all landscapes. It never ends.

Considerations in the Design of ACRES

The previous discussion provides a basic profile of the considerations that went into the design of ACRES. Or, rather, the key features of the design emerged logically and almost automatically out of these reflections. Consonance between the structure and the content of the program on the one hand and the characteristics of action research on the other was an obvious prerequisite. As learning about action research is not a matter of transferring formal knowledge, accord between the program and the practice in the field is not with regard to a body of knowledge that can be conventionally taught. It was very clear that the necessary relevance had to be provided by linking the learning process in ACRES directly to existing ongoing action research processes.

The solution chosen was that, as a condition for participating in ACRES, one had to be involved in action research and had to bring to the program a complete account of one's own project and be willing to make available, on an ongoing basis and in a systematic manner, one's experience with the development of one's involvement in action research. In this manner, the participants would generate the necessary relevant learning material for the program, the idea being that the structure, focus, and content of ACRES, together with the action research situations of the participants, should constitute a single learning environment.

The ACRES program consisted of four linked workshops (two in Norway and two in Sweden) of two and a half days each, spread over one year. The workshops offered opportunities for individual learning and, indirectly, became relevant events for the development of the participants' individual projects.

The logic underlying the principle of consonance dictated that the unit of learning should consist of a researcher and at least one relevant "other" from the action research project concerned. As discussed earlier, the epistemological stance of action research is based on the notion that the relationship between epistemic subject and empirical object is characterized by joint involvement and shared responsibility; the researcher and the researched are both knowing and knowledgeable actors. Accordingly, we seriously considered having such a unit be the unit of participation. Such an approach would have made the program much more complex from the point of view of structure and learning dynamics, however, and would have required considerable more time for preparation; it was therefore decided that that approach was not realistic at the time.

Although it was epistemologically and pedagogically flawed, the unit of learning had to be the individual researcher, who would bring his or her project to the program by means of a written report discussing the characteristics and development of the project, which would be updated for each workshop. In this way, workshops and action research practice were linked and the relationship between reflection, writing, and action made visible and mobilized.

The objectives of the program were formulated as follows:

- To give methodological and theoretical as well as practical support to action researchers in general and to provide specific learning opportunities for individual researchers (this was defined as the primary objective);
- To provide credits toward a doctoral degree in Norway and Sweden;
- To contribute to the development of projects;
- To contribute to the development of the distinctive competence of institutes;

- To learn about the interdependencies between institutes, projects, and researchers;
- To promote collaboration between institutes, researchers, and projects and to facilitate the development of networks.

Objectives 3 through 6 were seen primarily as spinoffs of the first objective.

These objectives were translated into four interdependent and overlapping perspectives, which formed the anchor points for the program as a whole as well as for each individual workshop.

First, the main focus of the program would be the participants' reflections on their actual practice in the field. It was expected that, as they interacted with other participants, these joint explorations would generate a very rich learning process with regard to the so-called evolving parameters in the various projects: the questions being addressed, the meaning of the various contexts in which the projects occurred, the rationale for the approaches taken, and the various assumptions underlying these processes. Also, it was expected that the dialogues would bring out the kind of issues and questions one encounters in action research that cut across these four dimensions — such as, the psycho-dynamics of joint involvement or the ethical orientation of a project — and help create a *safe* space for working through them.

Second, in accordance with the dialogical relationship between theory and practice in action research, the program had to have a very broad and open theoretical orientation. Focus on a particular theory would depend primarily on the way theoretical questions and methodological issues emerged from the case analyses. Discussions about the theoretical assumptions underlying the projects and the way they related to other kinds of assumptions would be seen as particularly important.

Third, in addition to social scientists, the staff would include an experienced philosopher to assist with philosophical reflections. Generally speaking, social scientists engaged in action research do not commonly engage in philosophical reflections; usually, one is driven too much by pressures resulting from the complexities of practical involvement with social change. This is somewhat paradoxical, since the very practice of action research confronts the researcher with questions having to do with knowledge, reason, logic, and language. Furthermore, on the whole, action researchers are not very good at identifying and explaining themselves in terms of their place in the landscape of the theory of science, which frequently leads to unhappy discussions within the social science "community" that seem to confirm to positivists that action research is not scientific and therefore not research.

Fourth, writing about action research would be an essential component of the program. As Björn Gustavsen has noted, although action research has "been on the scene for about fifty years, there is, on the average, less than one publication

per year from or about action research to be found in the scientific journals"
(1996: 5). This can be explained in various ways: action researchers do not write
because they are too busy with action; they just cannot write or are bad writers; if
they write, their papers are rejected because they do not meet the necessary
standards; and so forth. Whatever the reasons, writing about action research is
obviously a problem, which is exacerbated by the fact that publications about
action research are an essential part of the debate in and about the social sciences.

But writing is of great significance for reasons beyond the concerns just
mentioned. Apart from conveying an experience and producing a narrative, the
very act of writing is, in itself, at least potentially a powerful process of learning.
As a researcher reflects on the possible meaning of words — or, rather, behind
words — and becomes aware of the way one uses language and of the interrela-
tion between experience, thought, and language, writing becomes research. As L.
S. Vygotsky points out:

> The relation of thought to word is not a thing but a process, a continual movement
> backward and forth from thought to word and from word to thought. In that
> process, the relation of thought to word undergoes changes that themselves may
> be regarded as developmental in the functional sense. Thought is not merely
> expressed in words; it comes into existence through them. Every thought tends to
> connect something with something else, to establish a relation between things.
> Every thought moves, grows and develops, fulfills a function, solves a problem
> (quoted in Shotter 1993a: 43).

In writing about action research, one engages in a linguistic process in which
one learns about how to do action research — if, and it is a big if, one uses writing
as a transitional object and not as a comforter. It is a dilemma that in this process
one uses words in their formative sense, while, depending on the quality of the
writing, in our culture the reader is inclined to read them referentially. Nevertheless, the first step in the process of learning from one's experience by writing
about it (and in so doing enabling others to learn as well) is to be able to organize
and assemble intelligibly the various bits and pieces of information and experience dispersed in space and time.

Participants in the ACRES program were therefore required to prepare a
written analysis of the developments in their projects. These texts had to be
submitted and distributed before each workshop. During the workshop, participants would be given assistance with any difficulties in conceptualizing, organizing, and expressing their experiences in writing, so that at the end of the program
each participant would be able to submit an article for publication.

These four interdependent perspectives were seen as basic points of reference, as a sort of scaffolding necessary for building a learning environment. In
different ways, they determined the content and organization of the workshops.

In chapter 4, René van der Vlist discusses the various structures of ACRES
and the actual process of developing ACRES, what happened, how it happened,

and why it happened. I have focused only on the background and on the ideas underlying the design of the program.

Conclusions

I will, however, end this overview with a final comment about ACRES as a whole. The crucial question is, of course, the extent to which the envisaged ACRES emerged and, moreover, whether the program was effective. Many factors must be taken into account in answering this question, some foreseen and many not, a critical one being the particular manner in which staff and participants were able and willing to use ACRES and, most important of all, develop the ability to reflect on that process and thereby give meaning to their experience.

Ultimately, the program itself has many of the key features of an action research project. Staff and participants are jointly involved in and responsible for building a learning environment, and in this joint action — in addressing this question of learning about action research by means of reflecting on practice — knowledge is being generated. Also, the role of the staff is somewhat similar to that of the researcher. It has paradoxical aspects, such as jointness in a relationship that is basically asymmetrical and a shared responsibility in which both staff and participants also have distinct and different responsibilities.

All action research projects are, of course, unique, but ACRES was a rather special and complex case. First of all, it was concerned with action research on action research; further, in view of its international nature, the staff, the participants, and their projects (which together were the constituting components of the program) made for a great variety of nationalities, backgrounds, experiences, and social science orientations. ACRES represented a plurality of cultures, as well as a plurality of styles of reflection.

Combined with the different personalities of the staff and participants, this plurality generated a very rich and stimulating environment, but it also made complicated psycho-dynamic processes an unavoidable part of the program. The whole thus oscillated between being more as well as less than the sum of its parts.

As social scientists, those involved in action research represent an epistemological shift; we are part of it and are being formed by it. We cannot avoid "acting out," at least to some extent, the disarray in the social sciences. Similarly, the ACRES program could not avoid becoming the stage for an exciting and complex play with many plots in which the roles were heavily colored by the fact that there is always a strong relationship between definition of self and epistemological stance.

When reading, as well as writing, about ACRES, one has to remember, as Taylor (1985) argues, that the use of theory as self-definition has to be borne in mind when we come to explain and when we practice social science.

Notes

1. For a detailed description and analysis, see, for instance, Emery and Thorsrud 1976 and Gustavsen 1985.

2. Morten Levin was and still is the only one in Scandinavia overseeing a university-based Ph.D. program in action research.

3. van Beinum, Hans. 1996.

4. See Toulmin 1996a.

5. see Newcomb 1953, also van Beinum *et al.*1996

6. I am referring here to the epigenetic function of action research. See van Beinum et al.1996

7. A similar remark can be made about the term "collaborative inquiry" which is sometimes applied to describe action research. The notion collaborative inquiry actually comes from psychoanalysis and is used to characterize the nature of psychoanalytical practice. Also, the American inspired expression "participative action research", implying that there also exists a non-participative form of action research, is rather puzzling. My reason for mentioning these linguistic practices is not to question the professional competence of my colleagues but to illustrate the difficulty, if not the impossibility, of using a simple expression to indicate the complex dynamics of action research.

8. This is not the occasion to go into the very complex discussions taking place in the social sciences about communication. From the point of view of practice, however, I would like to draw attention to the very relevant points made by Adri Smaling made in the context of argumentation theory. He points out that a good dialogue is primarily not concerned with deductive validity or inductive probability, but more with degrees of local plausibility and tentative acceptability. That is: *does it make sense?* Reasoning in daily language will rarely be characterized by logically compelling conclusions. Furthermore, Smaling points out that the cogency of an argument is also dependent on personal, contextual, cultural and historical factors which cannot be fully explicated (Smaling 1997, p.143). It is not just 'logos', but also'pathos'and ethos' which play their role in dialogue.

9. See Lévinas 1991, Bauman 1993

10. Interplexity occurs, for instance, in the action research process when the parties concerned are trying to deal with a problem determined by the increase in the size of organizations and particularly by the interdependencies and their linkages across national and continental boundaries, or, what is even more "interplex", when these linkages consist of parts of different enterprises in different countries, where the parts such as R&D, production, distribution, marketing, etc., therefore are based on different traditions.

11. Winnicott, 1971 p.2 and 3

12. The concept of transitional object has a meaning in the context of action research which is more complex but also more significant and comprehensive than can be discussed in this chapter. See Winnicott, 1971.

13. Giddens, 1990, in his discussion on ontological security points to the critical importance of the use of the transitional object and transitional space for the development of basic trust, and the ability to be involved creatively. Also Shotter, 1993a, although he does not use the term transitional object, presents in his discussion on the special dialogical version of social constructionism, concepts which are not dissimilar to the notion of transitional space and which he considers to be of central importance for the way we construct both ourselves and our world in our conversational activities.

Chapter 2

Action Research Paradigms

Morten Levin

Action research (AR) practice is both multifaceted and intercultural. Research activity that carries the AR label ranges from liberating struggles in Third World countries to organizational change activity in industrial organizations in technologically advanced societies. Given the breadth of the AR field, there is no universal agreement about the necessary elements to include in a general AR paradigm. Still, certain common threads and themes can be highlighted and this is the function of the present chapter.

After a brief overview of the history of action research to provide some context for contemporary practice, this chapter discusses two different AR approaches that were central components in the ACRES process: the ABX model and the co-generative model. The ABX model conceptualizes the relationship between the researcher and the empirical object in a specific way based on the ABX model.[1] The co-generative model takes a constructivist and hermeneutic position as its point of departure and its central goal is the joint social construction of meaning. The two models have commonalities, but involve different emphases and diverge on particular points.

History of Action Research

A number of attempts have been made to write the history of action research over the last fifty years, but writing from different positions has, of course, resulted in quite dissimilar views. The current historical debate in the field can be found in books written or edited by Fals Borda and Rahman (1992), Gustavsen (1992), Reason (1988), and Whyte, ed. (1991) and in a special issue of *Human Relations* (Chisholm and Elden, eds., 1993).

Many professionals in the AR field trace the origins of action research to the 1940s and the work of Kurt Lewin whose main interest was in changing social systems using scientific methodology. During that period, social science in the

United States was dominated by a positivistic model of science and so being "scientific" was the core concern of social science activity.

Lewin's research on attitude change toward eating tripe (1943) was an early application of social science that could be labeled action research. He designed an experiment to test if it was possible to encourage American housewives to use tripe as part of their normal, everyday meals. This was an early attempt to develop scientific knowledge by initiating actions and recording the outcomes. In this model of action research, the researcher was highly visible and certainly influenced the whole experiment; the researcher was most assuredly not an external, objective observer.

Lewin's study also purposely raised methodological questions about assessing outcomes and controlling contextual variables. As such, it set a trend in U.S.-based action research. The controlled experiment, in which external consultants or researchers set up experiments and measured the results, became the ideal type and dominated American efforts for more than forty years (Pasmore and Friedlander 1982; Ledford and Mohrman 1993). The action research approach begun by Lewin thus gradually degenerated into positivistic experimentation in which a few variables were manipulated and only tangible, quantitative variables were accepted as results. Few attempts were made to go beyond this to look at the relationship between the researcher and the researched.

Why did U.S.-based AR end up like this? There are two possible answers, which, when stated briefly, paint too black and white a picture. Still they account for the main trends. First, the strong professional norms within American academia allowed little freedom to break out of the barriers defined by positivistic social science. Second, mainstream action research in the United States was linked to businesses competing in the marketplace. It was generally contracted and paid for by companies. In this context, action research soon became organizational development work in which the core interest was organizational change in support of a power elite's interests. The research part was subordinated to other goals and the open-ended inquiry dimension disappeared.

On the other side of the Atlantic, the post-World War II reconstruction period in the United Kingdom created room for organizational experimentation. The researchers at the Tavistock Institute in London, relying on psychoanalytical models, contributed substantially to the reindustrialization of England through AR.

The well-known study by E. Trist and K. W. Bamforth (1951) on the coal mining industry focused on the relationship between technology and social systems. This sociotechnical view underlined the importance of understanding how technology shapes social activity and that changing a social system depends on how the technology can support the intended changes.[2]

In essence, this view led to an emphasis on initiating social change activity where technology and social variables were linked. A change in one was supposed to follow from change in the other. By implication, if real change was to occur, the limits imposed by technology had to be dealt with. Industrial organizations thus became the dominant arena for action research — but working on sociotechnical change projects also required consensus among the participants, a cooperative relationship between employers and trade unions.

Eventually it turned out that AR projects could not be maintained in Great Britain because of a lack of institutional support and new locations were sought for the work. Norway, whose labor market tradition was shaped by social democratic governments, became a fertile ground for experimentation, and the Tavistock Group, in cooperation with Einar Thorsrud, developed AR projects focused on Norwegian work life (Emery and Thorsrud 1976). From the late 1960s on, sociotechnical research dominated international development within the field of AR. According to Elden (1979), who has identified three "generations" of sociotechnical research, this was the golden age in Norwegian work research, and it led to new approaches and new models for social change.

Active participation in the change process became a core value guiding the research, and the importance of having a national institutional anchor emerged as an increasingly important factor (Gustavsen and Hunnius 1981, Gustavsen 1983). Indeed, public and institutional support turned out to be the central factor accounting for the strong progress of AR in Norwegian work life.

An unfortunate weakness in the Norwegian work was a lack of systematic reflection and publications. That is, action was foregrounded and research was all but eliminated. Sociotechnical ideas for change spread to other countries by direct diffusion, among which the United States and Sweden were the most important (Davis and Taylor 1972). In the United States, the research component almost vanished as the emphasis was placed on action, whereas in Sweden, the research element retained a somewhat higher standing.

Parallel to — but almost decoupled from — this work life-based action research was the development of participatory research (PR) through the network of the International Council for Adult Education. Researchers associated with this group focused on the "liberation" of underprivileged people, on developing social organizational forms to support the underprivileged in their struggle for control over their own situations (Brown and Tandon 1983). The most important work in this field was done by Fals Borda (1987), Hall (1978), and Fals Borda and Rahman (1991).

Seeking to clarify the differences between mainstream AR and PR in the United States, Brown and Tandon argued that participatory research was value driven and had a strong ideological commitment: "The values researchers hold and the ideological perspectives that guide them exert a powerful influence on choices they make in the course of inquiry." (Brown and Tandon, 1983: 281) Action researchers, by contrast, were characterized as supporting consensus and

conflict-free theories of society, that is, adaptation to existing power arrangements rather than democratic social change.

Gustavsen (1992) refers to this argument in asking why the quality of work
life (QWL) movement failed to have a lasting impact on American work life. He
states that action researchers in the United States seldom have a broad societal-
based theory of work life change or an appetite for such change. Brown and
Tandon argued that AR is suitable in situations in which the power distribution is
accepted as legitimate and the relevant parties accept the researchers, while PR
strategies are appropriate when the power distribution is not accepted and the
involved parties do not accept the legitimacy of the researcher.

Whyte (Whyte and Whyte 1984; Whyte 1991) presents a slightly different
taxonomy in discussing participatory action research (PAR). Whyte, ed. (1991)
leaves out the ideological perspective, framing PAR instead as a process in which
participation is *fundamental* for action aimed at changing social systems.

Greenwood (1989) pays significant attention to the way research questions
are formulated. Contrasting the conventional paradigm-centered research dominating most social science activity with the client-centered research found in AR,
he proposes that participation in research be initiated by a dialogue on what
questions should be researched.

Paralleling Greenwood's work, Reason and Rowan (1981) developed what
Reason (1988) named the "human inquiry" paradigm, which emphasizes the
importance of involving all relevant actors in the research process. In the introduction to *Human Inquiry in Action*, Reason argues: "The simplest description of
cooperative inquiry is that it is a way of doing research in which all those involved
contribute both to the creative thinking that goes into the enterprise — deciding
on what is to be looked at, the methods of inquiry, and making sense of what are
found out — and also contribute to the action that is the subject of the research."
(1988: 1) *Human Inquiry* is quite comprehensive, including participants in conventional action research projects in the United States, researchers in the European QWL tradition, and PR and PAR researchers.

A core point that emerges from human inquiry is that there is a subjective
side to science. This statement has been debated in Norwegian sociology since the
work of Skjervheim (1974). His contention that social science researchers should
be participants in their research is supported by the scientific element of AR,
which, as Reason lays it out, supports the "objectively subjective side." This view
summarizes the European position.

A paper by Susman and Evered (1978), focused on legitimating U.S. action
research, using arguments and positions from the positivistic theory of science,
but it had little influence on conventional social research practice. This suggests
that mainstream AR in the United States remains very much mired within the
constraints of positivistic social science.

Action research frameworks in ACRES

There were two action research paradigms articulated in the ACRES seminars and both have roots in the Tavistock tradition. The ABX model is rooted in social psychology, while the co-generative model is built on a constructivist position rooted in sociology, anthropology, and cultural studies. In what follows, both models are laid out and then they are contrasted.

The ABX Model: The main feature of the ABX model is the conceptualization of the relationship between the researcher (A) and the empirical object, the researched (B), in the context of inquiry denoted as X.[3] To follow this discussion, the reader should refer to Figure 1 in Chapter 1 that diagrams the ABX model.

The general understanding is that this relationship, in a democratic society, is based on mutuality. Thus, the empirical object will, can, and should talk back, creating a discursive situation in which the empirical object becomes a subject along with the subjective researcher.

Action research, described in this view as the study of operating systems in action, is not a method in the conventional sense of the word. Action research refers to a way of understanding and managing an inquiry relationship — that is, the relationship between the researcher and the researched, between theory and practice. Further, in AR, that relationship is collaborative, which is contrary to conventional social science research that views the relationship as one of researcher authority over the research subject.

In action research, the role of the empirical object is changed from someone who merely sanctions the research, either as object or as client, to a position of active participant. The position of the researcher is changed from one grounded in empirical or descriptive research or critical theory to a position of active involvement based on constructivism. The relationship between researcher and researched becomes one of joint involvement and shared responsibility.

Any social relationship is about something. Person A is in relation to person B with respect to a thing, event, or situation X. The relationship between A, B, and X represents the basic structural characteristic of a social relationship (Newcomb 1953). The way in which these relations are perceived in the minds of the participants is indicated by the notation "pox" (Heider 1946); the *pox* thus refers to a corresponding *intra*personal system (*i.e.*, the interdependencies between the various attitudes and beliefs of an individual with regard to the ABX). In that A, B, and X are also interdependent, the relationship between researcher and researched or between research and project can be understood only in the context of the ABX system as a whole. It is the ABX and the nature of its interdependencies that is the unit of reflection and of analysis in action research.

In action research, choices about X are made jointly by the researcher and the researched. It is only because of their interaction in practice — that is, in their joint structuring of a project — that the content and other characteristics of X emerge and crystallize. Whether the X will develop as an *action research project* and make a contribution to social science will, of course, be greatly influenced by the content of X — for instance, whether it requires research or not, or if it will generate new ways of conceptualizing reality or produce new hypotheses. The skill and creativity of both the researcher and the researched will play an important role, but ultimately whether the research will make a contribution to science will be decided by the social science community.

Although a project may begin with a problem as formulated by the "client" organization, it is essential that the researcher and the empirical object take the reality of the empirical object as the point of departure and then begin their mutual engagement with exploring the way in which both perceive and understand that reality. This is a critical phase in action research for the following reasons:

- Joint understanding of the reality of the empirical object is a primary point of reference.
- It is only via the reality of the empirical object that the appropriateness and relevance of the focus of the research can be assessed.
- Joint understanding of the reality of the empirical object is a good starting point for initiating the essential process of moving between the elements in the ABX model.
- Joint understanding lays the foundation for building the necessary *common* ground between researcher and researched, enabling them to explore views about organizations and images of man. It provides each party with a basis for defining the values that should govern their joint pursuit.
- Joint understanding is also the obvious point of entry for the researcher, for he or she must develop a good understanding of the organization concerned. During this phase, the researcher will also be able to begin the process of "earning the right" to work with the empirical object. With each new project, the researcher has to be involved in such a process, as academic qualifications alone do not bestow that right.

In view of the interdependencies of the ABX, with its strong dynamic features based on joint involvement and shared responsibility, the quality of action research is determined by the quality of the communication between the researcher and the researched. Open communication is essential for developing a shared language and shared concepts in direct correlation with their practice. Only then will the researcher and the researched be able to fuse their existing knowledge as well as develop new knowledge.

In ABX relationships, we can identify two kinds of reality, which correspond with two concepts of knowledge. We can distinguish between an experiential reality and a representational reality and between knowledge that is "in the act of doing," directly engaging with reality, and knowledge that is "about aspects" of reality.

The experiential level in action research refers to the actual interaction between the researcher and researched, an event in which both are fully involved and by means of which the unique knowledge of that relationship is obtained and expressed. On this level, in the very act of interacting, subject and object are not independent: from a cognitive point of view, AB and X completely coincide and ABX forms a triune structure. Practice and research become the same thing. Who is the researcher and who the researched cannot easily be distinguished.

Conceptually, researcher and researched can and should be distinguished, but from an information-content point of view, they are indistinguishable on this level of reality. The interaction is a unique and nonrepeatable event and cannot be objectified; in a strict sense, the interaction cannot be *described* and it is impossible to make a model or an image of it. The only way of knowing this reality is by the events in which it reveals itself, (*i.e.*, *that* it is and *what* it is) (Stavenga 1991). Knowledge here is not knowledge regarding states or possible properties of the relationship but the relationship itself. Theory in this context is theory of this particular praxis.

In the other reality, the representational reality, we conceptually distinguish between subject and object. We may start with knowledge and facts and subsequently consider action (praxis follows theory). We can call this knowledge *instrumental knowledge*, for this is knowledge concerning the various *aspects* of the action research reality. As for the roles of the researcher and the researched or the nature of the research findings, AB and X are conceptually separate. It is on this level that researcher and researched express their individual understandings of the situation (*i.e.* the *pox*) and show their conceptual and theoretical positions.

The ABX and the *pox* are in a state of continuous interaction in which the representational level depends on the existential or the experiential level. Each has its own relational (subject-object) and structural characteristics (Stavenga 1991), and an awareness of both realities and their corresponding types of knowledge is a prerequisite for understanding action research and for engaging in it. Action research is an unfolding process and has heuristic characteristics; it is concerned more with "theorizing" than with the application of an *a priori* "theory." According to this view, the distinctive characteristic of action research is that it encompasses two different concepts of reality — and that gives it a special place in the ongoing dialogue between theory and practice.

An effective collaborative relationship, which is essentially a process of joint learning, must be based on open communication, on democratic dialogue. But although it is a necessary and critical condition in an action research process, just having a democratic dialogue is not enough. As Gustavsen points out, "The idea of democratic dialogue...must be converted into a set of more specific means, or measures, to become operational in actual workplace change" (1992: 4). The extent to which there will truly be democratic dialogue depends on the interaction between researcher and researched. The researcher bears a special responsibility for creating this condition, and it is the competence of the researcher that is important here. It is not sufficient that the researcher be an able social scientist in the traditional academic sense, be well acquainted with the relevant theoretical and methodological developments, and have the intellectual ability to conceptualize the unfolding dynamics of action research. These traits are necessary but not sufficient.

The researcher not only should be willing to be involved in a collaborative relationship but should have professional skills in social processes. For the researcher to gain distance so that he or she can reflect critically on the nature of the relationship between self and others, he or she must have a sensitivity regarding others and insight into such matters as his or her own cognitive style, values, and defense mechanisms.

An ongoing concern for the researcher is that he or she has to combine the professional responsibilities of a social scientist with involvement in a democratic, collaborative relationship, with its need for open communication. Consequently, he or she is faced with a dilemma: either the researcher provides too much input, becomes "the expert," creates dependency, and blocks the learning of the other, or he or she does not allow the other to profit from his or her knowledge and experience and is not quite authentic in the relationship. The researcher has to avoid sins of commission and sins of omission. In the ABX-*pox* process of action research, in the interaction between the experiential and the representational, this is exactly the dilemma with which the researcher and the researched are concerned. They do not solve the paradox; they do not do away with the paradox; in a manner of speaking, they *are* the paradox. The researcher and the researched jointly contextualize an unfolding process (Van Beinum, Faucheux and van der Vlist 1996, p. 196).

The Co-generative Model of Action Research

Among the many possibilities for modeling an action research process, the co-generative approach is based on understanding AR as a meaning construction process in which participants and researchers mutually work on solving pertinent problems in a local context. Given this initial formulation, an AR process obviously involves two parties: the *insiders* — the owners of the problem — and the *outsiders*, or professional researchers.

This arrangement shapes at least two distinct and different roles. The outsider has responsibility for supporting the continuation of the research process itself. He or she brings to the arena substantive skills as well as skills in keeping change processes going. The insiders own the problem and thus are the focus of

Table 2.1. The Co-generative Action Research Model

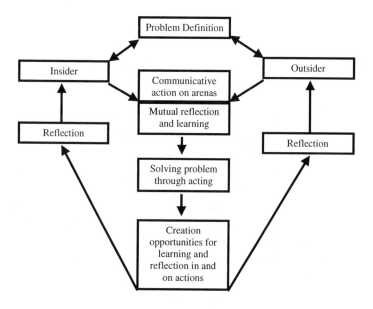

the action research process. (The figure illustrates the fundamental elements in the research process.)

It is useful to think of an action research process as consisting of at least two analytically distinct phases. The goal of the first phase is clarification of the initial research question, while the goal of the second and major stage is the initiation and maintenance of the change or meaning construction process. It is evident that the definition of the problem is never final. A good sign of development is how much the original questions are reshaped to include initially unknown dimensions, indicating that learning has taken place. Clarification of the research question is a crucial element in any action research process, as it sets the stage for the whole research activity. The question to be researched must be of major importance to the participants, and it must also gain leverage from the body of knowledge in the field (Greenwood 1989).

Even when the problem focus has been worked out, communication procedures must be established — to help in working through situations in which the insiders' knowledge and the outsiders' professional knowledge are in conflict. A working definition of the problem must come out of a discourse in which the knowledge held by the insiders and the outsiders co-generates an understanding that is created only through their communicative actions. The main challenge in the first stage is to search for the first good question that is shared to some degree by the involved parties.

Several obstacles can occur during the problem formulation process. The conventional traits of academics as capable debaters with strong conceptual models can easily create an oppressive situation. Bråthen (1973) calls this a "model monopoly," which he identifies as a situation in which one party dominates and, because of that party's skills in communication and in the handling of conceptual models, thereby constantly increasing the distance between insiders and outsiders.

The other trap that can occur in stating the initial problem is that the insiders and the outsiders can get locked into accepting the insiders' initial formulation of the problem, so that there is little use of outside knowledge. On the one hand, this situation is not detrimental to the action research *process*; it is certainly possible to start a project based on an initial, possibly limited problem statement and then to design a process whereby important reflections emerge through the communication and practical problem-solving activities of the project. Many AR projects have shown that this can be a successful approach. On the other hand, there are few positive outcomes when the researcher dominates the situation.

The insiders and the outsiders are equals, and they are different. They are obviously different because the insiders have to live with the result of any change activity, while the outsiders can leave the location at almost any point. In the co-generative model, another difference is that the insiders will have the final say in figuring out what the focus of the research activity should be, although the insiders and the outsiders are considered equal in personal and professional integrity and in the right to be heard. Listening and learning are important, for there is no way that a mutual learning process can take place if other people's arguments are not understood.

The challenge to integrity is also important. Researchers should not, in any respect, play the game of becoming natives. Researchers will always be outsiders from institutional and professional settings that make demands concerning professional praxis and that advocate ethical standards for behavior. The challenge in this unbalanced situation is to take advantage of the differences, because these differences can create the ground for new and important learning for all the participants.

In essence, an action research process is a collective effort to gain new knowledge. In a social context or in an organizational or local community, the working collectivity is shaped through people's interactions. The way people relate to each other to achieve a desired outcome shapes a theory of action about solving problems through social interaction. If the main purpose of action research is to support the solution of pertinent problems, then the research process itself must be built on the basis of planned social interactions. Accordingly, the main challenge is to shape these social interactions, and shaping them thus becomes the basic tool for facilitating co-generative learning.

As people interact in a specific spatial situation, an *arena* is constituted. An arena can be a meeting between two or more people, a team-building session, a search conference, a task force meeting, a leadership group meeting, or a public community meeting. Thus, a major challenge in an action research project is to design adequate arenas for communication, for discourses between the involved parties in the research is the major vehicle for learning.

Arenas are chosen according to what one wants to achieve. If the strategy is to engage a whole organization in an organizational development process, gathering all the people in a large room to work out the plans for the project might be a good solution — although conflicts between managers are best addressed in a leadership group. The point is that the choice of arenas should be made according to context and purpose. The selection of a proper arena certainly depends on the skills of the facilitator.

Similarly, the *communicative actions* shape the collective learning that is possible (Gustavsen 1992) and enable the members of an organization or people in a local community to understand how they interact, support, or fight each other in the struggle to achieve desired goals. Experiences shaped through communicative actions linked with collective reflection create the foundation for the development of new meanings. The struggle to solve important problems also creates the basis for new understandings to emerge. All outcomes of this collective reflection process support the creation of mutual understanding, shared knowledge that is equally accessible both to the insiders and the outsiders. The larger this shared ground is, the more fruitful the communication has been.

This shared knowledge, in turn, opens up possibilities for reflection for both the insiders and the outsiders. The participants can use this knowledge to increase their action capacity in their local context and to improve their goal attainment. In addition, if new insights emerge, this reflection, in turn, will open up new ways of formulating the research problem and thus change the communicative processes.

In the same way, reflections by the outsiders will create the space for new learning and for a link to be established between the action research process and the scientific community. Publications can be produced, but, unlike much traditional research writing, in our view, AR publications are built on a much more valid base. The essential difference is that in AR, the activity is based on long-term engagement with the field, and the researchers, by "living" the project, acquire personal experiences radically differentiating this research process from single-shot interventions. That *new understanding* emerges from discourses with participants and that it is identified as the *shared understanding* resulting from the AR process are fundamental differences.

In a successful AR project, it is also possible to have communications with the scientific community that are produced jointly by insiders and outsiders. Thus, the conventional dominance of the researcher is reduced, and the participants gain access to the valuable process of reflecting on and writing down the results of the project.

How different are these models of action research?

We have chosen to present ABX and the co-generative model because they played a dominant role in the ACRES program. But how different are they really? They clearly emerge from quite different professional contexts. The ABX model employs the language of social psychology while the co-generative model uses a sociological-anthropological contructivist way of speaking. Both models are similar in terms of building the learning process on the discourse between the empirical object (insiders) and the researcher (the outsider). In the co-generative model, seeking solutions to pertinent problems for the insiders through invoking concrete circumstances is the key to the whole process. This focus is less explicit in the ABX model. The language of the ABX model is also more interpersonal, while the cogenerative model builds on more sociological language about collective learning, arenas, and actions by the insiders.

Both models emphasize the important point of integrating insiders (empirical object) in the knowledge production process. This is constructed as a mutual learning process with to different feedback loops in the co-generative model, while this is not explicitly made clear in the ABX model. In the co-generative model the researcher feedback loop initiates the reflection processes that can result in knowledge and publications for the scientific community, while the ABX model does not emphasize this to the same extent.

An interesting hypothetical question is whether these two models would result in two different projects if they were applied in the same AR problem. Probably they would. However, we think that the differences would not just be a direct consequence of the models themselves. Our experience in ACRES suggests that the professional background and attendant professional languages of the researchers would exercise a major influence on this outcome. We learned, through our experiences in ACRES how powerfully our professional training and languages affect the way we conduct AR.

The action research tradition includes many different approaches; historical developments have led to many fruitful ways of working within the field. Although many different models of AR currently compete for space, most of the modern conceptualizations of AR center on communication processes as the key vehicle for knowledge production. In these paradigms, as illustrated by both the ABX and the co-generative models, the communication that occurs between the researchers and the researched creates the basis for gaining new knowledge and changing social systems. The same kinds of communicative process should be followed in the action research community itself. Open and free discourse between advocates of diverse positions should be encouraged, not limited.

Notes

1. The ABX model presented here is based an edited version of Hans van Beinum's 1993 paper, which was distributed, read, and discussed during ACRES. It is also discussed by van Beinum in Chapter 1 where the citations to where it was subsequently published are found.

2. This position was further developed in Emery and Thorsrud 1976, Emery 1959, and Trist 1953.

3. This entire section is based on van Beinum, 1993. This model of the action research process is based on Elden and Levin 1991 and Levin 1993.

Chapter 3

Research in ACRES

Claude Faucheux

One of the primary aims of ACRES was to assist participants in gaining a deeper understanding of the epistemological and methodological particularities of action research, with the ultimate goal of improving the quality of research and publication in the AR field. Helping participants in this way was especially important given that action research is such a demanding approach for researchers, is misunderstood in many academic circles, and good action research is urgently needed to support contemporary programs of social change.

An Emerging New Epistemology

Action research challenges the classical view of science currently espoused by the social sciences at the very time that physics is abandoning that scientific model. The classical view of science developed since the Renaissance, when Newtonian physics served as a model, and endured until the end of the nineteenth century, when the theory of relativity made some of the assumptions of Newtonian physics obsolete.

Quantum theory went further in causing the abandonment of classical views about science and knowledge as, simultaneously, critical debates arose about the foundations of mathematics and the validity of logical positivism, stimulating further growth in the fields of epistemology and the sociology of knowledge. Without going into too much detail about these debates, it is possible to focus on some aspects that are particularly crucial to understanding the difficulties AR aroused in conservative academic circles.

"Pure" Versus "Applied" Research

Classic science was considered a disinterested effort to know reality without polluting the activity with base, utilitarian interests. Pure knowledge could be extremely useful for practical purposes, of course, but these practical concerns were left to engineers. The bias was to develop knowledge for contemplative purposes. It was also assumed that reality was a stable situation, existing independently of us "out there," imprinting itself similarly on the senses of different observers, who could, if they conducted themselves rationally, agree on the descriptions of the object of their observation.

This absolute separation between subject and object, between observer and observed, which made sense to an astronomer in the sixteenth century, turned out to be less obvious to a social scientist in the twentieth century, particularly after quantum theory had questioned this basic tenet of classical positivism. Studying social reality as if the researcher could be aloof from the reality that he or she observed ultimately appeared to be impossible. As in physics — if not more than in physics — the observer had to be understood to be part of the process of observation. I say more than in physics because in social science we aim, as part of the enterprise, to study ourselves as observers. Social scientists are, in part, their own objects.

From this beginning, there emerged the sense that the "human being" was best studied not from an *external* vantage point but by using our capacity to access our inner experiences and make sense of them. This meant that researchers had to enlist themselves as co-researchers if they were to develop a genuine knowledge of themselves. It also meant that they had to study themselves in the act, in the very process of acting, because when we are transplanted to the laboratory, extracted from the situation in which our actions make sense, we become another kind of being. While human physiology can be investigated in the artificial, highly controlled environment of the laboratory, this is not so for the more symbolic actions that form human conduct.

Another reason reinforced this epistemological shift. As skilled, competent, effective actors, researchers put into practice knowledge that, for the most part, is tacit and cannot be made explicit without the active, conscious collaboration of others who also possess this tacit knowledge and use it as a particular mode of relating to their own environments. Hence, fundamental knowledge in the social sciences becomes knowledge used in action, reflectively known as a *knowledge of* action. This knowledge has to be studied *in situ*, in the very context in which it makes sense. It cannot be separated from this context without becoming dead and devoid of meaning.

So it is that we cannot develop a science of the actors along the lines appropriate for studying astronomy. We cannot adopt a purely contemplative attitude when studying ourselves, as we could, up to a point, when describing the orbits of the planets. On the contrary, we have to look at what we are doing and study these actions in their context.

This shift in fundamental epistemic attitude demands that we renounce the split between "pure" and "applied" research.

As Lewin (1948) said, "Nothing is more practical than a good theory." Not only is this new epistemic attitude bound to produce knowledge that is far more effective than positivistic knowledge, but this effective knowledge is also the only kind of "fundamental" knowledge in the social sciences.

A Science of Action

Contemporary critics have noticed that many social scientists claim that the aim of the social sciences is to study social action, while, in practice, they fail to do this. Giddens (1990) has been among the most articulate in voicing this critique, emphasizing that Parsons's *Structure of Social Action* missed the reality of action.

Garfinkel (1967) moved away from Parsons's stance by aiming to study our own social reality, as if we were from a different tribe, making the effort, as a researcher, to reach into the experience of the "natives" as ethnographers purport to do. Garfinkel aspired to develop an ethnomethodology for accessing the experience of the "natives" and demanded that the sociological researcher penetrate their phenomenology well enough to "pass" as one of them. This ability to "pass" is Garfinkel's touchstone for ascertaining the validity of the researcher's phenomenology of the native experience. In this way, ethnomethodology provided social scientists with a method for achieving a greater proximity to human experience.

Garfinkel refused to take a further step, however, and join the natives in their actions. That is, he refused to intervene actively with them in their own social reality, contending that pure science should not be involved in remedial actions. The sociologist, he argued, is there to provide us with an understanding of the reality of social actors; she or he is not there to fool around with it.

By contrast, proponents of action research believe that an understanding of social reality is achieved only while directly intervening effectively in it. Further, according to AR, understanding the tacit knowledge of local actors means understanding how they intervene in their own realities and transform them.

A Knowledge of Acting

The social sciences are moving toward a science of action, of acting. As such, they cannot be limited to purely descriptive science, and social scientists cannot evade the necessity of becoming more aware of and better able to state their aims, aspirations, and values for designing a social reality, as well as more aware of what they are actually doing in their practices, so as, in the end, to be better able to evaluate their actions and improve their effectiveness. They cannot evade their responsibility as actors. Action research is therefore a necessary dimension of their lives.

Operations and Representations

Logical positivism argued that science should be essentially about describing effective operations that can be described in univocal terms, understood in exactly the same way by all adequately trained scientists, irrespective of the context. In this, they were arguing that a description could be context-free.

Wittgenstein, who wrote the first bible of the neopositivists, later demonstrated that neopositivism was unfeasible. In a second phase of his work, he argued that no artificial language, such as symbolic logic, could be context-free and that, consequently, it was more sensible to study natural languages and natural speech to find out how the management of meaning in interpersonal communications is indeed achieved.

At the same time, Wittgenstein was implicitly criticizing "operationalism," which claimed that positive science was only about operations, objectively describable and repeatable. But clearly perceiving an operation — and describing it — entails more than logical correctness. It also requires being adequately in touch with the context in which the operation is being performed. It requires a certain interpretation of this context. The same operation may have different meanings in different theories and may correspond to different representations.

Operations have to be seen in their proper context as responses to a situation. Their instrumental side should not mask the conduct they serve, which gives them their meaning. Knowledge, therefore, is less a reflection of an external reality "out there," independent of us, than a reflection of what we can do with it, in our actions, to transform natural reality and to create cultural reality. Science cannot be separate from a project of cultural development, even if this drive is mostly unconscious. AR is an attempt to develop a better awareness of what we are actually doing, of whom we are trying to become, so as to become more effective at it.

To this extent, we are all involved as actors and as researchers, even if we would prefer to shy away from the responsibilities implied. Ultimately, fundamentally, we have to become responsible for ourselves, for the meaning of our lives and what we do, and therefore we have to participate actively in the debates about what we should be doing and in the construction of our futures. This makes the participative dimension of AR inescapable.

Action Research as Self-Development

Seen in this perspective, action research is more demanding than classic science was. It demands more than an intellectual exercise of rationality, more than a gathering of data, more than empirical generalizations. To become more effective managers of ourselves, we have to become far more critically reflective about ourselves and more conscious of the consequences of our acts.

Certainly, the evaluation of action and the generation of knowledge are both more effective when the actors themselves are involved. This insight was at the root of what was labeled the "training group" (T group) technique and the creation in the United States of the National Training Laboratories (NTL) at the end of the 1950s. Not surprisingly, a parallel insight was developed in England by a group of social scientists with a psychoanalytic background who later formed the Tavistock Institute of Human Relations.

During this period, it was realized that an actor learns, creates, and acts when he or she can participate responsibly in the action instead of being ruled entirely by a father, a master, or a manager. A developmental dialogue between authoritative figure and the evolving actor is necessary for the development of effective, responsible actors and for the generation of the knowledge we need to develop ourselves at group and societal levels. Thus, the effective practice of action research demands a higher level of personal development than is usual in ordinary organizational activities.

Doing Research

In any research process, we distinguish between three different activities — observation, conceptualization, and experimentation — requiring three different attitudes and involving three different methodologies. To different degrees, these activities also develop during the various stages of maturation of a discipline.

Observation

The observation phase is the very early phase in the development of a research process, when the researcher opens herself or himself to the phenomena being studied and becomes attentive to what is being experienced. The attention involved may be very broad and relatively unfocused. The observer tries to tune in to a context or a milieu, as would a nature lover strolling in a forest.

To become effective, such multidirectional attention has to become more focused, as, for instance, occurs when a bird watcher in a forest notices the general characteristics of different birds — their songs, their movements, and so forth. A zoologist will be even more specific, watching, for instance, particular behaviors, such as territorial struggles or mating actions, of particular species, looking for details not yet reported in professional journals and books.

During the early stages of research, which are essentially observational and descriptive, the instruments employed, above all, aid our senses: optical devices to magnify our sight and recording devices to enhance our hearing. These tools, when used skillfully, do not interfere much with what is being observed. It is left unspoiled.

Conceptualization

Accumulating observations requires making sense of them, organizing them, interpreting them into a story that integrates all the information meaningfully. This leads beyond the observable to what is behind it, which must be inferred by an act of conceptual imagination. Thus, concepts are created and intellectual elaborations for organizing the information are obtained. Sometimes they are mere taxonomies, tables, categories, as in the case of the early naturalists. Or, if the researchers are more insightful, as D. Mendeleyev was, they can order the physical elements into a table according to their chemical properties.

Observation is a powerful research tool. The observation of the stars and planets in the sky went on for a considerable time before astronomy developed into a scientific discipline able to provide explanations for those observations. These scientific explanations eventually transformed the meaning of the observations into a revolutionary theory that saw the apparent movement of the sun around the earth as an egocentric perception by earthly observers. Astronomy developed a "deeper" interpretation and formulated a theory that the earth not only revolves on its own axis in a day but orbits once around the sun in a year. This created the possibility of gaining a fuller understanding of the phenomena of seasonal variations, among other matters. This is a dramatic illustration of how far theoretical insights can go by mere unobtrusive observation, without intervening in the course of natural events.

Experimentation

As information is accumulated and conceptualization developed to organize it, the research process probes further and further into the phenomena and begins to address more pointed questions, which, to be answered, require more active intervention. No matter how sophisticated the observational instruments are, it is no longer sufficient to record the phenomena passively. It becomes necessary to intervene to see what happens systematically when some variables in the situation are manipulated. The experimental approach is then used, which represents a more complex stage of research.

Returning to the example of astronomy, it is only very recently that some possibilities for experimenting have emerged, as new technologies have enabled us to travel in space, to gain more information through astrophysical observations, to send observational probes into distant regions. These techniques have extended the possibilities of intervening in the astronomical world in order to understand its workings better.

Linking Observation, Conceptualization, and Experimentation

Although observation refrains from interfering with the object of observation, our minds are actively involved while we are observing. Further, our observing mind cannot remain for long a purely passive surface for "sensory data"; the very process of observation already contains quite a bit of interpretation, of sense making, of conceptualization.

Thus, in every attentive observation, there are tacit understandings that need to be made explicit if we are to come to know what we really are doing. As we progress in knowing, we thus invest more and more knowledge in our observations, which logically implies that they become ever more dependent on concepts, theories, instruments, techniques. Hence, conceptualizing and theorizing amount to making explicit the tacit knowledge built into our descriptive analytical efforts and then extracting or abstracting the more essential features. The aim is to account for both similarities and differences among phenomena using as small a set of variables as we can. This is "theorizing."

Theories are valuable because they enable us to separate the deeper structure of reality from more empirical formulations and thereby account for complex phenomena. Theories also enable us to intervene more effectively through our actions, since we have formulated a better understanding of what we are doing.

There is a dynamic cycle between theorizing and observing. On the one hand, we observe only what we can perceive. This is a function of our understanding, which in turn is a function of our theoretical grasp. On the other hand, theory progresses only through increasingly systematic observation and from having to account for more observations, some of which appear to present puzzles, contradictions, and paradoxes.

Experimentation is necessary because observation has to become more systematic and theory has to encompass puzzling, paradoxical observations. The experimental mind set is quite different from the taxonomic mind set. The taxonomic view aims to display a picture, a presentation of all that is known, in systematic form. This can be a voyeuristic device for a lazy mind that wants to contemplate without making much effort.

The experimental mind set cannot be that passive. It must play a more active and dynamic role, since it abstracts the relations between the variables in a dynamic way. The essence of the experimenting mind consists of modifying some variables while leaving the others alone and then observing the effects on those variables held to be dependent on the manipulated ones. Experimenting provides for closer scrutiny of deeper processes hidden from immediate observation. This closer scrutiny can be used for *probing* deeper into phenomena as well as for *proving* some assertions or hypotheses.

Experimenting is a very powerful way of gaining understanding, but it requires the discipline and the researcher to have reached a certain maturity. Some social science disciplines became experimental too early; they did not have the patience the naturalists demonstrated in investing in observation, description, and theoretical efforts. Premature experimentation often results in pedantically belaboring the obvious by testing trivial hypotheses that lack much theoretical meaning. This creates the illusion of participating in exact science through the intemperate use of quantification and curves, seasoned with statistical tests that, in the end, mean nothing.

Experimenting is much less an empirical grounding than an exercise in theoretical agility, a fact the positivists have often failed to understand. Experimenting is a mode of reasoning, of thinking, that helps us better sense the possible relationships between variables.

Different disciplines have different histories leading to their establishment as mature sciences. Astronomy developed earlier than physics. Chemistry came much later, but today chemistry has merged with physics, and physics has also, in a way, absorbed astronomy.

At the other end of the historical scale, the sciences of human realities are comparatively in their infancy. We are not yet truly sure of the very nature of our object. Many positivistic temptations still linger, reducing symbolic realities to physical ones.

Epistemological Self-Awareness

Epistemological self-awareness is a meaningful dimension in the maturity of a scientific discipline. It implies an awareness both of science as a whole and of the nature of other disciplines, as well as an awareness of the discipline's specificity in the context of other disciplines.

Into which context do the social sciences fit? It is possible to study human realities from the vantage point of biology and to seek to understand how we emerged through biological evolution and to examine our significance as a biological organism among other living beings. It is possible also to seek to understand our chemical and mineral nature, though this can only help us in understanding the ecology of our humanness at some point in the history of the universe. This process will help us understand to some extent where we come from, but it will not help us understand what we are becoming as cultural agents who construct our symbolic reality through a diversity of civilizations in the midst of a process of globalization.

Psychoanalysis brought about in the West a modest awareness of ourselves, which was never completely absent from Eastern civilizations. But this awareness was repressed in the West in favor of an overintellectualized and insufficiently self-reflective view of human rationality. This critique has been slow to progress from its beginnings in the Enlightenment. It has not yet been assimilated as a necessary component in the social sciences, which remain dominated by lingering behaviorism, particularly on the Anglo-Saxon side. Continental Europeans have been somewhat more appreciative of the self-reflective dimension, particularly in Germany.

The requirement that science be self-critical has been made particularly salient by developments in quantum physics that emphasize the active role of the observer upon the observed and end the illusion that observer and observed can be separated in any absolute way. This very scientific development brings to the fore the need to know better the knower, the observer, *us*, as an epistemic agent and as a cultural agent who continuously elaborates social reality.

The observation stage of social research has to deepen into self-observation, which entails a concurrent effort at self-conceptualization, before we can experiment sensibly with ourselves. The early naturalistic attitude cannot apply any longer. We have to develop a new posture toward the observation of reality by adopting an attitude of self-awareness and self-observation. This process cannot stop at the mere observation of the "data," of the "givens." It must extend to the consideration of the *possible*, contrasting what could have been done (but was not) with what was done and why.

The implicit ethical dimension of the "ought" is necessarily involved here. Deciding what ought to be done is an empirical issue, since it is a practical issue; it is also a theoretical issue, since it deals with a theory of human realities, or rather with alternative possible theories of what humans should be and do. We must reflect upon this before experimenting in human situations through action research.

If the Copernico-Galilean views shook Renaissance sensibility, we should not be surprised that some current developments in social scientific reflection will severely shake some of our most cherished assumptions and ideas about ourselves. After all, the development of the theory of relativity was seen as a revolution and the development of quantum theory as a further revolution. Yet Einstein experienced the latter as unacceptable because it did not accord with his sense of the world. So, when it comes to our core beliefs, we also should expect some nervousness.

Action researchers must decide for themselves what kind of science they are developing. Scientists in other disciplines cannot and should not do this for them. Action researchers in the social sciences need, of course, to have dialogue with other disciplines about their interdisciplinary interdependencies and about the changing significance of practicing science, but action researchers still must attend to their own scientific agendas.

Science has upset theological dogmas and established clergies and touched the whole of laity in proposing new world views conflicting with clerical ones.

Yet, apart from a few convulsive crises, as occurred as a result of the writings of Galileo, Darwin, or Freud, the general public has been concerned with science only from a distance. With action research, however, science enters into a new relation with the public, since every human being is able to become a responsible actor in some action research projects in almost every sphere of human activity. This is not only an issue for the whole of education but for our economic and political systems as well.

Action research is at the heart of the process of democratization, at the heart of the management of our own affairs. In this tradition, the sociotechnical approach has already emphasized that there are no such things as technological imperatives. We are growing increasingly aware that we have to exert responsible choices in organizing ourselves and to make defensible choices among technologies, in part by developing more humane ones. This implies a shift from a scientism without humanism to a science managed by responsible human beings researching together whom and what they will choose to become.

The passivity of Enlightenment humanism has to be transcended. It is our task to define and experiment more actively with feasible and desirable new concepts of humanism. We need a knowledge of ourselves and of what we do that we can use to manage ourselves more sensibly and to do what is most needed to transform our situations in wiser, more democratic directions. We need a science suitable for this purpose, and action research is a necessary dimension of that science.

Toward a Science of Action

It seems that the science we need is a science of action, directed toward the purposeful, deliberate transformation of ourselves, our circumstances, and our predicaments. Such a science requires not only a major epistemological revolution but a cultural, social revolution in the way we think and manage society.

Some germs of such an evolution can be observed already. Organizations of all kinds and states of all sizes are becoming more aware that the participation of all is required not solely because of democratic aspirations but for sheer practical effectiveness in an increasingly complex world.

Fortunately, it is not necessary to elaborate here on the methods specific to AR, since an excellent book has appeared on this topic: *Doing Naturalistic Inquiry: A Guide to Methods* by Erlandson and others (1993). It springs from two earlier books that, like Erlandson *et al.*'s, originated in the field of education — Lincoln and Guba's *Naturalistic Inquiry* (1985) and Guba and Lincoln's *Fourth Generation Evaluation* (1989) — both rooted in an earlier publication by Guba (1978). What follows is a brief look at the approaches behind these methods.

Naturalistic Approach

The word *naturalistic* is welcome here because it points to a patient observation of whole phenomena beyond superficial appearances, a penetrating way of understanding reality comprehensively and distinguishing the essential from the secondary. This attitude has been superseded in science by a more manipulative attitude exemplified by Galileo's experimental approach, codified by Francis Bacon, in which research is no longer a loving experience but a ruthless subjection of "Nature" to the inquisitorial rack of experimentation for the purposes of delivering the secrets of effective manipulation, the secrets of control.

The key issue at stake in naturalistic inquiry is being able to generalize the findings: can I extend what I have learned in a particular case to other cases? The approach is still valid in several established scientific disciplines, such as biology and anthropology, but it is much less appreciated in those disciplines aiming at superior scientific status attached to experimental approach and formal theories.

The naturalistic approach is also called constructivist, because it emphasizes the fact that the human condition is a human construction more than a mirroring or a picturing of nature. The naturalistic-constructivist approach recognizes actors' responsibility for transforming their universe and themselves in the direction of greater awareness, greater responsibility, greater emancipation of the human actors, and greater self-management.

The naturalistic-constructivist approach acknowledges its political nature above and beyond its technological dimensions. It requires, as Guba and Lincoln have clearly seen (1989), that there be a dimension of research built on continuous action, continuous reflection on what we are doing and whom we are becoming. During this process the actors become more aware of themselves as responsible authors of what they do, knowing that their action needs continuous correction, in the light of the continuous discrepancy between intended and actual outcomes.

Psychodynamic Approach

The naturalistic approach points to a need for collaborative work in which all actors can be responsible. The realization that this was necessary emerged contemporary with the realization of the need for action research. Shortly before his death, during a two-week workshop with educators, Lewin discovered serendipitously that the participation of the learners in the reflections of teachers on their teaching process was beneficial to the understanding of the deeper processes at work and consequently instrumental in the improvement of the teaching-learning process. This led in the United States to the development of "sensitivity training," the T group technique, and the NTL (Marrow 1969: 210–14).

This development paralleled an independent and even earlier British effort that used an approach to group dynamics inspired by psychoanalytic thought to select officers during World War II. These activities eventually led to the "Leicester Conference" in 1957.

These efforts, on both sides of the Atlantic, aimed to develop sensitivity to the deeper psychodynamic processes taking place in groups. A similar dynamic is at work in the search conferences action researchers use, in which all concerned stakeholders participate actively and responsibly in a project aimed at self-transformation. To become truly effective at managing these processes requires significant sensitivity to the psychodynamics of groups, indeed, a higher level of skills in interpersonal relations and group dynamics than is usually found among social scientists today.

Evolutive Approach

Traditional positivist research seeks to structure as much as possible *a priori* and is fond of grids and categories. By contrast, the evolutive naturalistic approach begins by defining only the broad scope, the main direction of the inquiry. Initial findings are interpreted to help define further what needs to be done next, letting the material suggest the dimensions that will be most meaningful in its analysis. Since early research findings "feed back" into the design of the next steps, they actually "feed forward." Content analysis becomes a recurrent, ongoing, self-defining process.

As deeper understanding emerges, the earlier tentative categories are refined, and the whole data array is looked at again in a new perspective. Several such cycles might be necessary, obviously a time-consuming process and one demanding analytical skills ordinary research assistants may not have.

Ljungberg van Beinum has used this approach very successfully, enlisting the collaboration of participants in her research as well as in testing and assessing the meaningfulness of her categories (see chap. 11). Such an approach was also used by Moscovici in the 1960s in his pioneering study of social representations. Goethe took this approach — the antithesis of the positivistic Newtonian method — in his study of plants (Bortoft 1986), rejecting the superficial, easier taxonomic approach preferred by most botanists.

Contrary to positivists' claims, theoretical knowledge is not cumulative: new theories become incommensurable with previous ones. Operational knowledge, know-how, remains valid, although it may, in the process, become purified of irrelevant, ineffective components, but meaning cannot be decontextualized so as to be treated mechanically. Research on meaningful behavior requires more dialogic communication with the researched than the Baconian method allows. It demands a different attitude toward reality, toward nature, toward other beings, because deep understanding does not come with rape but with dialogue and thus is essentially evolutive.

Research as the Breathing of the Mind

Research is a characteristic feature of the mind, a creative dimension of our symbolic reality that has been systematized in the history of civilization but has been there since the beginning of human development. An organic metaphor is better here than a mechanical one, because what is at stake in research is a particular quality of interaction with the environment that is a symbolic interaction, not a mechanistic one.

The basic significance of research in human life makes it close to the organic cycle or pulsation of breathing, essential for life. In research, there is a taking-in/moving-out dialogue with the environment that is akin to a symbolic metabolism.

We can distinguish three basic steps in research: search, reflection, and reconstruction or re-creation. During the search stage, the mind is oriented toward the environment, vigilantly trying to perceive or "apperceive" some new aspects of reality, while another stream of the mind keeps in touch with what is known, maintaining this knowledge as flexibly as possible. This is a state of double mind — on the one hand, minding what is there that is worth observing more carefully and, on the other hand, remembering what we know already, while keeping it subject to review in the light of possible new experience.

The process of reflection enables us to ponder upon whatever it is we are perceiving in an effort to grasp its real significance and the various ways in which it can be interpreted and understood. Finally, we reconstruct existing knowledge by integrating the new discoveries, which, more or less, affect our prior knowledge, sometimes confirming expectations but sooner or later requiring deep changes in our views and ways. Whether done by bushmen in the Kalahari Desert or by theoreticians in universities, these steps are always followed in the minds of inquiring people when they are not frozen by conventional thinking into operating mechanically.

Key Dimensions of Action Research

To understand the specificity of action research, it is necessary to disentangle its key dimensions. Although these dimensions are interdependent, they need to be distinguished conceptually.

The *autopoetic dimension* is the self-organizing or spontaneous creative aspect of oneself that the self — the organism or the organization — manifests, in contradistinction to physical mechanisms. The autopoetic dimension has garnered the attention of chemists such as Prigogine, biologists such as Maturana, general system theorists such von Foerster, Varela, Luhman, Zeleny, and Mingers; sociologists such as Touraine and Hegedus; and logicians such as Kampis.

The *reflective dimension* is a state of increased self-awareness, as a result of a process of recurrent feedback. This awareness is of what one is doing that is more or less explicit, more or less conscious of itself, aware of its awareness. This awareness is a secondary phenomenon derived from the autopoetic dimension.

The *self-designing dimension* pushes the research process into the future by deliberate action toward self-transformation as a result of having a plan in mind, or at least a conscious intention that is more than just a blueprint. The self-designing dimension is at the core of Ricoeur's reflections (1990).

Research as a component of action requires that an investment be made in exploring reality in search of *better* knowledge and *deeper* understanding. Research as a component of action is the facet most often looked at by actors who undertake research merely to serve the needs of practical everyday action.

Action as a mode of research is the phase in which action is taken as an object of research in a search for a deeper understanding of oneself as an actor.

As a cultural innovation that contributes to the emancipation of social actors, action research can be compared on these grounds with the cultural innovation brought about by psychoanalysis in seeking out the motivation, the autonomy, of the personal psyche. Of particular note in this regard is a very unusual AR project being conducted at the Scottish Institute of Human Relations in which this institution composed of psychoanalysts working on societal issues has undertaken a review of itself (see Raffaelli and Harrow 1995b).

Action Research as an Active Minority Movement

As with so many social movements that took time to gain broad appeal, action research cannot expect at this early stage in its development to be recognized for the sheer strength of its arguments. It will gain recognition first as a result of its practical achievements on the social scene. It will gradually be recognized that the transformation of social reality cannot be achieved with *a priori* planning and a hierarchical ladder but requires an evolutive design resting on participative research with all concerned stakeholders. This is much more than a scientific issue; it is a political one that entails an evolution of the current representations of reality in society as a whole.

Action research, with its new paradigm, will be influential on the social scene to the extent that it articulates explicitly what it does. Increasing the *effectiveness* of action research should, therefore, be the major concern of practitioners, and a professional community of action researchers should be formed so that thinking and experience can be shared and discussed in a climate supportive of this effort. A forum conducive to creative debates should be designed, along with journals that offer outlets for publication in the field and workshops such as ACRES, aimed at developing specific skills.

Public support will become accessible when the social significance of AR for *social* transformation is visible in national and international political circles. For now, action researchers are too scattered and ignorant of one another for a critical mass to be reached.

Being an innovative movement in the social sciences, action research is bound to remain a minority view for as long as the dominant positivist view of science is not transformed. AR is the strong arm of a paradigmatic transformation of the epistemology and practice of the social sciences and of science as a whole. As such, it cannot feel at ease within the prevalent contemporary institutions (universities and other academic circles, scientific journals, discipline boundaries), which still reflect an obsolete paradigm. At the same time, action researchers must not shy away from confrontations with the majority viewpoint. For these efforts to be successful, however, action research as a field has to be much more aware of itself than has usually been the case among scientific disciplines.

Nor can action research be solely a movement within science. It aims at cultural transformation by seeking more collaborative action between the actors concerned so as to become more conscious, more reflective, more effective, more authentic, true architects of themselves within reality, within life. It aims to pursue the emancipatory goals of the Enlightenment, its democratic ideals and humanistic aspirations, within a renewed vision of science and humanity. Thus, it cannot be a neutral bystander, watching what is happening with detachment. It is bound to be the militant practice of a new way of being and acting. It is bound to be a movement within society seeking to transform our relationships with nature as well as with ourselves.

Science and conscience can no longer be separated. Action research can bring them back together. Hence, action research is as much a transformation of human reality as it is a transformation of science.

Chapter 4

Organizational Processes in ACRES

René van der Vlist

The structure of ACRES — as intended — was basically very strong, and, in fact, was perhaps the only possible one, given the set of objectives we had in mind when we started, especially "to give methodological and theoretical as well as practical support to action researchers in general, but in particular to provide tailor-made learning opportunities for individual researchers." The fact that the outcome of ACRES was modest can only be understood against this background.

This chapter, which provides an overview of the organizational processes of ACRES, is taken from my personal account of what happened, extracted from contemporaneous notes made as the events occurred.* It is always possible, of course, for others to give a different account of the "facts." But by framing these events as "issues" that affected our outcomes, followed by my own reflections, I hope my assessment will help us better understand what happened — and lead to conclusions that may be relevant whenever a program like ACRES might be attempted elsewhere.

Preparatory Period

The original planning group for what was then called the Scandinavian Action Research Development Program (SCARDEP) consisted of Davydd Greenwood, Björn Gustavsen, Morten Levin, Thoralf Qvale, René van der Vlist, and Hans van Beinum. According to a paper drawn up after the first planning session in Stockholm in January 1992, day-to-day responsibility for the "design and organization of the program" lay with a "management committee consisting of Hans van Beinum and Morten Levin. The selection of the combination of institutes, projects, and researchers for participation in the program will be done by means of a process of consultation between candidates and the management committee

---

* This chapter was edited by Davydd Greenwood on February 17, 1995.

and may also involve members of the faculty."

From the planning group, van Beinum, Greenwood, Levin, and van der Vlist would be on the final faculty or "staff," along with Claude Faucheux and Kjell S. Johannessen. To Johannessen, action research was a new term, but it was of major importance that we asked him to join the staff. Although he was not familiar with the AR concept, he is a philosopher (University of Bergen) and an expert on Wittgenstein's later philosophy. To the planners, there was a strong convergence between the epistemology of Wittgenstein and the epistemology on which action research is based — in fact, by inviting Kjell we implicitly agreed that this epistemology was at the very heart of action research.

Design of the Workshops

As eventually developed, the program consisted of four connected workshops of three days each, spread over one academic year: September 9–11 and December 9–11, 1992, and March 10–12 and June 16–18, 1993, two in Sweden and two in Norway. The planners envisioned that each workshop would be composed of four parts. The first part would consist of in-depth analysis of the field projects of the participants, which would constitute the program's learning material; the analyses would focus on the relationship between theory and practice in action research. The second part would focus on theoretical inputs pertinent to the meaning and practice of action research in our present society and emerging from the case analyses. The third part would concentrate on philosophical reflections, especially with respect to the theory of science. Finally, the fourth part would consist of a writer's workshop, in line with our stated objective that "at the end of the program each participant will be able to submit an article to an international journal."

The planners kept redesigning the agenda for the first workshop over and over again. In a way, one could say we tried hard to visualize the workshops in advance. Given the objectives of the program, the costs involved, and the attention the program had drawn in Scandinavia and elsewhere, it had to be successful. This led to an almost ritual process of redesigning the agendas (a ritual we repeated at each workshop). By doing so, however, we risked at least once, but probably more often, estrangement among staff members or subgroups within the staff.

At the first planning conference, in January 1992, we decided that, in addition to having plenary sessions, the participants would be broken into six smaller work groups, each led by a staff member. The hope was that the groups would be as heterogeneous as possible in terms of experience with action research, home country, gender, and familiarity with staff.

Early on, we also concluded that "pairing" participants could be a very important way to keep the program alive between workshops and valuable in the development of projects, as well as in writing progress reports for future workshops. Pairing also fit well with the "societal" objectives of the program, since creating bonds between representatives of institutes of different countries seemed to be vital to the program. This decision would become rather important.

Overall Objectives

The final statement of the program's objectives, as sent to participants before the first workshop, is detailed in chapter 1 of this book. Of those six objectives — seven when "writing" is included — objectives 4, 5, and 6 were more or less forgotten in the planning discussions as early as January 1992 but certainly by the second planning meeting in April.

As we focused on the content of the workshops to come, our general objectives were drawn from a memorandum of "Questions and Issues" and a general "Outline," both written by Hans van Beinum after discussions with Björn Gustavsen and Morten Levin.

As explained in the memorandum, it was important that "above all we should realize that SCARDEP by definition will have itself the characteristics of an action research project. It is concerned with the learning about and the development of interfaces." By this, it was meant that SCARDEP would foster societal developments by linking researchers' projects and institutes and in itself could be a "transitional space" as well as contribute to the generation of such transitional spaces at the macro level.

This objective was hardly discussed during the program. Instead, the idea developed that learning that took place within the program should be dealt with as if it were a participative action research project. As later events showed, this view influenced developments from the beginning right to the end.

Increasingly, the only concrete goal became writing. At the first preparatory meeting, the staff had a lengthy discussion on the writers workshop, based on a note prepared by Davydd Greenwood. This "Preliminary Plan for Scandinavian Action Research Group: Action Research Writing Project" stated that action researchers did not publish enough and "varieties of solutions" were needed and ended with "specific proposals in the context of SCARDEP." It was already becoming clear from our preparatory discussion that writing would play a major role in the program and seemed to be the second way in which the staff came to see the program itself as an action research project.

At the second preparatory meeting, in April 1992, in Amsterdam, Davydd presented a revised version of his plan that included structuring the three days of each workshop to put more emphasis on writing, by means of specific writing exercises during the workshops and assignments to be completed between workshops.

Davydd recommended several books on writing, which were later sent to all participants, including Coles's *The Call of Stories* (1989) and Lauer et al.'s *Four Worlds of Writing* (1991), along with examples of good AR writing he selected;

these books never played a notable role in any of the workshops, however. Given these efforts, it is disappointing that at the end of the final workshop, it was estimated that only ten or so participants had succeeded in writing an article suitable for submission to an international journal.

The SCARDEP program was, of course, eventually called ACRES, short for action research, but as an acronym also reminiscent of the French word *accres*, meaning "increase" or "growth." As such, it nicely summarized the objectives we had set.

Participants

Thirty participants gathered for the first ACRES workshop in Trondheim: ten from Sweden, eleven from Norway, three from the United Kingdom, and two each from the United States, the Netherlands, and Finland. Their ages ranged, rather evenly, from twenty-seven to fifty-seven.

A number of participants were well acquainted with one another from previous conferences or from working together, and we generally satisfied our goals for heterogenity. Included in the group were Ph.D. students as well as full professors; academic backgrounds ranged from a B.A. in education to a Ph.D. in cultural anthropology, from a degree in civil engineering to an M.A. in business administration to training in psychoanalysis. Employment status varied from consultant or researcher to director of a service institution or research organization. A few participants had abundant experience in action research. Writing experience ranged from none at all to some experience in a native (non-English) language to authorship of books and articles in English. Quite a few participants had acquired some writing experience through preparing their project reports.

Criteria for Participation

Though we had planned to send out application forms by the end of February, they actually went out in April. The document stated that except for travel expenses, all costs of the four seminars would be covered by the program and that participants had to commit themselves to the full schedule of four workshops.

The document also stated that candidates should have at least two years of experience with action research and that they were *required* to bring their actual field projects to the program. The written applications, due before May 1, were to include a short *curriculum vita*, a statement explaining why it was important to participate, a three- to five-page description of the project to be discussed, and information about the primary tasks and mission of the person's home institute.

How Participants Were Chosen

In fact, the program was not open to everyone who might have been interested. Hans van Beinum and Morten Levin contacted institutes and stimulated researchers to apply. Given my Dutch context, I was very much in favor of sending application invitations to a fairly large number of Dutch institutes, both to publicize the program and to foster a wide selection process. This never happened; the application process was almost completely a closed system in which Hans and Morten had a large say.

Quite a number of participants were accepted only because the rules were changed, so to speak — and many never even wrote an application letter. In the end, because of this "closed system" for applying, almost a quarter of the participants did not bring an ongoing AR project to the workshops and, based on the original criteria, about half would not have qualified.

Of the projects brought to the workshops, at least eight were already finished. (In these cases, the workshops could be seen as an aid in writing about the results.) And, ultimately, a few others could not even be viewed as action research projects but were pure consultancy or classical research projects.

Many projects focused on the improvement of work organizations, and six dealt with change and/or improvement in educational institutions. Two projects dealt with development aid in Zambia and the Philippines. Others were focused on improving the organization the participants came from. To illustrate some of the difficulties emanating from the selection process and qualifications of the participants, I would like to detail the events of my first two small-group sessions on the first day of the first workshop.

My group of six spent the first meeting getting acquainted with each other and with each other's projects. Each person gave a verbal summary of his/her project, followed by questions and discussion. This laid the groundwork for real work.

In the afternoon, I suggested that we again talk about the six projects, this time from the point of view of the question "In what way is this project an action research project, or, if it is not, in what way could this project benefit from becoming an AR project and how could this be done?" This question could open up discussion on action research itself, as well as on the introductory lecture on the ABX model given by Hans van Beinum at the morning's plenary session.

The discussion proved to be difficult. In one case, the participant was working on a consultancy project that originated from an institute that actually did not want its projects to be research projects at all. Another was a traditional applied research project, brought by a participant who was not familiar with action research and found it very difficult to see how AR could improve his work. Yet another participant had not yet begun his project. In his application letter, he had written that when he was chosen to be the department chair, "This opened up the rare opportunity of developing a social science and action research-oriented profile at a traditional computer science department." His concern then was "how to develop as an active node in an interdisciplinary action research network." Indeed, an ambitious project plan.

The fourth case was a development aid project in Zambia. It could become an action research project. The other two projects were clearly AR projects, one involved with the redesign of education in a city school in New York State, the other having to do with the evaluation of a consultancy program for small manufacturing companies with fewer than twenty employees.

Thus, only half the projects fulfilled the application requirements. Experience with research was modest, experience with action research even more limited. This situation was more or less the same in the other groups, too.

Criticisms from the Participants

At the end of the first workshop, each small group presented a general evaluation of the ACRES structure. From notes taken by Davydd Greenwood, the criticisms that were voiced included the following:

- The time was too segmented, the sessions too many and too short.
- There was not enough time for reflection. They were interested in a secondary structure (added to what we already had). Some wanted the small groups formed around important issues, such as power, conflicts, and leadership, with the themes chosen in advance, discussed in these small groups, and then taken up in the plenaries.
- Some wanted staff members to rotate among the small groups.
- The plenary sessions were characterized as "poor process and poor design" and suggestions made that participants become active presenters in the plenaries and that the staff have a plenary debate on a paper Hans van Beinum had written on the ABX model.

Other problems — often major issues — shall be considered in more depth.

"Pairing" Process

Our plan was that participants would form pairs on the second day of the first workshop, enabling each participant to work together with one other participant, both during and between workshops. The staff — and especially Hans, Claude, and I — felt that participants would thus learn to help and support each other in the difficult task of writing. Discussions in pairs could also lead to suggestions for themes to be discussed in plenary sessions. The plan was announced at a plenary session the first evening.

At our staff meeting after dinner, to which each small group sent a representative, it was quite apparent that the idea of pairing was rather anxiety-provoking, probably because the process could lead to a situation in which some participants might feel like second choice or, worse, no one's choice at all. Morten and Davydd exacerbated the situation by comparing the forming of pairs to choosing a marriage partner. I emphasized the importance of forming pairs not against the background of a marriage as a metaphor but with the goal of creating a promising learning situation. I emphasized that it was irrelevant whom one worked with, that the concept was that each participant would have *one person* as a "first outsider" with whom to discuss activities and writings and who would serve as an aid in opening up closed minds and making others aware of taken-for-granted presumptions. The pairing also could be the first step toward the creation of an active network of action researchers and cooperation between institutes. I won the argument, but it proved to be a Pyrrhic victory. The pairs never worked as I meant them to.

The way in which the pairs were to be formed was not discussed at length, and when each group was subdivided the next day, the process could best be compared with casting dice. Further, because the issue had caused emotional difficulties, the groups did not really discuss why the forming of pairs was felt to be important. I think this was a serious mistake indeed.

ACRES as an Action Research Project

The participants expressed complete incredulity at the thought that ACRES was an action research project itself. They also complained that they were not previously informed of this intention and thus raised questions about the kind of contract between us. Some demanded to take part in the design of the program.

It was evident from the participants' critiques at the end of the first workshop that they saw the plenary sessions as defective as learning opportunities and that they were troubled about the role of the staff in this respect. The participants, of course, sensed that there were certainly differences among the staff with respect to the concept of action research, and this also influenced their feelings on this subject.

Emphasis on Writing

As should be obvious, the staff had become committed to the objective that participants would complete ACRES with a publishable article. On opening day, Davydd Greenwood lectured on "writing as a skill in action research" and on the "rhetoric of writing," and in that evening's staff meeting, we decided to have an early start the next morning to allow more personal writing time. At a later meeting, we agreed that participants would rewrite their project descriptions as the first draft of an article and have their partners give feedback before sending the draft to Morten Levin prior to the second workshop.

The second workshop proved to have an embarrassing start. To our surprise and disappointment, only seven people had sent in a rewritten paper. We thoroughly discussed this unexpected result. In my notes, Davydd's reaction was the most clear. Although angry, he noted that seven did write and asked, "Why did that group succeed where the others did not?"

Claude said, "We are responsible for confronting the participants with this state of affairs."

Hans said, "If you have difficulties in writing, you may have difficulties in doing research." Thinking about my own small group, I wondered whether it could be a language problem.

We concluded that this "nonwriting" by the majority of the participants forced us to redesign the program so the "writers group" would not suffer from the laxity of the others. Presumably there would be a group of "late deliverers," so we thought we would have to make a design that would enable this group to catch up with the writers. The nonwriters were the real problem, and we decided that this group should use as much time as needed to produce a rewritten paper.

We redesigned the agenda three times. The "final" schedule called for the problem and its proposed solution to be presented in a plenary session, followed by small-group discussions without the staff, to enable the participants to discuss the possibility that the staff had contributed to the problem. We then would have a plenary session "to finalize the design," which called for separate schedules for the "writers/late deliverers" and for the "nonwriters."

The first two groups would have topic presentations on day three, and the nonwriters would have an optional program for the plenaries on the second day. ("Optional: if time needed to write, write!"). This group's third day was also to start with individual meetings with van Beinum and Levin to discuss "future involvement in ACRES workshops," a rather frightening formulation. The schedule ended with a "writing assignment for all participants" specifying that "a paper of 20 pages in 12 point Courier type, double-spaced" had to be sent to Morten Levin by Monday, February 1, 1993. "This is an absolute requirement for continued participation in the ACRES program," the document stated, adding that the paper should define the problem; show the impact of the action taken; analyze the role of the action researcher, including the assumptions used; show the research dimensions of the project--beyond data construction--and discuss matters of general value that could be learned from the project.

When I explained the situation and planned schedule to my small group, I noted the following comments:

- "In January I am going to do interviews. At this stage there is no reason to do any writing."
- "The interval between workshops was too short."
- "A paper, is that what it is about? For me, it was the group of participants. How to develop AR skills."

- "Writing was not my main objective."
- "For me, writing was a means to know — not an end in itself."
- "The prime objective was networking."

The climate had grown quite aggressive by the time I left my group as planned.

The plenary session that followed, planned "to finalize the design," was, in fact, used to blow off steam. Participants made it clear that writing was not their prime objective. Some documented this with the original invitation to the workshops, written by van Beinum and Levin, in which five objectives of the program were mentioned, writing being a secondary goal. One group collectively declared itself a nonwriters group.

Summarizing the main undertone of the reactions, the proposed schedule was now called — I think Morten said it first — "the fascist model of writing." It was not accepted. The groups did not want to split according to "writers," "late deliverers," and "nonwriters," expressing a feeling that might be summarized as "We are here to learn about action research. This may or may not include writing." We decided to redesign the schedule.

The new schedule included reading time to catch up with developments in the various projects (a number of participants had brought rewritten papers and other material with them); discussion of redrafted papers in small groups; a presentation by Kjell Johannessen on concept formation, as well as presentations by Morten Levin and me on our views of action research.

To summarize: this second workshop was a lively event. It could be seen as a successful workshop, but it also made clear that the one concrete objective — "to write a submittable paper" — would be out of reach for the majority of the participants.

Disappointed that only a few participants had submitted papers in advance, the staff overreacted and designed a schedule that was seen as punishing the "late deliverers" and "nonwriters." This impression was not wrong, as can be seen from the pronouncement that the nonwriters would have to meet individually with van Beinum and Levin to discuss "future involvement in ACRES workshops" and that fulfilling their "writing assignments" was "an absolute requirement for continued participation."

The ensuing discussion led to redesigning the schedule and resulted in a less rigid contract with the participants. I personally think that the function of this discussion was to create an escape route for the nonwriters.

On December 14, Hans van Beinum wrote a letter to the staff, which I read as a peace-making letter. In his "remarks and observations about ACRES," he said, in part:

> Generally speaking, the second workshop was a good event. The problematic start, due to the fact that we as staff expressed our concern in an unfortunate manner, triggered off a good process of clarification, involvement and correction.

> We all learned a lot. The participants were very much engaged during the workshop; they worked hard and although there are still many problems with writing and understanding research, they came with some good "products." The workshop also ended on a promising level of commitment. The atmosphere has become more relaxed and relationships are more open. ... However, having said this, we should also recognize that the increased transparency has made other aspects of the process more pronounced and visible, among which issues such as the heterogeneity of the participants and questions of power and control are, I think, the most dominant ones at this stage.

Van Beinum once more summarized the objectives of ACRES but spoke of writing as a secondary objective, as "an important learning process, as well as a critical research tool." Referring to our original statement about producing publishable articles, he said: "This sentence, in which the emphasis should be on "intention," must of course be read as an expression of an ideal which will be pursued, but which may or may not be achieved, at least not by everybody... Participants who are unable to conclude ACRES with an article have not failed and should not be seen as having failed."

I must admit that looking at writing as only a secondary objective can be documented by the invitation letters and that this was probably the best way to deal with the poor performance of so many participants. But it was certainly contrary to the psychological contract made during the first workshop — and, consequently, one may wonder about the meaning of such a psychological contract.

Six participants did not attend the third workshop; five had not written anything. Of the remaining twenty-four participants, nineteen had written something. Altogether, at least twenty participants were supposedly still planning to write something that might be publishable. My impression then was that the majority of the participants were now convinced that writing was a serious objective of the program. The disappointment the staff expressed so openly during the second workshop may have had its effect after all.

In line with the wishes expressed by the participants during the second workshop, our schedule called for plenary sessions on two participants' papers and for staff members to comment in detail on other papers in small groups.

The first participant's paper presented at a plenary session was entitled "The Scandinavian Model — An Achilles Heel for Development of Participative Organizations?" by Karin Aslaksen, who was aided by Morten Levin in preparing her presentation. The case concerned an organizational development project in a Norwegian metallurgical plant called Elkem Fiskaa Werk. The focus of the project was twofold: (1) to develop a participative work organization and enhance the capacity for further organizational change, both to increase productivity and to improve the quality of the work life; and (2) to diffuse results from this plant to the trade union and to the employer's national confederation.

The concept of democratization in this project (part of a larger program) was related not so much to ownership patterns, board composition, or any other form of formal democracy but to participation in decisions with respect to everyday conditions on the work floor. During the 1970s and 1980s, representative participation in Norwegian work life had developed in the direction of having union representatives on the companies' boards of directors, as "the strong leg in the democratic system," according to Aslaksen. A participative work organization would generate another kind of structure in the plant, and a competence-based, horizontally organized structure could become threatening to the traditional vertically organized union system. An interesting aspect of the project was its attempt to find out if the traditional democratic system, often called the Scandinavian Model, would be a hindrance, "an Achilles heel," in developing a participative organization and the necessary management procedures.

Aslaksen worked throughout with a "vertical slice group," which designed a strategy and the methods for the first step. The project formally started with a search conference in June 1990, organized as described in the AR literature (see, for instance, Gustavsen 1985) and attended by seventy participants, half of whom were shop-floor workers.

Through the search conference, both management and the workers realized their differences in their understanding of the problems of the plant and gained insight into new possibilities for worker participation. Twelve task force groups were established to determine areas for improvements and change, and follow-up conferences were arranged every six months for discussions, reflections, and decision making. Eventually, the change process was successful indeed.

In November 1991, Elkem's financial situation deteriorated rapidly. Management decided temporarily to lay off about 40 percent of the workforce to reduce stocks and labor costs, using traditional rules and regulations as a guide. The workers reacted immediately and accused the management of being back "in the old culture" and being unwilling to use a more participative problem-solving strategy when faced with a difficult situation. The rates of departures and of absenteeism increased dramatically.

As a result of Aslaksen's efforts, in the middle of that period, top management, middle management, the head of the union, and a group of workers met to discuss the problem and the feelings of distress. For the first time, all sat together and reflected on their own practices in critical situations. Management's willingness to admit it had been thinking about cost reduction in traditional ways and not in accordance with the intended new culture kept confidence at a level that made it possible to continue the participative development process.

It was a nice case to discuss, and for the first time the audience was highly involved. Claude Faucheux, who chaired the plenary, held a completely different opinion: To him, this was a finished project and a straightforward example of social engineering in which long-known principles and knowledge were applied and did not lead to any new insight. As he was the only one who voiced this diverging opinion, he soon became silent.

I found the second presentation less stimulating, perhaps because discussing two papers intensively is probably too much for one day.

On the last day, I attended Kjell's group. We had a long discussion of one paper, a good session that helped the participant to focus on one question only. Meanwhile, I met with two other participants the night before and then with another on Sunday morning after the workshop's closing. I sensed that participants now moved more freely and felt free to discuss their papers with staff members and other participants. I found this a hopeful development.

In the staff meeting following this third workshop, we had the first lengthy discussion on "life after ACRES" and the possibility that the staff would write a book that would also contain papers written by participants.

By our staff meeting before the fourth workshop, it had become clear that we would have at least sixteen papers and perhaps more. The papers we had received so far were graded from A to D based on their likelihood of being published; grades were assigned primarily based on the judgment of the staff member who had worked with the person's small group.

We were astonished when Claude reported that he had given an A to one paper that had not yet been produced. Claude was so convinced that this person in his group would eventually write a publishable paper that he had put him in the A category. We had to convince him that the only thing we could do at the time was to add a question mark to the participant's name.

In total, it looked as if we would eventually have four to thirteen publishable papers — four if we just counted the As and thirteen if we could get Bs and Cs to publishable levels. So, seven or eight papers would make it, 25 to 30 percent out of a total of thirty participants. Not exactly much, given the investment.

By the fourth workshop, the question of writing or not writing had more or less resolved itself — and, indeed, was overshadowed by concerns about "democratic dialogue" and how to choose the publishable papers and by a particular incident related to one person's writing. This incident is discused in detail below.

In November 1993, nine participants attended a meeting in Holland with the staff to choose papers that might be included in a book, and four who could not attend also submitted papers. (These submitters were appointed a "godfather," who would convey comments back.) Final manuscripts were due to Morten Levin by April 15, 1994, and the staff was to decide whether a paper would be accepted by May 15. Eventually, eight papers, all included in this volume, were accepted.

Complex Incident with Possibly Far-Reaching Effects

Five participants did not show up for the last workshop, which caused one small group to have only three participants. Two of these had interesting "live" projects, and they were, according to this group's staff member, true action research projects.

The third person was engaged in a consultancy project and had not yet been able to convert it into an AR project, at least not in the eyes of his staff member.

During the preceding workshops, relatively little group time had been spent in discussing this consultancy project (or, for that matter, the project of the fourth participant). But time and again — and this is a sad but not unimportant detail — this third participant had proven himself to be in the "writers group," since his revised papers had always been sent around in time. The quality of his writing was perhaps a little bit disappointing, but he nevertheless had shown himself to be an eager learner. In retrospect, one has to wonder if the lack of attention given to this project may have contributed to the poor quality of the writing.

The other two participants, active in interesting projects, were well looked after, though both were nearly always "late deliverers." In fact, during the second workshop, when only one participant had delivered anything and that was late, the staff member said in a note that this late deliverer "qualifies fully for the writers group" and that he intended to work with the other late deliverer "so that he can integrate into the 'writer's stream' as quickly as possible."

His December note continued: "I have now a new categorization of the various papers: those which lack proper relevance as a contribution to Social Science and are not even useful for the local users. ... They need a lot of help, but might distract staff investments from more promising endeavors." The staff member evidently made this clear to the third and fourth participants and spent all his time on the two "late deliverers." To our suprise, when we met after the second workshop to try to estimate which papers could reach a publishable standard, he put the two late or nondeliverers in the "publishable" category. We made it clear that this was nonsense indeed, but we did not discuss his "pedagogical" approach.

The Incident

Then, on the second day of the final workshop, during a small-group session, Y, the participant with the consultancy project, demanded at least some feedback on his writing. And that is what he got. It must have been quite shocking.

In a letter the staff member later wrote to me, he stated:

> Our situation in ACRES was different from that of a Ph.D. program: We were assuming that we were dealing with already experienced researchers and were guardians, as a staff, of a certain integrity, of the process of Science. It turned out that the level was less solid than we expected, especially among the junior participants. Some, like Z [the fourth participant], did not know the difference between "applied" research, or engineering research, and genuine contributions to science. Y was among them in a worse way: He is confusing consulting with research, and worse, his consulting is shallow. Had he not insisted to ask my assessment in order to fight it, not in order to learn from it, it would not have been an incident. His rebellious and counter-dependent strategy forced me to be unequivocal in this context.

In another letter, this staff member is even more precise:

> Y, however, had not progressed much in his understanding of what makes a paper publishable in a scientific journal. He had unrealistic views about the state of his paper, which he felt was considered more favorably by other staff members. He wanted again to check my opinion on this point, and when we sat together, I realized that he also wanted to confront me, arguing that I must hold some grudges against him since, in spite of his considering himself an experienced researcher and skillful process consultant, having been through many Tavistock conferences and other staff members looking favorably at his paper, I persisted to say that not only it is not yet in a publishable state, but unlikely to become so until he has learned to become a researcher. I had to tell him that indeed he had to learn that research is not consulting ... and that I had also to deflate his arrogance on another point by asserting that his process skills were not as high as he was assuming, and if he were aiming at such a level of skill, he would be wise to invest in psychoanalysis.

This last point caused misunderstanding. Y came to me at the time, complaining about his staff member and stating that this staff member had said the person needed a few years of psychotherapy. That sounded odd and harsh, so I asked his staff member what had happened, explaining that I had the impression that he had been rather unfair. Within a few moments, I understood what had happened, but before I had time to have another discussion with the participant, he had already talked to two other staff members and quite a number of other participants, including a few he had gotten to know well during a summer school on action research that preceded this fourth workshop.

The two staff members mentioned were rather annoyed, perhaps furious. Both said that this treatment, as Y had described it, was unacceptable and that they would do their utmost to get his paper into publishable shape — that no one should be allowed to treat his students as this staff member had done.

When that small group (of three) had a final evaluation of ACRES and the small-group process, "We went all over the incident," according to the staff member, "not trying to retrieve the precise words exchanged, but working from what each of us had to say here and now. I repeated my arguments and statements uncompromisingly. A [one of the other participants] said he had felt personally a little embarrassed by my having perhaps idealized his project and pitted him against the others," in essence putting the "good ones" on one side and the "bad ones" on the other. The staff member's summary went on as follows:

> When I stood uncompromisingly by everything I had told Y, A asked candidly: "But then it means that you have not learned anything from our evaluation?!" The underlying assumption was that, indeed, I was wrong in what I did and should have been able to perceive it from our discussion. I had, according to A, given differential treatment — rewards for my preferred members, punishments for those I did not like as much, this being "unfair" because not legitimate.

These notes make it clear that Y was not complaining about trivialities. The members of his small group felt embarrassed by the differential treatment.

It is worth noting that this staff member had expressed two different goals for ACRES: (1) scientific, epistemological, critical reflection on AR with the more senior or experienced members in which junior researchers could participate in and learn and (2) a "summer school" component for junior researchers, who could benefit as well from the discussions with the senior researchers.

Given his small group — two "senior" researchers with live AR projects and two "juniors," one without a live project and the other with a consultancy project — this staff member's feeling was that the juniors should listen carefully and try to learn a lot but should not take too much time for their own projects as they were not worth bothering about. But these juniors did not accept this role. To this staff member's dismay, both wrote on time and felt they had the right to some feedback. When Y insisted on feedback at the last workshop, the staff member still felt he did not want to waste his time, and that possibly made him less articulate in his critique than in other situations.

In his comments on the group's evaluation, the staff member adds:

> This shows how a managerial analysis may differ from a psychoanalytic perspec-
> tive in an organizational situation. Either from an educational vantage point or
> even from a consulting vantage point, I am asserting that I have a professional
> responsibility in not colluding with some illusory process moving away from
> reality. This, of course, is discussable in terms of professionalism, between
> competent professionals, in an appropriate setting with sufficient time available,
> and I am open to the possibility that I have been professionally wrong.

Disquieting Effects of the Incident

The incident gradually created severe problems among all the participants and triggered already existing, or at least perceived, differences among the staff. It made the final plenary an unhappy one, as both A and Y, in mature, detached ways, summarized and openly criticized the situation.

I also have to mention some unforeseen aftereffects. Shortly after the post-ACRES meeting in November 1993, where we discussed the publishable papers, an international group of action researchers formed in the area of Halmstad University in Sweden. The group has at least nine participants, the majority of whom had met for the first time at the ACRES program. Included in this group was Y, who felt he had been the subject of "abuse" during ACRES. In fact, he is one of the most active members.

That Thing Called 'Democratic Dialogue'

The concept of "democratic dialogue" was familiar to at least the Scandinavian participants in ACRES through the Swedish national program "Leadership, Organization and Codetermination" (LOM) and the Norwegian Center for the

Improvement of the Quality of Work (SBA) program, in which quite a number of participants had been active. Other participants had been exposed to democratic dialogue through literature that was distributed and discussed during ACRES, especially Gustavsen's book *Dialogue and Development* (1992). The term was also used in an article by M. Elden and M. Levin (1991) reviewed in the second workshop and in the paper presented by participant Karin Aslaksen, who referred to Gustavsen's work.

The Elden and Levin article states that Gustavsen sees the researcher's job as guaranteeing that the procedure that is followed maximizes democracy in dialogue. As Elden and Levin express it, Gustavsen thinks the researcher should "control procedures, but is not supposed to participate in creating content" (1991: 136).

Elden and Levin's own approach is rather different: "Our theory, based on our practice, is that we intentionally and strongly influence content. We are always seeking opportunities to bring forth more self-managed forms of organization. Our experience indicates that, if we do not contribute ideas from socio-technical systems thinking and organization design to the dialogue, then they tend not to appear in the results" (1991: 136).

Elden and Levin are aware that by actively influencing dialogue, they may monopolize the content. The solution to this "expert dominance," however, is not very clear. They see the generation of "local theory" — practical theory integrating the general knowledge of the outsider (the researcher) and the local knowledge of the "insiders" — as being "empowering ... because those who create it learn why things are as they are, and this naturally leads to ideas about change" (1991: 138). There is a connection between their ideas and those of P. Freire (1970), who argues for a liberating dialogical relationship characterized by subjects who meet to name the world in order to transform it (Elden and Levin 1991: 134).

From the book *Industrial Democracy as Process* (1992), by Greenwood and González, also distributed to participants, I gather that Greenwood shares the ideas put forward by Elden and Levin. I came to this conclusion based on the strategy Davydd used in his research and the references his book makes to the article by Elden and Levin. Those ideas may explain why Davydd and Morten again and again emphasized that participants should "co-design" the workshops and have an important say in how each workshop should be organized. It also explains why both were very much in favor of topic-oriented plenary sessions that included the staff's views on action research, insofar as these sessions would enable them to fuse their expert knowledge with the knowledge participants might have had from their experiences with AR projects.

Such an approach, however, can confront participants with responsibilities too early — and allow a traditional teaching process in which the expert tells how things are and what should be done, as in a recipe. It is, indeed, as Hans would say, a difficult dilemma: "The researcher either provides too much input, becomes 'expert,' creates dependency and blocks the learning of the other, or does not allow the other to profit from his or her knowledge and experience, and is therefore not quite authentic in the action research relationship. The researcher has to avoid sins of commission as well as sins of omission (Van Beinum, Faucheux, and Van der Vlist 1996).

Given the staff's authoritarian reaction to the nonwriters at the start of the second workshop, I wonder in what way our approach to them had been "liberating" or whether we had created a stifling dependency. Was it a phony democracy after all?

A Misunderstanding on Democratic Dialogue

The final workshop included a discussion of Milgram's book *Obedience to Authority* (1974) and of comments on this work by Argyris, Putnam, and Smith in *Action Science: Contents, Methods and Skills for Research and Intervention* (1987). The comments on Milgram's obedience studies fulfilled their function — advising ACRES participants that when obedience is studied in the way Milgram did, it remains unclear what actually causes obedience behavior. The presentation also gave the staff an opportunity to emphasize a set of values connected with doing action research.

More important for my understanding of the ACRES processes, however, was a discussion my small group had on democratic dialogue and its practical content. In a peculiar way, though, this may be seen as linked to the Argyris, Putnam, and Smith study. The case in question, as reported in a paper by one of our participants, concerned evaluation research with respect to a Norwegian program "to improve the competitive strength and the learning/developmental potential for Small and Medium Sized Enterprises that have to meet international competition" and then the subprogram for small companies.

The main program, called BUNT, focused on using external (organization development [OD]) consultants to conduct strategic analyses of companies. The BUNT program "did not function very well" in small companies (five to twenty employees), however, because they apparently "needed some training before they could use a consultant." So SBB, BUNT for small companies, was launched. The main objective was "to initiate strategic development processes"; the main tools were "company seminars" and "OD consultancy."

The two action researchers "started out as more or less silent observers, but as time went by they became more active, discussion-oriented, and suggestive." The participant's paper then asserted that "catch words," metaphors, and "phrases" had especially powerful effects. This led to a lengthy discussion in which I expressed the feeling that when one deliberately uses catch words, metaphors, and so on to convince others of a point of view, a "theory," or a preferable set of actions, one is in fact manipulating the others. In so doing, one is a long way from a "democratic dialogue," which to me (and to Argyris, Putnam, and Smith) implies a *sincere* relationship in which one does not debilitate the other — or create a situation that would, indeed, be the opposite of "empowering."

In hindsight, my comments may have been stated too strongly. When Elden and Levin state that "we intentionally and strongly influence content" in a dialogue (1991: 136), then one may think they are inclined to manipulate (and Levin was this participant's Ph.D. supervisor). What Elden and Levin advocate strongly deviates from the way Argyris and Schön (1977) understand dialogue, and Elden and Levin know this (1991: 136).

Now, I do not think that Elden and Levin intentionally try to manipulate their audience. But to avoid being manipulative, one has to be really skillful and to realize that "handling" and *understanding* the relationship is very central in the ABX-model of Hans van Beinum. If approached in the way advocated by Elden and Levin, however, the dialogue may easily become manipulation.

Democratic Dialogue Once Again

On the first day of the last workshop, two voluntary groups were formed, one on evaluation and one on publication, to consider ways the writing done during the ACRES program could be converted into something that could be published. By now it was clear that we were discussing a possible book for the Dialogues on Work and Innovation series, published by John Benjamins. One or two papers could perhaps be published elsewhere, but such a book was a realistic possibility.

The publication group's plan called for "anyone from ACRES" who was interested to submit papers by October 12, 1993, and for both staff and submitters to be involved in deciding which papers would be in the book. The deliberations had to take the form of a democratic dialogue, and if there were any differences of opinion, each participant would have an equal vote. The discussion on the plan made it clear that the majority of the participants thought it fair and just and in line with the values of action research.

This is, I think, a clear misunderstanding of what a democratic dialogue is meant to be. The misunderstanding may be rooted in the nature of the Swedish LOM program, in which a number of participants had taken part, and in Gustavsen's book *Dialogue and Development* (1992), which had been distributed to all ACRES participants at the first workshop. In this book, democratic dialogue is presented as a "concept of communication to function as the key theoretical underpinning" (1992: 3-4) of the LOM program, and Gustavsen lists a set of thirteen criteria a democratic dialogue has to meet.

This set of criteria is the result of a formal argument only; it is put in almost legalistic terms. What is missing is that such a dialogue can be democratic in the true sense only when it is based on an attitude of sincerity or authenticity. Only then it is possible to exchange ideas and arguments void of self-interest, or to avoid having one person get his or her way just because of the rhetoric used, as can be the case when metaphors or catch words are used just to win a debate. Because that basic principle is missing in Gustavsen's criteria, one can easily come to the conclusion that a decision can be based on taking votes, on the principle that all participants are equal.

But although it is certainly possible to have such a dialogue on publishing possibilities, the results of the dialogue should be disconnected from the decision on exactly what to publish. Such a book has to meet international academic standards — and many ACRES participants had only faint ideas what these are. Participants in a dialogue that may lead to organizational change are equally responsible for the results, equally dependent on the quality of the results, but publishing a book is a different issue altogether. An additional difficulty was that action research and publications based on or about AR have a weak status in academia anyhow, which made it even more important to meet a high standard. We knew that such a book and its editors would be judged on the basis of the poorest chapter. Nonetheless, the plan was accepted.

Obviously, most of us on the staff were not too happy with the selection process to be used. In our staff meeting after the last workshop, Claude said that "given the difficulties," he was "reasonably happy" with the plan but that "it reflects, however, the immaturity of the majority of the participants." I felt that competence and democratic values were all mixed up, and Kjell, Hans, and Claude agreed.

Davydd saw "an element of distrust. The book is a pedagogical enterprise in itself. It will be a learning experience. The debate will probably concern only a few papers."

Morten responded, "Indeed, there is a distrust with respect to the staff. In order to regain confidence, we have to follow the plan."

When Hans argued that that logic was wrong, Morten replied, "Sure the logic is wrong, but from a pragmatic point of view it is all right."

When I questioned whether the problem was distrust or misunderstanding, Claude said, "The ideology of some participants is such that they find it difficult to allow for differences in competence."

Davydd added, "It is our own doing: we did not deal with our own differences. We acted as participants *and* as powerful authorities which leads to distrust. We have not been able to make our own roles clear."

Differences of Approach among the Staff

Some tension or distrust arose among the staff members even during the planning meetings. For example, Davydd's notes for September 8 refer to "tension between the psychological and the sociological-anthropological perspectives on action research" to sum up what are complex and deeply held convictions. Additionally, there probably was some rivalry between Morten and Hans about the "ownership" of the idea of the ACRES program. At the planning session in Leiden in June, for instance, when Morten learned that in his absence Hans and I had worked on redesigning the intended agenda, Morten seemed to become so annoyed and suspicious that we backed off and kept the program as it was.

The differences between the psychological approach (Claude Faucheux, Hans van Beinum, and me) and the sociological-anthropological (Morten Levin and Davydd Greenwood) also coincided with long-standing relationships between Morten and Davydd on the one hand and Hans and myself and Hans and Claude on the other. Hans, Claude, and I had extensive experience with what might be called "Tavistock thinking," in Hans and Claude's case including a strong inclination to emphasize the importance of psychodynamic aspects of relationships in action research.

To look more closely at these perspectives and the way they surfaced during ACRES might be illuminating both as to the approaches and as to some of the events that occurred.

On Pairing and ACRES Agendas

At the staff meeting the day before ACRES began, Davydd Greenwood proposed a slightly altered program for the first day. The main alterations he suggested were that the small groups would, in their late afternoon session, "identify common issues and dilemmas participants want these workshops to deal with." The plenary to follow, he suggested, would focus on the "presentation of issues and dilemmas emerging from each group's work; identification of common themes and issues; decisions about the structure of the rest of the workshop presentations, group work, and use of staff, including formal presentations, etc." and the "creation of agenda for day two." The staff then would "organize response to requests."

Looking carefully at the suggestions, one may conclude that Davydd preferred the participants to play a more important role with respect to the content of workshops and the drafting of agenda. He also questioned the agreed-upon "pairing" of participants. We more or less decided to follow the program as originally designed. In hindsight, I think we should have taken more time to find out why Davydd suggested these changes, which now seem to me to have been aimed at creating a more conventional but participant-friendly teaching program.

In that September 8 meeting, we also had a long discussion on the research dimension of ACRES and especially what we wanted participants to have learned when the program was over. In this discussion, the participants' projects and ACRES as an action research project became confounded issues. Using a "before/

after model," we asked, "What is unique about what we could learn in this process?" Some of the answers were as follows:

> *Claude*: What kind of change in the vision of the participants has been created by the participation in the workshop? What kind of change in vision has taken place among the staff?
> *Hans*: How they understand and manage their relationship with the empirical object in the field and how the ACRES program has changed it.
> *Morten*: How did writing improve the meaning construction process of the students?
> *René*: Testing the hypothesis that treating this "live project" as an AR project is necessary to its success.
> (My notes do not show a comment from Davydd.)

The questions put forward by Hans, Morten, and René are especially illuminating about their points of view. For Hans, understanding and managing the research relationships is a dominant feature in action research. For Morten, writing means reflection and thus is important in constructing meaning. For me, action research is important for some projects, such as those in which answers have to be found with respect to problems a "client system" is dealing with; however, it may not be a relevant research strategy in other situations.

We also discussed a note Hans had written entitled "Remarks on Action Research Learning and Critical Issues." There was rather severe criticism of the note, especially that the rhetoric employed was too reminiscent of positivistic language: the "dyadic" representation of relationships in AR projects; the use of terms like "irrational" and "fear" as vehicles for resistance to the "democratization of work," and of a term like "analytical" where "representational" would be much more correct.

We concluded that the overall discussion focused on the possible tension between the relational constructivist approach and the remains of positivistic language (like "empirical object") and that the discussion could be seen as exemplary for the work of comparing text and experience or text and reality, as we intended to do in the workshops. In other words, it became quite evident that differences existed within the staff with respect to action research. It was less clear what these differences were and whether they could harm the program or learning possibilities of participants. We decided not to press the point at that stage. After all, we had to make a start.

The participants' critique at the end of the first workshop focused on the defective nature of the plenary sessions as learning opportunities and the staff's role in this; the divergent views on action research within the staff (which could not yet be discussed openly); and the status of the program and the character of the learning opportunity if ACRES was considered an action research project.

In retrospect, I think these three topics hang together. In our diverging ideas about the program as a possible action research project, Davydd and Morten were the most outspoken in favor of the idea, and I was inclined to reject it. Hans and Claude took an intermediate stance, but, I think, were closer to Davydd and Morten than to me.

My main points were that if ACRES was an AR project, what was its focus, what was the research question? If the answer was, in Hans's terms, that the staff could be seen as A, the participants as B, and the program as X, then the question would be how to understand and manage the relationship with the participants and how to transform the participants from students into "co-researchers" — that is, how to enable "cogenerative learning" to take place (Elden and Levin 1991). And, if that was indeed possible, how?

As noted earlier, SCARDEP could be seen as an AR project "to foster societal developments by linking researchers, projects and institutes." With ACRES, that possibility was lost. We did not discuss it any more, although the idea of creating "pairs" was seen during the planning phase as an instrument for this process. Another possibility would have been to examine how a program like ACRES could be organized to enable optimal learning that might make any second opportunity more successful.

A third possibility could be phrased as follows: If a participant's project were a problem for him or her, how could we discuss this difficulty and what could the participant do between workshops to solve this problem? What could be learned this way that could be relevant in other projects? This approach would have led to a multitude of AR projects within the program. Organizing the plenaries intelligently could have created possibilities for joint learning and allowed for a combination of learning opportunities that could have been carried forward on their own.

Of these, the second possibility is, I think, the worst. Following Hans's view, X has to be a "psychological reality" to both A and B. That is, X is not an abstraction from that reality. Part of that complete problem can be — or can become — a more abstract understanding of the problem, but it is never dissociated from its context. If we follow the reasoning of this second possibility, however, then concrete problems — the live projects of the participants and their lack of experience with action research as a means of solving and describing them — are immediately translated into abstractions. The participants are placed in the position of saying "I want to learn more about action research, so teach me." Pursuing this second possibility would lead to a situation in which participants demand lectures, thematic discussions, and abstract exchanges of opinion between staff members. This is what happened. And in line with this "cogenerative learning," the dynamic was translated into "co-design of the agenda" and false, ineffective, participative decision making.

The design, as originally planned by the staff (and especially by Hans, Claude, and me), implied the possibilities mentioned under the third option. This was based on understanding ACRES as an educational problem rather than as an action research project. We felt that true learning could take place only in a situation in which the pursuit of knowledge was not dissociated from experience. That is why live projects, discussed in small groups and in pairs, and not abstract lectures and theme discussions, were meant to be the backbone of the program.

In line with this analysis is a reflection written by Claude on September 15:

> Quickly enough emerged the differences of approaches between Hans and Davydd: Hans was defending a design which allowed the process of maturation of the participants for joining in co-designing with us without confronting too prematurely the participants with responsibilities they would have been unable to discharge at a serious enough level, running the risk of a phony formal democracy at a superficial level. Davydd was defending the view that we had to open up the designing process to the participants as early as possible, almost implying that the design as initially proposed reflected too much of an insistence to maintain a power relation, a teaching relation.

From Davydd's minutes of the staff meeting on September 12, just after the first workshop, it is clear that the program took a more traditional teaching course: "We agreed that there are indeed different schools, and that we need to expose the participants to these differences in a constructive way. ... [and] agreed that the notion of theme groups was reasonable. The issue is how to surface themes for the groups to work with." It was decided to have some staff presentations on our views.

Davydd also sent all the staff members a "reflection," dated September 27, 1992. For him, the first workshop had produced both ecstasy and agony — agony "because of our ways of handling some important issues." He goes on:

> There was a tendency of staff discussions to slip into Model I organizational behavior and position bargaining ... battling positions and control of the agenda. I personally see the substance of the disagreements to have to do with initial lack of or willingness to recognize and deal with the legitimate and real heterogeneity of viewpoints about AR within the staff. ... Other causes of considerable discomfort for me were the processes by which we executed pair formation, structured the plenaries, and sought participant involvement in co-design.

> Given our commitments to AR and the fundamental role we espouse for co-design in all AR projects, the difficulty we had in recognizing the role of participant co-design in ACRES and the lateness with which this showed up on our agenda should again give us cause to reflect on our own practice. ... It took us a long while to recognize the inconsistency in excluding the participants from the planning and the research.

Again referring to the "pairing," he states:

> I experience what I would tentatively define as a split between sociology-anthropology and social psychology in this matter. It is clear to me that action researchers from these two traditions really differ. ... I experience the social psychological view as being extremely dyadic in form. ... The continual emphasis on the rhetoric of interpersonal relations ... suggests a different world view

from that in sociology and anthropology. ... We see a great deal of force in the
structure of causal-functional social systems and logico-meaningful cultural systems.

I disagree with Davydd's diagnosis. Hans van Beinum and I are both sociologists
by training, and as far as I can see, Davydd's point is irrelevant. The real point is,
How do you think learning can take place, and in what way could this process
benefit from defining ACRES as an AR project? The split within the staff had
much more to do with this than with differences in world view based on disciplinary training. By the end of his comments, Davydd came to this conclusion, too,
and said that his goals for the rest of the program would be "to help participants
learn what action research is going to be for each of them."

The main lesson I learned from the first workshop was that somehow we had
not been able to solve the question of whether the program could be an AR project
and, if so, in what respect. That we were unable to do so may have been the result
both of our divergent backgrounds and of the insufficient time the staff had to
come to grips with these differences. Hence, workshop two started without a clear
view on the question, and because our problems were exported to the participants,
in the form of helping the staff co-design the agenda, the second workshop was to
be one in which we had to execute a crippled design. To quote Claude here, we
had reached "a phony formal democracy."

Differing Views of AR

At the opening session of ACRES, Hans van Beinum explained his view of action
research as an ABX model. He emphasized that action research — that is, the
study of operating systems in action — is not a method in the traditional sense of
the word but refers to a way of understanding and managing the relationship
between the researcher (A) and the "empirical object" (B) (the researched), and
the "problem" (X). (For a fuller explanation, see chapters 1 and 2.)

The second workshop included a presentation by Kjell Johannessen on
concept formation, as well as presentations by Morten and myself on our views
on action research, as well as Claude's comments on Morten's talk and Davydd's
comments on mine.

Kjell's presentation was very articulate. To him, it was clear that AR is much
closer to the Wittgensteinian philosophy he adheres to than "positivism" is. He
emphasized that concept formation is in fact an inductive, experience-based
process, enabling one (or a community) to make sense of these experiences and,
in so doing, to develop a body of practical knowledge.

To some of the staff, it seemed a good idea to increase our understanding of
AR along the same lines by studying and discussing "good examples" in the
literature. I was opposed to this idea, but there was not enough time to find out how

examples could be beneficial or to find out what negative effects this might have. To be exact, I agreed with Kjell that it is from examples from our own experiences that a concept evolves and that some sort of anxious need for identity was behind this call for studying good examples (rather then personal experiences).

Several staff members had the impression that a lot of participants were not doing any research. I believed we had to be aware of the possibility that the "nonwriters" could decide their research was not action research after all and that that was why they did not write. They could even decide that they were in entirely the wrong camp, a camp that they did not want to identify with — and in that case we would lose participants. Obviously, I could not explain this during the plenary session. To the others, studying "good examples" seemed a natural and good idea, and the proposal was accepted almost immediately (except by Hans van Beinum, who felt uneasy with it but consented to it).

During our staff meeting that evening and in a letter to the staff dated December 14, 1992, van Beinum explained that, as we have learned from history, "the good example will not be followed: It is naive to assume that the diffusion of, for instance, new forms of work organization will take place through good examples. To the contrary, both the successful case and the failure are being rejected and encapsulated."

I entitled the paper I had written for this second workshop "Research, Action Research and Consulting." It had been sent to participants well in advance. Assuming that everyone would have read it, I summarized the main points. These were as follows:

Positivist science states that it studies reality. Reality in this tradition is anything that can be known objectively. And anything that can be known objectively is subject to the laws of cause and effect. Positivist social science states that we should study behavior in this way.

But reality is more than what can be known objectively, and subjective experiences play a dominant part in the way people behave, as goals, purposes, values, attitudes, and intentions do. That positivism is so tenacious, so persistent, especially in the social sciences — even more so than in the natural sciences — may be related to the fact that, to stay alive and function reasonably well, human beings have to adapt to a changing environment, and this is possible only when this environment is reasonably stable and changes follow regularities that can be understood, so changes can be anticipated. Put another way: human beings need order and predictability.

This view easily leads to conceptions of science and knowledge that tend to favor determinism. There is nothing against determinism as long as one does not want to apply it to all spheres of life. Most of us see ourselves as free agents, at least in some respects and some of the time. What most of us apparently find more difficult to accept is that other persons also claim some independence, or free will.

It is as if it is easier for each of us to see ourselves as free agents, but we act under the presumption that the rest of the world, be it physical objects and processes or human beings, is subjected to an order, a set of laws, that may be known and put to our advantage.

To understand other human beings, we have to know their intentions, purposes, goals, values, and skills. We also have to understand their inductive reasoning processes, forged out of experiences and observations as well as conversations, and based on their need for order on the one hand and their assumption that events are predictable on the other. In other words, we have to understand how local and tacit knowledge developed and to accept that a positivist inclination is natural.

To help people, we have to convince them of three things: (1) not everything is predictable and subject to a limited set of laws that can be understood; to some extent, people do have a free choice; (2) each (local) theory is based on a limited set of observations and experiences, and other theories and understandings may be used to explain/summarize this same set of observations and experiences (theories tend to be deceptive — they tend to create their own truth; and (3) observations and experiences may refer to a reality called into being by external conditions, which can change.

In his comments on my paper, Davydd Greenwood emphasized the following differences between his views and mine. (The following is from a letter to me dated November 15, 1992.)

> (1) I disagree with your implied history of social research. I do not believe that the positivist model was "traditional." I believe that social research arose from an effort to improve society and that it has deviated radically from that into positivism. Further, I see a one-to-one relationship between positivism, scientific management, and bureaucratic control systems. So, for me, it is important to explain that action research was where social research began and positivism is the deviant outcome.
>
> (2) While I agree that humans are always collecting and interpreting data, I don't agree that humans are "scientists." I prefer to reserve science for organized attempts to discover that trial formulations are incorrect with the consequent substitution of better formulations. That behavior is exceptionally rare, including in action research. Yet, doing this is an option that action research offers that is far better than what positivism can do.
>
> (3) Our clients in ACRES are powerfully confused about the meaning of "research" itself. Your paper does not address this. We need to decide together if we are going to take this on in the second workshop. I suggest we need to clarify what the variety of meanings of "research" are and how we intend to help them understand how to engage in activities that can count as "research."
>
> (4) Your discussion of leadership and then the AR as leader leaves me perplexed. [I had made a comparison between an action researcher and a democratic leader.] I understand the empirical example you gave, but not the unilateral authority model it implies for action research.
>
> (5) You don't say anything about the desired overall direction of organizational change. In my view, a major aim of AR is to engage the energies of insiders and

outside experts in organizational transformation in the direction of creating a learning organization and thereby enhancing the capacity of participants to contribute to the overall future of the group. This is important to me in principle and also because it has a great deal to do with my image of the role of the expert in action research as combined devil's advocate, research expert, and democratizer.

It should be evident by now that Davyyd and I were not completely on the same track, but the differences seemed manageable. The discussion after my presentation did not bring up any new points.

For his presentation at the second workshop, Morten Levin did not write for the occasion but instead presented the article he and Max Elden had written for a book edited by William Foote Whyte (1991). I quote from the article:

As Scandinavian PAR [participatory action research] professionals aiming to contribute to major reforms in work life, we are a long way from being detached, "value-neutral," individual scientists. For us and many of our colleagues, PAR in Norwegian work life means researchers who have (1) clear value commitments to democratization as well as economic improvement: People have a right to "good"-quality jobs; (2) a vision of "the good organization" — that is, one based on self-management, development of human potential, power equalization, and democratic principles; (3) well-developed and proven tools, concepts, and ways of working founded on sociotechnical systems thinking that can be used to (re)design organizations to achieve our visions and values; (4) a shared tradition of a way of working, as vocabulary, and a network of collegial relations and support structures, mostly in the form of well-financed public or nonprofit research institutes; (5) a researcher role of "co-learner" rather than of "expert in charge of change" in which the researcher's expertise includes the ability to "fade out" as participants take charge of their own learning; and (6) an extensive formal political infrastructure supporting participation in work life as reflected in specific labor legislation, national labor-management agreements, and industrial relations and traditions in Norwegian work life. ...

Our model of PAR rests on "insiders" (local participants) and "outsiders" (the professional researchers) collaborating in co-creating "local theory" that the participants test out by acting on it. The results can be fed back to improve the participants' own "theory" and can further generate more general ("scientific") theory. ... The basic idea behind our version of PAR is that those who supply the data have their own ideals, models, or frameworks for attributing meaning and explanations to the world they experience. ... The researcher has no legitimate monopoly on explaining social worlds or making sense of reality interpretations (Whyte 1991: 128-31).

In his commentary on Morten's paper, Claude Faucheux explained that he fully agreed with the main thrust of the argument. For Faucheux, "Action Research is required for basic fundamental knowledge of human conduct ... which cannot be studied from an external objectivist position and therefore necessarily involves understanding the experience of the actor as an author of the acting" ("Comments on M. Elden and M. Levin," Nov. 16, 1992). From this, it is unmistakable that Claude does agree with Elden and Levin but places action research in a wider context in which the democratization of society is an important objective.

I personally felt uneasy with Claude's comments — and up to a point with Elden and Levin's view. For me, "traditional" (positivist) research is not without value. But by making a sharp distinction between subject (the researcher) and object, traditional research is able to see "reality" only in a certain limited way (or only part of the reality, we could say). At the same time, conducting this traditional research is much more difficult than many researchers seem to realize.

In most research designs, it appears impossible to create a situation in which subject and object are completely separate. In those cases in which the researcher succeeds in this objective (as possibly occurs when "unobtrusive measures" are used in natural environments), it appears that the researcher can explain only a small part of the studied behavior, as a rule far less than would be needed to formulate a "law."

Behavior is caused largely by factors that are unobservable (such as experience, emotions, understanding). Action research is a research strategy that should be able to grasp more of the reality than traditional practices, but it truly *requires* close cooperation between the researcher and his or her "object."

To my surprise, the discussion that followed did not bring up new perspectives. Apparently, Morten's position was well known.

As should be evident from the above (and as the participants had already sensed), there were certainly differences among the staff with respect to the concept of action research. To me, AR is a way of doing research that might unravel a larger part of the "reality" than more traditional forms of research. More than traditional positivist research, action research takes into account that behavior is determined largely by the way individuals and groups construct and reconstruct their experiences in order to make sense of the world in which they live. In no way does this mean that other methods of research should be denounced. It only means that each research strategy has its advantages as well as its shortcomings and that the choice of a strategy has to be made carefully.

To Davydd Greenwood, as well as to Morten Levin, action research is the only possible way to do any research in the social sciences. To Davydd, it means even more. He states that social research arose from an effort to improve society and that positivism was a deviation from that course that has to be overcome (some historical evidence on this can be found in chapter 9, by John Puckett and Ira Harkavy, in this volume). To Hans van Beinum, AR is a way of handling the relationship between the researcher and his "empirical object," and within the context of AR, it is possible to do traditional research as long as the AR partners agree on this. To Claude Faucheux, AR is the only possible way to do research that contributes to the true (democratic) development of society. These differences in opinion were not discussed at length, and this fact itself may have caused uneasiness among the participants.

These differences arose again at the third workshop (March 1993) during a plenary session on the famous article "Some Social and Psychological Consequences of the Longwall Method of Coal-getting" by Trist and Bamforth (1951). The study was to be analyzed as an outstanding example of good, or even impressive, action research.

Trist and Bamforth's article has always been seen as a landmark in the development of the sociotechnical systems approach at the Tavistock Institute of Human Relations. Authors today still refer to and quote from it. We discussed it initially in the plenary session, starting with reviews by Morten Levin, Claude Faucheux, Davydd Greenwood, and Kjell Johannessen, and followed that with discussions in four smaller groups and, finally, in a concluding plenary.

Morten Levin judged the article to be very important but "not at all" action research. He found only three passages referring to the research dimension: two footnotes on the first page and a passage on the fifth. The second of those footnotes reads: "The field work necessary for this study has been lessened by the fact that Mr. K. W. Bamforth was himself formerly a miner and worked at the coal-face for 18 years." To Morten, the "modesty" of this footnote was disingenuous, its function being to stifle any critique. He felt that Bamforth had approached the longwall method, an operational invention that "industrialized" the traditional way of getting coal, from a common meaning construction perspective, a perspective disconnected from what happened at the pit itself. To Morten, the authors had followed a straightforward traditional social research procedure, and he concluded that the article was "extraordinarily conventional" and had no arguments on the validity or reliability of the data but was an important paper because it showed in detail that work processes can be designed in different ways and that the actual work process in operation is the result of an explicit or implicit process involving choices. He did, however, acknowledge that the article heralded the beginning of sociotechnical systems thinking.

Claude Faucheux said he agreed with much Morten had said but that he thought that Trist and Bamforth's study was nevertheless an important action research project. He explained that he took a broader view, based on epistemology, and thought that the research done derived from normal science and led to a deeper understanding of social reality and that the relationship between the technical (operational) and social aspects of work situations was clarified for the first time. Whatever Trist and Bamforth's research strategy was, Faucheux felt the study could be seen as an example of fundamental research that has made a major impact on the way we look at organizational design questions ever since.

Davydd Greenwood proposed to retitle the article "Durkheim in the Dark." To him, the study contained no fundamental research at all. He noted that the article uses evocative rhetorical language and is full of moral arguments. The credibility of the study seemed to him to be based mainly on that second footnote saying "trust me, I am a coal miner," with the scanty data the article provides actually going against the authors' argument. To summarize his review, he felt it is a poor article, morally prejudiced, and uses rhetoric in a false way and that the study is not an example of action research at all.

Hans van Beinum tried to explain the significance of the piece and its impact on practical as well as theoretical matters. I myself am much in agreement with Claude and Hans. If you take a careful look at the article, many questions do arise. It is certainly possible to criticize it from a research point of view, as well as from a theoretical point of view, but my conclusion is certainly much more generous than the verdict of Morten and Davydd. After all, one should take into account that the article was written in 1951 and that it opened up a completely new perspective on the effects of structural-technical design on social and psychological phenomena. This was all discussed.

What in hindsight is most astonishing is that we did not do our utmost to find out what caused these affective attitudinal differences (Kjell, of course, being unfamiliar with action research, distanced himself from the argument). The issues coincided with Davydd's earlier remarks about the difference between the "sociological/anthropological approach" and the "social psychological approach." This difference had/has to do, according to Davydd, with whether one places more importance on small-group and relationship phenomena (Hans, Claude, René) or institutional phenomena (Davydd and Morten). Davydd, in fact, despises the group dynamic/psychoanalytical approach and sees it as moralizing, paternalistic, and, up to a point, dehumanizing, while Claude and Hans feel that unless one understands organizational and group phenomena from a psychoanalytical perspective, one has not understood these phenomena at all.

These differences are so encompassing and fundamental that one may wonder what the effects would have been had we tried to discuss the issue in depth. It could have ended what cooperation existed among the staff. Not discussing it was probably the only possibility left. The effects on the participants are hard to estimate, but the problem certainly did not foster a better understanding of action research.

A memo written by Hans van Beinum in January 1993, concerned with the evaluation format for the fourth workshop, also noted the disparate views:

> This is not necessarily a bad thing. Differences are not only part of reality and should be tolerated, but are necessary and desirable for a creative and mature process of learning. Of course, if differences are too big and with regard to fundamentals, then they invite manipulation and result in confusion. These differences have been discussed to some extent in the staff, and have sometimes been labeled as the psychological versus the sociological/anthropological perspective. Frankly, this does not ring true to me. As a matter of fact, I think this is a false dichotomy.

The dichotomy was, of course, labeled as such by Davydd and Morten back in September, just before the first workshop. Among other things, the situation then had to do with my insistence on creating pairs, which had caused quite some commotion during the first workshop. The issue also had to do with the fact that

Hans, Claude, and I were very familiar with the Tavistock approach to action research and the three of us knew each other, while Davydd and Morten formed a pair who had worked together for a long time.

While the dichotomy label may be false, the differences in background and outlook certainly are not. This can be illustrated by another point in Hans's memo:

> Personally, I would be inclined in the future to consider a tighter intellectual link between plenary and group sessions. Also, I think that there can be a more explicit form with regard to two dimensions, that is, on what I call the evolving action research parameters of a case and on the psychodynamics in the actual research relationship. As far as the former is concerned … it means:
>
> - The focus of the research and its objectives.
> - The nature of the contextual setting of the focus; the wider reality from which the research question has been distilled.
> - The assumptions (theoretical and otherwise) underlying all this.
> - And above all, the nature and the actual and potential interdependencies between these dimensions.
>
> As far as the psychodynamics of AR are concerned, it is interesting to note that although they are of crucial importance, they are not very much discussed, described, or analyzed. This is, of course, understandable, as things are getting close to the bone along this dimension. … We need to focus more on what is really taking place in the dialogue between researcher and researched.

What this actually means is that Hans (and I) would have preferred plenaries around topics that emerged out of discussions in small groups, instead of plenaries like the one on the Trist and Bamforth article. Hans's interest in group dynamic and psychodynamic aspects of AR are more or less shared by Claude and myself. The three of us would have liked rather different schedules, which would have led to a rather different teaching model. I think that when ACRES was defined as an AR project without formulating what the research question was, we had completely dissimilar concepts in mind. Instead of defining ACRES as a research topic, we should have focused on the kind of pedagogical model we wanted to apply.

Hans's memo was not discussed in this way. Instead, we took some ideas from it for the evaluation process.

Ending

During the final plenary, each staff member was asked explicitly to comment on the whole ACRES process and on the final workshop. Claude refused to do so.

In our final staff meeting, we discussed this too:

> *Davydd to Claude*: Why didn't you want to evaluate?
> *Claude*: Ending up, I didn't want to take part in an illusory process. I am
> suspicious in giving a hand in covering up. We were very close to the end. I did
> not want to collude; I reject that.
> *Davydd*: Illusory process? Covering up? You pretend to see through the matter.
> So you find that I collaborated in the process?
> *Morten to Claude*: I cannot at all understand the basis on which you judge papers.
> You are not constructive, you simply chop off heads. Other papers, that are not
> even there, you marvel at.

Claude asked if we thought he used a double standard.

> *Kjell*: In a way, you might say that you used a double standard. You were positive
> about a paper that had no problem formulation. You were even positive about a
> paper that wasn't there at all.

Claude explained his behavior and the fact that he felt that we should make a very
clear distinction between action research and consultancy or, for that matter,
social engineering. The two projects he was positive about were truly action
research projects. The others were not.

This debate had no happy ending. The gap within the staff was a fact. We
decided to finish the whole exercise in a businesslike way, without indulging in
personality conflicts.

Reflections on AR

This account of the organizational processes of ACRES has been rather critical.
Though this impression is not incorrect, the picture needs some retouching, or,
rather, it needs to be completed.

The chosen structure was, in principle, a very strong one, although it was
difficult to operate this "perfect" vehicle. The basic structure consisted of preparatory staff meetings, to build a joint identity and a thorough understanding of our
task; small working groups of four or six participants, each with its own staff
member; pairs within each working group, enabling support during and between
workshops; plenary sessions to exchange experiences and joint concerns; leisure
time for participants to meet in a more relaxed state of mind; the study of ongoing
action research projects in which participants were actually engaged; staff meetings before, during, and after each workshop to fine-tune the intentions of the
program and link them to concrete developments.

To explain why I believe this is a very strong structure, I have to paint a short
picture of what action research is to me.

Basic to Kjell's philosophy of science is that establishing knowledge (of
social matters) is essentially a form of human activity performed in an
intersubjective space of "shared tools": knowledge is dependent on the context in

which it is produced. Based on Wittgenstein, he concludes that there is an internal relationship between forms of human reactions and activities, concept formation, and the "reality" that emerges as "our" reality by virtue of the concepts we have formed based on our (often implicit) reflections on activities. Concepts are embedded in "practices," established ways of acting. To do action research, one must accept that to understand the reality of the person, group, organization, or society studied is impossible without the collaboration of the person, group, and so on, so that we may see his or her or its point of view and bring to the surface tacit local knowledge (its contextual knowledge), as embedded in practice and based on experience.

Humans are naive scientists. Humans are constantly trying to understand the world in which they live. Each of us develops a personal set of constructs that we revise and refine on the basis of our experience, as Kelly says: "Man looks at his world through transparent patterns or templates which he creates and then attempts to fit over the realities of which the world is composed. ... These patterns that are tried on for size ... are ways of construing the world" (1955: 8-9).

Kelly emphasizes individual differences (1970: 12) more than I would, since evidence suggests that this individuality is bounded by the fact that individuals are social beings. Social factors at least partly shape our understanding of the world in which we live.

In *Method in Social Science*, Sayer states that the problem of induction "is probably the favorite puzzle of philosophers of science. It concerns the fact we are not logically entitled to assume that because a particular sequence of events has always been observed to occur in the past, it will do so in all cases. ... Valid inferences about infinite sets of events cannot be made on the basis of finite sets of observed events" (1992: 153-54).

But humans are not philosophers of science; humans are naive scientists — better still, naive "applied scientists." Humans are forced to *act* in order to stay alive, and our actions are based on our "understanding" of the world as developed on the basis of our experience and our conversations with other human beings. This does not imply that our understanding of the world is correct; it does not even imply that our understanding of the world is not, eventually, harmful to ourselves. Dealing with uncertainties in the everyday environment is part of the "human condition." To survive, humans (organizations, groups) have to make "guesses" about regularities and changes in our environment, using inductive reasoning, based on experiences and conversations with others (indirect induction).

The correspondence of this with Wittgensteinian epistemology is striking. The difficult task of an action researcher is to try to understand what kind of experiences and conversations form the basis for the notions and practices of "the researched" with respect to the relevant problems confronting the researched and the difficulties the researched meets in dealing with the world as the researched sees it. On the basis of our own knowledge and experience, the action researcher may make the researched aware of the "bounded rationality" of the researched's local knowledge. Together, they may come to the conclusion that existing difficulties can be solved in certain ways. In this process, new concepts can be developed that are practically relevant and scientifically useful.

Doing AR is difficult. What may be especially exacting is to fuse one's own expert knowledge with local knowledge or to create situations in which "sets" of local knowledge can confront each other to create an awareness of the relative character of local knowledge and arrive at a deeper understanding and possibly changed practices.

Given this demanding task, it is clear that only in situations in which ACRES participants had live projects did the possibility exist of helping them understand this task in their ongoing AR situations. The forming of pairs of participants familiar with each other's projects would have enabled them to consult with each other and to ask for help. Discussions in small groups, again and again focusing in detail on each participant's projects, with the process repeated in plenary sessions, would have enabled them to understand AR in its essence. Over and above this, it could have created a situation in which participants could have used these experiences to form meta-concepts — concepts with respect to *understanding* action research.

Why were we not able to harvest all the potential possibilities of ACRES? I think there are at least five reasons:

1.   The staff did not sufficiently discuss the original objectives of the program — or the implications of accepting participants who did not meet the criteria set. Nor were the objectives sufficiently discussed with participants.

2.   Quite a number of participants did not bring live projects, and quite a number had only limited experience with doing research at all. Perhaps the eagerness with which Hans and Morten tried to build firm relationships with and between institutes made them less aware of the possible negative consequences of selecting participants through their "closed system."

3.   As to the different views on action research within the staff, it is not so much that the two views are at odds; it is that the statements may hide where we were essentially in agreement: on the epistemology — and thus the art — of doing action research. For example, Davydd's letter on the "split between sociology-anthropology and social psychology" was a rather clouded discussion of values that conceals the fact that what is essential to AR is understanding human reasoning.

4.   Right to the end, I sensed a certain rivalry within the staff about the "ownership" of ACRES. I have not before voiced my full concern that this was a factor

— perhaps because we were not immediately aware of it, or perhaps because we underestimated its disruptive effects.

5.   Certainly there was the irritating "incident" described above. In itself, it was not too important, but it led to serious discomfort, within the staff and among participants.

The results of ACRES are modest. To arrive at a "definite verdict" on the effects of ACRES in general and on its impact on the participants and the staff, a much more elaborate study is needed. For me, the program has indeed deepened my own insight into action research.

Chapter 5

The Rhetoric of Action Research

Writing in the ACRES Program

Davydd J. Greenwood

Most practitioners in the field of action research agree that writing about AR is difficult and that getting the results published is equally challenging. Including a writing component in the ACRES program was therefore viewed as critical.

This chapter and the next form a dialogue between the member of the ACRES staff most responsible for the design of the writing component and four participants. We hope it conveys some of what we learned together about the process of writing about action research and that it encourages others to work on the rhetoric of AR as a central element in the improvement of AR practice.

Development of the Writing Component

The writing component was introduced to the participants in the ACRES program by its co-director, Hans van Beinum, in a statement about the overall aims and structure of the program:

> Writing is seen as an important learning process as well as a research tool. Participants will be required to prepare themselves for each workshop by means of a written description and analysis concerning the developments in their projects. These texts will be submitted and distributed before each workshop. During the workshop, by means of tutorials, assistance will be given with any difficulties participants may have in conceptualizing, organizing, and expressing their experiences in writing. It is the intention that at the end of the program each participant will be able to submit an article to an international journal.

From the outset, I envisioned the writing component in a larger context: as both an element within the ACRES curriculum and an overall thread in our collective attempts to reform and promote action research. Further, I defined the problems of AR writing as quite serious. There are few publications reflecting our complex experiences and the excellence of AR. Some of the best practitioners and examples fail to get recognized in print. The behavioral and political priority placed on action leads to weaknesses in reflection, which ultimately lowers the quality of the action.

Writing is a major tool of AR. Since "writing is thinking," not writing reflectively deprives projects of the analytical clarity and effective action designs writing can create. And since writing is communication, not writing reflectively deprives projects of commentary and the opportunity to hear suggestions from outsiders. By directing attention away from writing, the behavioral and political priority placed on action undermines the political and economic support action research might receive. By putting off writing, practitioners fail to consolidate their own learning for themselves and other AR practitioners. By failing to write, AR practitioners fail to convince agencies supporting AR of its value and success. Failing to write also limits the range of organizations that might come to action researchers for help. Thus, in my view, the writing component is central to the success of AR in general.

Before the workshops began, I had already been thinking about the fundamentals of rhetoric as they apply to AR. In my teaching, I argued that writing is thinking, politics, and communication. In particular, I emphasized the importance of the author maintaining control over the text, believing that AR practitioners need to take a more aggressive posture toward writing. I also encouraged experimentation with a variety of rhetorics, including first- and second-person writing, which has greater immediacy and possible connection to action than use of the third person.

Reflections on Writing in Action Research

Mondragón

By way of background on how I came to link my concerns with rhetoric to the subject of action research, it is worth recounting a bit about my involvement in the Mondragón project, which dates to 1984, when a series of circumstances initiated by William Foote Whyte combined to place me in a collaborative relationship with the labor-managed cooperatives of the Fagor Group at Mondragón in the Spanish Basque country. (For an analysis of this project, see Greenwood and González 1992.)

As part of a process of developing a four-year collaborative research and writing project on Mondragón with members of the cooperatives, I had the opportunity to learn a good deal about rhetoric in action. At the outset, to create a context that would surface members' views of the cooperatives, I had the group read what both outsiders and insiders had written about them. We emphasized both the analytical strategies that had been used and the way the studies were structured by means of particular tropes and images. These works created the context against which initial writing about the Fagor group was done.

In an effort to create a definable product that would demonstrate to the members of the Fagor team and management that we had accomplished something, the members of the project team and I co-authored a monograph on some of the most important and traumatic episodes in the history of the group. Through the writing, we attempted to express a vision that was different from that found in the works we had read together. The combination of time pressure and our desire to express an opposing view made the writing flow rather easily.

Later in the project, I suggested that we write a book together, since we had developed a vision of the Mondragón cooperatives that was so fundamentally different from that expressed elsewhere. Surprisingly, the members of the group, including people who routinely write extensive reports and argue complex issues in public assemblies, found the notion of writing a book with a professional social researcher quite intimidating. Though the intensity of their reactions differed, clearly the hegemony of the academic model of a "book" was disempowering to them. This reaction was so out of character with the risk-taking and adventurous spirit of this group that it caused me to wonder how and why the concept of academic writing was so disempowering. Clearly, the idea of writing a book lay at the opposite end of a scale stretching from action to reflection.

The members of the group eventually agreed to write the book, but the process was often difficult. With the exception of José Luis González, the Director of Personnel for the Fagor Group, everyone needed support and encouragement. The process also caused concern because it continually aroused conceptual issues that had seemed clear in discussion but were not clear enough to be written about effectively. In the end, the group felt that a major portion of the learning took place during the writing process, and the members were proud of the result. Without continuous pressure, however, it would not have happened at all.

Subsequently, the book had a very difficult publication history. Reviewers produced radically opposing reviews of the manuscript, loving and hating it in succession. Many of the reviews, in one way or another, noted that the rhetoric departed from ordinary academic rhetoric and treated this as a defect. They complained that there was too much about the research process, as if findings could and should be presented as divorced from the actions that had produced them. I learned later that our experience was a very common one action researchers encounter in attempting to publish their work with conventional academic presses.

Having talked the group into writing the book and as the one responsible for getting the manuscript published, I anguished considerably about our publishing problems. Here we were having difficulty getting one of the most extensive studies of this important group published because it did not conform to some predetermined academic form of writing. They equated the differences in rhetoric with defects in conceptualization rather than with the uniquely participatory research process that produced the results. After years of delay, it was finally published (Greenwood and González 1992).

Programs for Employment and Workplace Systems

During this time, I became engaged in a six-month project with a group called Programs for Employment and Workplace Systems (PEWS) in the Extension Division of the School of Industrial and Labor Relations at Cornell University. As part of that project, in collaboration with two other action researchers, I worked with two PEWS team members on a kind of "model" intervention. The purpose of this effort was to find ways the interests and capacities of professional social researchers could be made to work on behalf of improvements in the management and documentation of action projects in industrial settings.

Although the effort was very brief and the project only partially completed, it confirmed a number of the lessons I had learned in Mondragón. The two intervenors were both very talented and effective but experienced their own work as distant from the academic reflections that engaged the rest of us. Yet, when we joined forces, it became clear that social research could provide useful support for the action project and that the action project involved a variety of very important issues of social theory. At the same time, the action requirements of the project and the view of PEWS as an action organization made this project unique and in many ways militated against the development of such a dimension in most research projects. Including such a dimension would threaten the hegemony of the academic social science community that is not engaged in extension activities.

Work Research Institute

During a seminar at the Work Research Institute in Oslo, I mentioned some of the difficulties encountered during the Mondragón writing project, and for the remainder of the seminar, writing problems became the focus of the participants' questions and expressions of anguish. Several of the most creative senior action researchers there acknowledged that they had difficulty writing. Others said they could not find the time to write. All were apologetic. Clearly, the failure to document the work of the Institute effectively in reports that the Norwegian government and public could evaluate was contributing to difficulties in the organization.

Increasingly, it was becoming clear to me that the issue of writing and action research was a far more serious one than I had realized. That writing and publishing creative and important work on action research is difficult while an endless outpouring of essentially meaningless academic trivia flows unabated raises a basic question about the meaning of social research itself. I sensed that most AR practitioners experienced a direct conflict between action and reflective writing that made no intellectual sense to me but was a very real feature of their lives.

Given the steely discipline of many of the individuals I have met, their explanation that they lack the time to sit and write struck me as totally improbable. I noted instead a sense of self-disempowerment and a fear in the face of writing, as if it were more difficult than, say, running a complex project involving hundreds of people in conflictive change processes.

Interim Conclusions

I had come to believe that there were a set of generic problems surrounding the rhetoric of action research. To the extent that action research is different from orthodox social research, it must have its own rhetoric. Through this rhetoric, it must become clear that AR practitioners view authority as a community property, that facts are produced by collectivities, and that social research itself is a social process. The rhetoric must not hide the actors behind the impersonal "it"; it must allow the "we" that conducts social activity to speak with the diverse, dynamic, and often conflictive voices that we experience in the real world. I came to realize that the ideal rhetoric would be one that is collaborative, analytical, and yet affective and richly ethnographic.

ACRES Experience

Shortly after the end of my involvement in the PEWS project, I attended a conference in Aske, Sweden, organized by Björn Gustavsen. The conference dealt with the philosophy of action research and engaged eminent philosophers and action research practitioners from the Swedish LOM project in an attempt to look for a common ground between them. It was here that I met Hans van Beinum for the first time.

Within a short time and to my astonishment, Hans asked if I would be interested in developing an action research project with him in Scandinavia. I was greatly flattered but, to my surprise, responded by suggesting a different direction for my participation than what Hans had outlined. I reviewed my concerns about writing in action research and made it plain that I wanted very much to explore this dimension as a major element in my participation. Hans listened, though I could not tell at the time if he thought this was a good idea. In the time since, I have discovered that he took what I said on good faith and has supported the development of this unusual dimension in the project in a way that no one could have expected.

In the time since that conference, the Scandinavian Action Research Development Project (ACRES) took form, and writing was given a very important role. As part of the terms of acceptance into the program, it was stated that participants had to be involved in an important ongoing project in their organization and that they would be expected to produce a publishable analysis of the project by the end of the course. Throughout the year, the writing, critique, rewriting, reading of the projects of others, and the analysis of rhetorical strategies appropriate to these cases were core elements in the program. In short, the project bet on the vital importance of addressing the writing issue directly and challenged itself to develop rhetorical standards that would liberate the considerable capacities of the participants to engage in more fluid and experientially real writing. This was a daring bet and a fascinating experiment, a piece of action research in itself aimed at transforming our collective practice.

As we began to move through the workshops, it became clear that our ideal with respect to writing was both too abstract and too homogeneous. Reflecting this, Hans van Beinum sent a memo to the participants on December 14, 1992, entitled "Some Remarks and Observations about ACRES." In it he stated the following:

> The importance of writing in ACRES is reflected in the statement: "It is the intention that at the end of the program each participant will be able to submit an article to an international journal." However, this sentence, in which the emphasis should be in "intention" must of course be read as an expression of an ideal which will be pursued but which may or may not be achieved, at least not by everybody. We should distinguish between learning about writing as a tool and the kinds of writing which results in an article in an international journal. Participants who are unable to conclude ACRES with an article have not failed and should not be seen as having failed. People who write easily but do not learn or do not make a contribution to the learning of others are more appropriate candidates for being labeled in this way. . . . The significance of the writers workshop lies in my opinion in the fact that it provides a unique opportunity for people to become aware of "what is going on" in the process of writing and to learn about the way they reflect in their practice and engage in concept formation. These four components together form the building blocks for each workshop. They are of course highly interdependent. No single one can be understood without the other three; they all need each other. No single one should be maximized at the expense of the others as this would result in a suboptimization of the learning process as a whole.

From this document, it is clear that considerable pressures had built up around the writing component. For one thing, rather than treating the writing component of the program as a matter to be handled by one staff member, the participants were divided into groups, each of which had a staff member who worked with them on issues of theory, method, and writing. In this heterogeneous situation, approaches to writing and to the teaching of writing could be expected to vary a good deal;

nor would the writing experiences of the participants be homogeneous.

In responding to van Beinum's memo, I expressed the view that I had incorrectly conceptualized the writing component of ACRES. I concluded, pessimistically, that I thought we had practically no projects that I would define as action research. I continued:

> We have action projects and action plans, but the "research" component is either nonexistent or so poorly conceptualized as to be nullified.
>
> This is a major discovery for me. My previous view was that the participants were action researchers who needed some help to clarify and improve their thinking and writing. Now I see them as action agents with either no understanding of the concept of "research" or no clarity about the relationship between research as they were taught about it and their own work in projects. Thus, I now understand our task more as the creation of a research dimension in what are mainly just fascinating projects being carried out by intelligent and committed agents.
>
> The writing component also is aimed at the creation of an action research COMMUNITY with some agreed-upon standards by which they can communicate their learning and defend their collective interests. In this way, writing is part of the larger social ecology of action research that Hans is concerned about. This dimension of writing is essential.
>
> Clearly we should not hold all accountable to a single mechanical standard of writing. I don't think this means special attention to those with difficulty alone. I believe we are obligated to map the differences among writers in different states. Some need help in fashioning the very kinds of publishable articles we envisioned. Others are trying to learn how to conceptualize their work as research for the first time. Still others simply do not know how to write at all. We need to serve them all. I think this is a major design problem for any attempt to integrate writing into action research.
>
> I don't think that an entirely relaxed approach to writing is politically reasonable. Support for action research in Scandinavia is evaporating in a rain of criticisms about the failures to do "good" research and to write up results in a timely and convincing manner. For there to be a future for AR in the increasingly negative economic climate, the action researchers have to elbow the pseudo-social scientists aside aggressively enough to make their own case. If the participants do not understand this, we will not have given them an honest appraisal of reality. That each of them will have to approach this differently and with different levels of competence is fine, but the issue affects them (and us) all.

Thus, I had come to change my view of the writing problem radically on the basis of my experience with the action researchers in the workshops. I had initially assumed that action researchers were researchers who simply had not found a "voice" and an organizational matrix in which to write about their research. I now had a more complex view of the problem and had begun to recognize that many action research practitioners lacked basic training in research itself.

As a result of this recognition on my part and others', the staff devoted time in plenaries to the basics of the scientific method, the methodologies of action research versus those of orthodox social research, and the development of community standards. These standards were developed by criticizing the writing of such exemplary figures as Eric Trist and analyzing the arguments of the psychological researcher Stanley Milgram. They were also developed in plenary sessions in which a number of the workshop participants' projects were discussed.

Thus, the staff came to realize that the process of writing about action research was far more than a mechanical one. It involved issues of training, theory and method, rhetoric, and the creation of organizational environments conducive to the development of a persuasive personal voice for action researchers. It turned out to be true in a new sense that "writing is thinking."

Of course, the participants were not inert during this process. We now turn to their views.

Chapter 6

The Rhetoric of Action Research

Views from ACRES Participants

Siv Friis, John Puckett, Øystein Spjelkavik
and Agneta Hansson

The ACRES participants were an active force in shaping their own learning about writing and research and in teaching the staff as well. They actively expressed their confusion and frustration with the goals the staff had set. They rebelled against the staff's overzealous attempt to press them harder about meeting the program's writing goals, which had been laid out on the basis of what had been a misdiagnosis of the writing problem. And yet, by the end of the series of workshops, the participants had developed a considerable stake in the quality of their writing. Not only were issues of publishing the results important to them, but the creation of a book about ACRES led to both new opportunities for discussions of writing and tension about who would and would not be published.

Long meetings followed among interested ACRES participants, which led, ultimately, to the design of this book. In a presentation at a final plenary session on the book, these participants explained that the proceedings of the ACRES workshops would include everyone's work, guaranteeing everyone a publication. They also indicated that they hoped to produce a peer-reviewed, high-quality manuscript for publication, for which only some papers would be selected.

All participants who wanted their manuscripts to be considered for the book would have to submit their papers by a particular date. The submitters and the staff would then review the papers and determine which to include and, whether included or excluded, make suggestions for revisions. The participants suggested that a set of standards be applied in making these judgments and insisted that the submitters be treated on a collegial plane with the staff. After the selections were made, the remaining collaborators would form the editorial team. When the manuscript was completed, the staff would see to its publication.

It is hard to imagine how the participants could have taken the writing process more seriously. They not only developed a good design for the publication process but they did so while addressing the needs of those participants whose work would not be included in the book and asserted their right to an equal "voice" in the publication process. Further, they asserted, their learning and experience had given them a kind of "expertise" that qualified them to take such an active role. In response to the participants, Greenwood and others on the staff who were to write chapters for the book encouraged participants to become collaborators — as evident in this chapter.

The previous chapter by Greenwood lays out the writing dimension of ACRES from an analytical, external point of view. This chapter, by contrast, provides reflections on the writing process from the view of participants. In all these reflections, the importance of writing is evident, but so too are the connections between writing and research and the conflicting professional responsibilities that intervene to make the time and motivation to write less strong than it must become for action researchers.

All those who chose to participate in the writing of this chapter agreed to criticize drafts of Greenwood's chapter and then write a brief reflection of their own. There were no instructions given about the content of these reflections. They have turned out to be so rich and varied that they have been given a chapter of their own. They reveal some of the experiential dimensions of writing action research.

The order in which the reflections are presented is not significant. The last one is much longer and reviews the whole ACRES project and thus seemed to work best as the close to the chapter.

Storytelling as an Action Research Tool by Siv Friis

In my youth in Sweden, in the 1950s, the art of writing was taught very early in school. The emphasis was on grammar and spelling because grammar was deemed more important than content. I was an inventive girl with a big imagination and I did not have any difficulties with spelling, but, looking back, I realize that the strict discipline of grammar hemmed in my creativity. Fortunately, I had a teacher a few years later who deemed that storytelling was as important as grammar. I loved storytelling, so this teacher and I got on very well, and he encouraged me to continue to write stories. He claimed that people who have stories to tell contribute in many ways to others. He often stated that "we can always learn from a story. Writing your own story is to reflect upon and sort out your own ideas."

What is storytelling then? In my view, it is the process of very clearly describing the context in which events take place, enabling the reader to recognize both the mode and the route of the story in this context. One need not worry if the story is a meta-story (which may be applied to more than one context) or a story set in a specific context. In the act of recognition, the reader finds certain universals in the story. Authors should be open and honest in the way their stories are told, showing both bright and dark colors. They should use metaphors and tell anecdotes, but they should name the anecdote a saga if it is. A story must have a final point. One should not simplify; most readers are more clever than most authors believe.

I have continued telling stories and have used storytelling as a tool in my research. Sometimes I have been criticized for it, especially by research committees. Many researchers claim that storytelling is characterized by crude language, in the sense that it is not scientifically precise. Yet often the critics themselves are not very specific or precise about what science is — whether the natural or the social sciences.

My research falls within the social sciences and concerns the design of computer-based information systems in work organizations. Such research often involves strenuous empirical work done in cooperation with the future users of a new system. The empirical work is performed within the action research tradition, and the methodological rules are derived mainly from Glaser and Strauss (1967). I extend their discussion of grounded theory to encompass discussions of local theory by Elden (1983). My point of departure is that every development in a change situation is unique, and only the people within the work situation are in the position to tell the true (*i.e.*, relevant) story of that workplace. They are the local experts who know and recognize the problem to its fullest extent (Elden and Levin 1991). Hence, I claim the local experts are the actors with the relevant stories to tell.

My main research objective has been to develop and test a model for an approach to information systems design. Most design approaches today derive their mode of action from a traditional and linear science model. The design approach I have advocated is more process-oriented and has strong similarities to AR methodologies. In action-oriented organizational change, the people in the change area take active part in the change process. I believe the future users of new or changed computer-based systems should also be very active during the design and construction stages of the proposed approach (Friis 1994).

In an ongoing research project, we are testing the approach used during the construction of some "local planning systems" for foundry workers. Since it is claimed that the local experts know the truth about their own work, they should be allowed to own the development of change. It follows, because they are the actual problem owners, and, as such, they should also be the problem solvers. In an AR project, this means that the workers should be co-researchers (cf. Reason and Rowan 1981 and Elden 1983) and as such have the possibility to tell their stories (Friis 1991).

Thus, together with my co-researchers, I continue storytelling in my field-work. These stories are documented in logbooks. Each researcher keeps his or her own logbook, and there is one for each research group. We document actions, developments, and decisions made, and we attach stories to them, sometimes angry, sometimes funny. All logbooks are open for all to read. We even write comments in each other's logbooks. Thus, we also evaluate the development work, the work process, and the resulting actions, providing a continuous valida-tion process. When we state something in writing in the logbooks, we take responsibility for that statement. In this way, storytelling becomes an instrument for documenting and communicating, for taking responsibility for one's actions. It is also a first step toward systematization and research evaluation.

During most of my empirical work, I have found that my co-researchers did not want to engage in any strict scientific analyses of their workplaces and/or of the communicative patterns of their work systems. Rather, they wanted to tell stories — stories that may have been critical of management, or hilarious stories about future possibilities (*e.g.*, genuine decentralized planning). We have even used stories to identify problems. Later on, the researchers in charge of the empirical work systematize all the logbooks.

To me, one of the actions in AR involves the dissemination of what we have experienced and learned during our work. The dilemma is how to reach the research community fully. I do not think scientists (except for mathematicians) know enough to be truly precise, and I doubt that formal logic is an appropriate tool for explaining the development of change in a social system (*cf.* Churchman 1979). Thus, I try to do it in storytelling — although often in a systemic framework.

As Greenwood mentioned in the previous chapter, van Beinum claimed that writing was an important AR tool. I fully agree. At the same time, I believe that storytelling is a significant AR tool. I'll go on telling stories, not only to research-ers in my own discipline of information and computer science but to expert practitioners and participating nonexpert co-researchers.

The ACRES Writing Process by John L. Puckett

The paper Ira Harkavy and I worked on during ACRES (see chapter 9) went through four iterations, largely as a result of critiques from staff and participants at the first three ACRES workshops. Here I discuss the major points of critique and how we addressed each point.

As a result of the writing process, the focus and content of the paper changed dramatically between the December and June workshops. Comments and criti-cisms provided at the March workshop also led to the development of a second paper, "Lessons from Hull House as a Model for the Contemporary Urban University" (1994).

Paper #1

The original paper was directed toward the professional social work community. Our intent was to stimulate a rethinking of social work training and research, using the University of Pennsylvania's school- and neighborhood-improvement project in West Philadelphia as a model. We argued that the West Philadelphia project built upon the social work tradition represented by Jane Addams, the leader of the early social settlement movement. We also described the applied research focus and engagement in civic affairs of the University of Chicago and the University of Pennsylvania in the Progressive Era (1890-1914). On the strength of these historical examples, we then described Penn's current approach as a "neo-Progressive" attempt to reinvent the American university. We concluded the paper with an extensive description of the West Philadelphia project, including activities undertaken by the West Philadelphia Improvement Corps (WEPIC) and the Center for Community Partnerships.

Critique of Paper #1

The first paper was criticized on two counts. First, the prose, especially our depiction of the condition of American inner cities and the failure of universities to respond to the urban crisis, conveyed too strong a sense of urgency. Second, although we conceptualized the West Philadelphia project as an action research project, we did not provide any concrete examples of action research; consequently, our claim that action research advances general knowledge was unsubstantiated.

Paper #2

Between the first workshop in December and the second workshop in March, we toned down the rhetorical urgency of the writing, although grudgingly, believing that the major shortcoming of American social science is its lack of engagement and its posturing as an objective, value-free enterprise. We titled the paper "Back to the Future" to make a stronger appeal to the social work audience.

We faced a dilemma regarding the second criticism — that the paper lacked concrete examples of action research. Although action research projects were emerging in West Philadelphia, writing about this work had not yet been submitted for publication or the projects discussed in conference papers. Consequently, we decided not to alter the current description, which included a brief statement about each research project that was under way. We also believed that reviewers would accept the general direction in which we were headed.

Critique of Paper #2

The major critique was that the paper suddenly leaped from a discussion of the decline of action-oriented, reformist social science after the Progressive Era to current efforts at the University of Pennsylvania. A suggestion was made to include an examination of Kurt Lewin as a bridge between Jane Addams and the West Philadelphia project. Readers also recommended that we limit our discussion of Jane Addams to a brief description of her approach and the definition of science, that we include a statement of action research epistemology, and (once again) that we provide some illustrations of action research in our own work.

Paper #3

Our attempt to bridge the gap between Jane Addams and the West Philadelphia project resulted in a major recasting of the previous draft and a decision to develop two separate papers for publication. In the paper for ACRES, we dropped the social work emphasis and refocused the piece by adding a survey of the action research tradition from 1930 to the present, highlighting, on the one hand, the ameliorative, reformist social science of Jane Addams and her Chicago colleagues and, on the other hand, the action research of Lewin and his legacy after 1950. (The second paper, "Lessons from Hull House as a Model for the Contemporary Urban University," retains the focus on social work.) At the outset, we realized that simply interposing a statement about Lewin's action research between our discussions of Addams and the West Philadelphia project would be inadequate. We also had to answer the question of what happened to action research after Kurt Lewin. Two books assigned as workshop readings, Bjorn Gustavsen's *Dialogue and Development* (1992) and Davydd Greenwood and José Luis González's *Industrial Democracy as Process* (1992), helped.

We decided not to shorten the section on Addams and Hull House because we believed that material strengthened our case for an alternative social science. Finally, we added a description of action research epistemology, drawing upon ACRES workshop papers by René van der Vlist and Hans van Beinum.

Critique of Paper #3

The major recommendation was that we delete all discussion about Jane Addams, the women of Hull House, and Chicago sociology that did not explicitly address their particular approach to social science. Presumably, this would give the paper a tighter, more explicit focus on the historical development of action research. The readers also requested a more precise definition of Progressive Era social science, and they reiterated their recommendation that we furnish concrete illustrations of action research in the West Philadelphia project.

Paper #4

We revised the third paper, entitled "The Action Research Tradition," to incorporate each of the recommendations made in the third round of critiques. The final version also benefited from the comments and criticisms of colleagues at the University of Pennsylvania. The paper now includes concrete illustrations of the various stages in the action research tradition and concludes with an explicit statement of how the social science approaches of both Addams and Lewin are embedded in action research in West Philadelphia.

Overall, the process of writing, reflecting, receiving criticism from other action researchers, and rewriting greatly sharpened the focus of the paper and brought forward an explicit consideration of the action research dimensions of the West Philadelphia project in a way that would not have been likely to occur during the usual process of drafting and revising professional papers.

Fighting the Time Bandits to Develop an Article by Øystein Spjelkavik

When I received the invitation to participate in ACRES, I saw a good opportunity to concentrate on my writing. For a long time — in fact, since coming to the Work Research Institute — I had been waiting for an opportunity like this. In everyday life, there are too many time bandits, including meetings, telephone calls, and other interruptions that break my concentration. To put it simply, I am always writing and thinking, but, because of the interruptions, I seldom arrive at any conclusions.

I didn't have a definite subject to write about, but I did have a desire to discuss and reflect on my research. My starting point was diffuse: a general paper describing some experiences from my particular field, with sketches for possible future research strategies.

Input

For a long time, I had observed what seems to be a basic need among many action researchers to see themselves as extraordinary or at least different from the rest of the research community. At ACRES, my attention was immediately drawn to this emphasis on AR versus other forms of research. At the same time, mainly because of the staff's focus on writing, I devoted a lot of attention to producing an article.

In my group, we focused on the importance of addressing a clear-cut problem or question and developing a well-defined argument. I realized rather quickly
that my initial paper did not meet these conditions.

After lengthy discussions with my partner and in the group, not least during
some rather extensive tutorials with our staff member, I began to reflect on my
own research methods and strategies — and to connect this reflection with my
growing concern about the tendency to regard AR as different from other research. As we presented our papers in the group, we discussed forms of research
and degrees of participation. I also began to discuss these issues with colleagues
at the institute and elsewhere and to search in the literature for answers.

Going through ACRES

During ACRES, especially in the group sessions, new concepts emerged that
shed light on my own research. For example, I had always taken the importance
of informants for granted and had viewed the concept of co-researchers as AR
rhetoric. Gradually, I came to realize that empirically there are degrees of cooperation and participation and that this was the case in my own project.

By touching upon epistemological questions, forms of knowledge, and the
question-answer logic of the research process, I was also able to develop a more
critical view of AR as a version of applied research. Eventually, as I worked with
these issues, I felt challenged to develop a systematic argument and to be explicit
on one or more main points within the framework of my article.

The ACRES program was not always a pleasant experience; it produced
problems and frustrations. One such problem was that between the ACRES
meetings, the time bandits always were about to attack. Another was that it was
unclear how much emphasis to put on writing. Because I wished to use the
ACRES program as an opportunity to write, I came to find some of the plenary
sessions boring and uninteresting. Eventually, I skipped a few of them, locked
myself in my room, took a beer from the mini-bar, and wrote.

While carrying out the writing, I derived growing confidence from the group
sessions. My co-members certainly helped me to develop the necessary thinking
to carry out the writing process.

Dealing with the Short Supply of Time

Since time is in such short supply, I am convinced that the main condition
one needs to write an article is a way to fight the time bandits. One way to do this
is to stretch out the workday from ten hours to fourteen. I tried this and nearly got

divorced. A better way is to arrange seminars for the purpose of writing, provided that the focus is on writing. ACRES was such an event. It made clear to me the importance of question-answer logic to purposeful, effective writing.

The third way to fight the time bandits is probably the most general. Every research project must have — or generate — a clear question. From the beginning, time must be set aside to develop this. Having such a question is important in all research processes, but obviously even more so in AR projects, where so much time and energy is put into conducting the work in the field.

ACRES and the Writing Process, by Agneta Hansson

When Hans van Beinum came to Halmstad University in the spring of 1992 and invited our research group to apply for the ACRES program, I felt that this was certainly something for me. I had been to seminars, summer schools, and AR training before, and although these sessions had been interesting, they had also confused me, because I had found it difficult to connect the theories of action research with my own experiences in practice. Defining what it means to be a good action researcher was still not clear to me. In ACRES, we would have the opportunity to learn and be trained in writing, something concrete that I hoped would enable me to better understand action research as a phenomenon.

My work experience, my interest in people and communication processes, my involvement in union work, my struggle on behalf of women's rights, and my overall concern about the problems of inequality and the misuse of power were among the incentives that drew me to the field of work life research. When, through my colleagues and the LOM program, I found out that research could be focused on bettering work life through direct interventions, I felt this field of research was right for me.

It was not until later, when I started to write about my projects, that I encountered difficulties in sorting out theory and practice. Whom was I writing for? Whom had I worked for? What had been action, and what had been research?

According to Hans van Beinum, a condition for participating in ACRES was that one had to bring an ongoing action research project on work life development to the workshop. My contribution was an organizational redesign project being conducted at a regional laundry.

First Workshop

The first ACRES meeting was a fascinating experience. About forty researchers from all over Europe as well as from the United States met outside Trondheim. There were young doctoral students as well as senior professors, and many disciplines were represented: anthropology, philosophy, sociology, education, psychology, engineering, and business management. What we all had in common was our interest in and experience with action research.

I went to my working group with great excitement. Who was in the group, and how would we cooperate? Kjell S. Johannessen, a professor of philosophy, was our tutor. In all, there were six participants in the group. I was the only woman. We came from different countries, different disciplines, and had widely varied experiences to share.

Compared with the others' projects, I felt that mine — on a small regional laundry in the southwest Swedish forest — was platitudinous and uninteresting and that I had nothing to contribute to this male seminar group with its mass of experience in conducting large projects. When I was paired with an experienced colleague, I considered dropping my project to discuss one of the more spectacu-lar projects our research center was involved in.

We were the only group whose staff member didn't consider himself an "action researcher." Kjell was very interested in learning more about action research and saw ACRES as a good opportunity to do that. As a result, we spent all the time during the first meeting discussing the epistemology of action re-search. Using Kjell's great experience to conceptualize the production of knowl-edge from practice, we generated fruitful models that helped us map out the different dimensions of action, research, and participation.

As we were summing up the first seminar, I was inspired to use these models to write a report about another project I had just finished involving a tool company. I promised the group I would concentrate on this project during the next three months.

Between Seminars 1 and 2

Returning from Trondheim meant coming back to the day-to-day problems of administration, letters, telephone calls, meetings, and so on, leaving little time for reflection about the epistemology of action research. I felt that if I started my writing in November, I would certainly have time enough for reflection. But the time flew by and suddenly, in the middle of November, I received a note from my discussion partner, reminding me that I had only a month left.

After the first seminar, I read articles on action research referred to at the seminar and written by the staff. The common message seemed to be that (participative) action research was the only way for social science to democratize working life. These articles challenged me to shift the focus of my ACRES writing once again. I decided to discuss three questions that I had been reflecting on while reading about and practicing action research: Is it possible to do "research together"? Who "owns" the project? What do we mean by "broad participation"?

I thought that ACRES would provide a good opportunity to focus on these questions and to relate them to what I had experienced in my own organizational change projects. Also, while I agreed with the values of (P)AR, I felt challenged by the excessive polarization of (P)AR in relation to other forms of research methods and theories. It did not seem very democratic to claim to have the only right way to do research.

I decided to write a paper entitled "Action and Research — Is (P)AR a PARADOX?" I intended to structure this new article by starting with a discussion of the above three questions and then relating them to my own experiences. I did not know if it was acceptable to question what every action researcher seemed to agree about, but I felt that I had to raise these questions before I could present myself as an action researcher.

I outlined the article but succeeded in writing only a few pages of the introduction before the second ACRES seminar in Stockholm. I did not mail my pages to the ACRES staff before the meeting since I wanted to discuss my work first in my small group.

Second Seminar

I entered the second ACRES seminar in Stockholm feeling guilty for not completing my "homework." The evening before the start of the seminar, I had learned that I was not the only one who had not been writing and that the staff was very disappointed.

The seminar began with an "accusation." Why hadn't we been writing? Why did we join ACRES if it wasn't to be writing? But there was also a sense of division among the staff members. Davydd Greenwood demonstrated this by positioning himself in the audience, away from the other staff. These contradictory messages gave me an unpleasant feeling of insecurity about what was going on. What was the essence of the disappointment with the nonwriters? Was the conflict between those favoring an action orientation versus those favoring a process orientation or between those used to an Anglo-Saxon research culture versus those used to a continental research culture? Was the conflict between those favoring the sociotechnical view, represented by the anthropologists and the sociologists, and those favoring the interpersonal view, represented by the social psychologists?

We were being treated like children and blamed for not having respected the ACRES agreement. Wasted hours were spent in that session, most of them in silence. It was not until we were told to spend all of the first seminar day on individual writing that the seminar participants launched into an open and constructive discussion. The participants asked why we should have spent time and money and traveled for days if we weren't going to learn about action research (writing included) and be interacting with other action researchers. After some hours of frustration, this "therapeutic process" ended and we came to a democratic decision that we should continue to work in our small groups and that we should make a better effort to write before attending the third seminar.

After this, rejoining my small group was a relief. We all seemed to have reacted in the same way to the plenary meeting and were all happy to be able to continue to work with Kjell as our tutor.

Some in the group had rewritten their papers, but I was not the only one who had made only modest progress. My paper was the first to be discussed, and it was somewhat difficult to get the others to understand my intentions. This discussion led to an examination of the relationship between participation, action, and research. We agreed to question those canonical statements about action research that had bothered me.

I was also advised not to use expressions that were too strong if I wanted to be taken seriously. It is a style I got used to while writing journalistic texts and still causes me difficulty. In general, however, I was encouraged to continue the paper and to follow up empirically on my case studies.

After the disturbing start, the second workshop turned out to be very fruitful. We hardly wanted to break out of our small groups to meet with other participants. But obliged to form new groups, we realized the advantages of the new ideas and contacts. It was through these "semi-groups" that I realized that other ACRES participants faced the same questions I had. It also proved to be very useful to meet with another tutor. Another good idea, with respect to the group design, was that any ACRES participant could attend staff meetings, an option introduced at the second workshop.

We all noticed how the group feeling got stronger and stronger through the year, not only in the small groups but among all the ACRES participants. It made clear the importance of forming groups in sensible ways, giving them time to flourish, and knowing when and how (and if) to intervene.

My own observation was that the ACRES staff, at least in the beginning, did not treat the participants as mature "co-researchers" who "owned" the ACRES project as much as the staff. This may have happened because the staff did not have enough experience in group process work itself or because the members of the staff came from different cultural backgrounds. Whatever the cause, the group process evolved positively over time.

One incident occurred at the end of the second seminar, which, although motivated by good intentions, nonetheless provoked me and indirectly made me once again change the focus of my paper. Because of a complaint from the participants, we were informed at the closing plenary session that the staff had decided that it would invite one woman to a staff meeting that would take place in Stockholm the following day. I might have overreacted but I found this insulting. Extending this invitation at the moment when all the participants had their planes and trains booked and it was impossible for anyone to accept seemed insincere. If the members of the staff had really wanted a woman's perspective, they would have asked at least one female senior action researcher to join the staff from the beginning. Or do these "animals" not exist? Ultimately, this episode had a positive outcome for the women in ACRES because we decided to meet at the next seminar to discuss what united us and whether we could take advantage of these commonalities in some way in the future.

Third Seminar

Another three months passed, and in March we met again in Trondheim. Morten Levin invited all the women to come one day before the others, "either to work on their own or to participate in the staff's work, or possibly to do both." I could not get to Trondheim early because we had invited John Puckett to Halmstad for a seminar. This was unfortunate but also reflected a positive outcome of ACRES, since I would never have gotten to know him if it weren't for the ACRES workshops.

I had worked more on my paper, and it now had three parts. The first part ended with the three questions I had posed in the first version but also included questions regarding the distinctions between action, research, researcher, and practitioner and between content and process. The second part described the two different organizational change projects in which I had been engaged. My aim was to focus in part three on the core questions in participative action research, based on my own research. Unfortunately, when I went to the third ACRES seminar, I had not yet started to write the third part of the paper.

In my small group, I focused on how I had found that men and women were treated differently during reorganizations and, in particular, that women were made invisible. I asked my group in what way gender issues could be included in my cases and in participative action research in general. I worried that by not bringing in the gender perspective, there was a risk that women would became invisible to action researchers.

The group encouraged me to highlight the gender question. I was advised to introduce the paper with a discussion of feminist theory, then to describe my findings, and, finally, to discuss them from an action research perspective. Even if I didn't exactly know how to do this, I was content because I had reached the point where I saw the possibility of combining feminist theory with theories and methods in action research.

During the third workshop, the collective, group feeling became stronger. New, small, informal groups were created, and we learned more about each other's lives and working conditions beyond ACRES. We also had a women's meeting (in the bar), where we discussed possible ways to highlight issues related to being a woman action researcher, as well as issues of equality between men and women in democratic change processes. We agreed to build a network of women action researchers, with the goal of arranging a conference on the theme of women in action research. This came to fruition quickly because there was an international conference in Finland later that year where Anneli Pulkkis from Helsinki arranged a workshop on action research from a gender perspective.

Between the Third and Fourth Workshops

After leaving the workshop in Trondheim, my core question was, If the new paradigm for organizing work is the same as the way women have traditionally organized their lives, will future work life arrangements automatically be good for women? I decided that I should compare the new paradigm with feminist research on men's and women's values and their different rationalities. When I started to write again, my introduction to this version ended as follows: "Out of these reflections about the ongoing structural change in working life, I will below focus on organizational change and the development of working life and discuss this from a gender perspective: (1) How will organizations change? (2) Will women's values influence the 'new' work organizations? (3) What are women's conditions in working life from a feminist point of view? (4) How does participative action research make women visible?"

I wrote at least half a dozen versions of this introduction before I sent one in to be discussed at the final seminar. I asked a number of people around me to read and criticize it. Though I received conflicting advice, I strongly felt that my writing had improved.

Fourth Seminar

My male colleagues in my small group seemed to find the results of my action research cases interesting and gave me positive feedback. Finally, through the case examples, they could understand what I was trying to say. I was most proud of the way my theoretical analysis connected feminist theory with the new organizational paradigm. I had the feeling that my colleagues had not been able to understand my feminist perspective and my message until I could give them examples from everyday working life. We agreed that gender was a "black hole" in the action research literature. Again, I was advised not to use strong rhetoric if

I wanted to be taken seriously. The balance between awakening an interest and irritating an audience is a delicate one.

I learned a lot about myself during the writing process. I became more aware of my thoughts and more stimulated to write. I also found out that I have difficulties modulating and compressing my writing. In the process of revision and learning, I had written hundreds of pages before time pressure finally forced me to accept a final version.

I think we all felt sad when the ACRES seminars came to an end, for the group feeling was strong in the ACRES group overall, as it was in the small groups. One issue in which there was disagreement, however, concerned the book being developed about ACRES. Specifically, the participants did not agree that the staff should have unilateral control over which papers would be published. We wanted to meet again later in the fall to make this choice more democratically.

My overall impression is that ACRES succeeded in its mission to develop a strong network among action researchers that will broaden and last for a long time. Already, a network has been formed of researchers interested in gender in action research, and in February 1994, a seminar was held in Halmstad on action research for doctoral students.

Between the Fourth Workshop and the Amsterdam Meeting

At this point, I faced a choice. Either I could let the paper remain as it was and have it published as part of the proceedings of the ACRES program or I could continue the writing process in an effort to have the paper selected for publication in the ACRES book. A decision to do the latter would cost some more months of writing and there would still be the possibility of negative criticism and revision.

Although I realized that I had only a slim chance of having my paper selected for the book, I thought I had such an important story to tell that I still had to make the effort. So, after our summer holiday, I took up the writing process again, wrote new drafts, and, the night before the deadline, faxed an updated version of the paper to Morten Levin in Trondheim.

Amsterdam Meeting

In the middle of November, six of the ACRES participants and the staff, minus Davydd and Kjell, met again near Amsterdam. We came from Norway, Sweden, the United Kingdom, the United States, and the Netherlands for two intensive days of work. In all, there were fifteen papers to be discussed. Together, we set up at least ten criteria to use in analyzing the papers.

It was a genuine pleasure to attend this meeting since the learning environment was so dynamic. In an ordinary Swedish doctoral seminar, one professor and a handful of students discuss one's paper. Here, I received the attention of four professors and a group of qualified researchers.

My paper was discussed right after two brilliant papers. Compared with the discussion of these papers, I felt, first, that the criticism of mine was massive and, second, that nobody agreed with my argument. As the discussion went on, however, I realized that there was strong agreement on my core issue, the importance of including the gender perspective in action research. Through their questions and criticism, the staff and the participants forced me to stand up intellectually for my arguments. My writing was given great attention, and in the final judgment my paper was placed in the second group, which meant it had to be partly rewritten. (Papers in the first group were accepted as they were, and papers in the third group had to be completely rewritten to be acceptable.) Once again, my rhetoric was found to be aggressive, and I had to modify my tone and strengthen my arguments. My new deadline was five months later.

Being part of the selection process taught me a lot about the academic way of thinking and evaluating work, though I am not certain I learned as much from ACRES about the rhetoric of writing research as I could have. At the very least, I now have a worldwide network of action researchers who are struggling with the same questions I am.

PART II

Chapter 7

Applied Research or Action Research?

Different or Complementary Methods

Øystein Spjelkavik

> A method is a way of doing something and a means to solve problems and to amass new knowledge. Any means that serve this purpose belong to the arsenal of methods. — Aubert, *The Hidden Society*

Since I came in touch with the action research community a few years back, I have been puzzled by the creeping feeling of having joined a sect whose members claim that their way of doing research is fundamentally different from other forms of research and by the somewhat rancorous attitude among action researchers toward "academic" research and common scientific procedures.

An important challenge in the action research field must be to improve the research component in our projects so as to increase the legitimacy of action research in the social science community. There are at least two ways to achieve this. One is to focus on the differences between action research and other forms of research. Another way is to demonstrate to the scientific community that action research is simply a variant of other applied scientific procedures.

Many features of what is often labeled "applied research" can also be called "action research," at least in a broad and unorthodox sense of the term. I shall develop this argument by showing through, the use of a case study that normally would be described as applied research, that several principles of action research are at work.

The orthodox view of action research holds that an action research project must be clearly defined as such — and commitments made — before the researcher enters the field of research. As my project shows, action research can be more of an on-the-way process.

After some brief definitions of applied and action research, I shall describe the stages in my research project, which focuses on fish farmers in a coastal community of northern Norway. I hope through this discussion of my methods and findings to shed light on my assertions that (1) action research is a variant of applied research,

(2) that the most important difference between common applied research and action research is the evolving contract between the researcher and the researched, and (3) that there are no decisive distinctions between applied and action research strategies that make a particular epistemology of action research necessary.

Action Research Defined

Emery (1986) states that the aim of action research is to help integrate the social sciences and to advance social science through direct involvement in practical issues. On a more ethical level, the aim, according to Emery, is to underpin the democratic values in society.

Orthodox sociologists tend to be skeptical not only of action research but of the notion of applied research: "The notion of applied sociology is neither a discrete and developed area of the discipline nor a term which is commonly used by sociologists. It raises problems of ethics and professional autonomy" (Abercrombie et al. 1988: 12).

As Aubert (1985) points out, however, the sociologist is also a member of society, not only an observer, and he finds it meaningless that describing society should be more valuable than changing it or, alternatively, preserving it (see also Kalleberg 1989). Aubert thus labeled his approach "problem-oriented empiricism," in opposition to positivistic sociology.

As in orthodox sociology, however, there is a one-sided relationship in most applied research between the researcher and the informants.[1] In action research, by contrast, the development of solutions to local problems is a primary goal.

In general, action researchers (*e.g.*, Palshaugen 1992; Sorensen 1992a, 1992b; van Beinum 1993) view the participatory aspect of action research as absolutely different from traditional empirical research and action research and empirical social science as two different activities. Thus, Hans van Beinum describes action research as "the study of operating systems in action, . . . not a method in the traditional sense of the word" (1993: 190).

Whatever they prefer to call themselves, most social scientists are, in one way or another, studying "operating systems in action." It is the methods used, more than the object of study or the epistemological reasonings, that distinguish action research from more traditional applied research. Viewed from this perspective, the participatory aspect of action research supplements the applied model.

Models for Organizing Fish Farming

I started my field research on the coast of Helgeland in northern Norway in 1987 while I was pursuing graduate study in work and organizational sociology with a particular interest in rural development and survival strategies in marginal or remote areas. Personal involvement, time spent in the field, and the frequency of contacts have varied over the years, but a stable relationship has developed with about ten people in the area around Helgeland. In the last two years, the project has taken on a more regional perspective and my contacts have broadened to include neighboring "communes" on the coast. At present, researchers at various applied research institutes and universities are also among my most valuable contacts. In the reports from the first part of the project (Spjelkavik 1990 and 1992), the development of fish farming in Helgeland, one of the strongest aquaculture communities in northern Norway, is described and analyzed. Two models for organizing fish farming--"peasant" and "industry" — are presented, and the main analytical concern is the role of the peasant model in the development of the business.[2] The main conclusion is that fish-farming units were established as an element of the occupational pluralism that characterizes the local economy and that created the basis for remarkably strong economic growth throughout the 1970s and 1980s. The analysis focuses on the interaction between business life and the local community by investigating the importance of local entrepreneurial activity, capital investment behavior, processes of succession, and the organization of work.

Households in which income comes from multiple sources are still the norm on the Norwegian coast, where fish farming was one of several dominant occupations during the 1970s.[3] The structure of fish farming changed throughout the 1980s, but not because the residents were unsuccessful at adapting. Rather, the fish-farming businesses became the main source of income, sometimes the only source. Similarly, the business units no longer followed the peasant model not because they had failed at small-scale production but because individual households of fish farmers had become so successful.

Fish farming became a local opportunity in Helgeland as part of a process of income adjustment in which people with various income sources raised or consolidated their incomes by putting some fish into a net in the water and feeding them until they reached slaughter size. Most, if not all, of the fish farmers in this community began their careers in this way.

The established peasant model disappeared simply because the actors quickly found themselves with several incentives for expansion and few hindrances. Running a fish farm while also pursuing other occupations became so profitable that it soon became unnecessary for households to combine incomes.

Role of Opportunity Situations in Fish Farmers' Career Decisions

The main purpose of my research was to isolate the conditions in the fish farmers' opportunity situation that generated the existing form and structure of fish farming. It is difficult to specify a single mechanism that has been important for every person; rather, several factors stand out.

An important feature in the fish farmers' career course is that their opportunity situations changed after each decision about their careers was made. Thus, conditions changed on the basis of choices made earlier. From this, it follows that the choice to start fish farming was a preliminary result, or the aggregated effect, of a series of short-term decisions. Opportunity situations changed after each choice was made — leading to more and more reasons to choose fish farming as a source of income.

My intention was to explain how and why the occupational structure in fish farming emerged and changed through a variety of processes working in combination. The career analysis enabled me to explain the institutionalization of new patterns of behavior in a local community. The analysis was process-oriented, in that the changes in life situations involved everyday situations — how people created and ordered their own society and how one decision followed from another.

The main methodological strategy involved was fieldwork; I lived and worked with the fish farmers and their families in order to capture their life stories and understand their opportunity situations. By investigating their life histories, I was able to propose "hows and whys" about the observed social structure and to develop empirical data about the genesis and workings of the models in question.

This first part of the project, which can be labeled the applied research, was anchored in the following questions: When we look at the fish farmers' careers, what model best explains the emergence of the local business? And what model might be most fruitful for the local community, given that we wish to improve the possibility that other local actors will be able to undertake similar careers by using the free natural resources available to them? By raising questions like these, the project is part of an official debate on the aquaculture business.[4] It is also easy to see that there is only a small step from these questions to practical suggestions or conclusions.

Role of Co-researchers

The next step in the research project involved taking a more participatory or action-oriented approach. In particular, passive key informants were transformed into more active co-researchers.[5] In traditional interviewing, structured or informal, an informant is an object from whom the researcher collects information as part of the data-collecting process. By contrast, a co-researcher is a member of the organization under study who, together with the researcher, is part of the research team. Although the co-researcher's role may be unclear, this strategy obviously creates the opportunity for joint meaning construction of the available data.

In the participatory part of the project (Spjelkavik 1993, 1994), the goal was to link the process of internationalization that was occurring in fish farming with the local situation. The most important features of this development were made clear through several central actors, who represented various official bodies and banks. Questions were raised about the hindrances and possibilities for increased cooperation between municipalities as a strategy to meet the rapid changes in the market and the increasing internationalization of the economy. It was argued that local economies increasingly are integrated with and dependent on international economic development and, further, that the ability to compete depends increasingly on having access to and investing in expertise.

The report for this part of the project (Spjelkavik 1993) argued that expertise must be generated from the inside rather than from outside the region. A vital challenge for local and regional development and competence building is small-scale business units that are horizontally organized. Closer integration with the European Community would make the conditions for developing local farming more uncertain. Further, remote parts of Norway are more dependent on natural resources than ever, and the only way to bolster local career possibilities would be by developing a strategy for locally controlled resource regimes.[6]

Kalleberg (1992) claims that the most important component in a research project is the question, since it fixes the general orientation of the project. Kalleberg suggests that there are three kinds of questions in social science: ascertaining questions — those we ask when we engage in finding out how a phenomenon is, was, or is going to be; valuating questions — those we ask when we are interested in what value a social reality has; and constructive questions, such as "What can and ought a set of actors to do to transform a given social reality into a better social reality?" (1992: 33).

In the first part of the project, ascertaining questions were raised more or less purely for their intellectual interest, while the methods used raised more valuative and applied issues. In the second part of the project, there were no clearly defined research questions at the start but rather a theme: the implications of internationalization, possible membership in the European Community, and so forth. The questions were chosen and defined by the local actors to be the most important ones. Before releasing the report, some of the local actors made comments and criticism, stating what they found interesting and not and where they did not agree with my analysis.

Thus, both questions and analysis were developed in a different way than in the earlier part of the project. Earlier, I depended on key informants. Now, questions were generated through extensive discussions with local actors, and the analysis was very much part of the process of exchanging views with these informants in a form of cogenerative learning; the relationships involved had changed, and as the participative part of the research became more important, the project became closer to action research.

I found this participative strategy extremely useful, in that it provided a good foundation to raise the "right" questions and to develop as qualified assumptions about local conditions as possible. The notion of the "right" questions needs some clarification, however. I believe it is impossible to do research, no matter whether we call it applied or action or not, on an organization or a local community without having extensive substantive knowledge about the field in question. The necessary knowledge must be of three kinds. First, there must be general, perhaps even abstract, knowledge of the organizations, local communities, economy, business, organizational learning, fish farming, and whatever. Second, there must be local lived-in knowledge about the particular features of the local conditions that generate opportunity situations. Third, there must be a theoretical framework and the ability to analyze data.

According to Meløe (1992), the good social scientist is a person with experiences from different worlds. To raise questions that are constructive both from a scientific and a practical point of view, knowledge from all three worlds is necessary. In my project, I had gained substantial knowledge through indirect learning, by studying theory and by learning from other researchers' contributions. The theoretical framework was very much provided from extensive work in libraries. Local, lived-in knowledge was gained through fieldwork, interviews, and conversations with key informants, which eventually generated a sort of co-research relationship.

In one case, a co-researcher and I may even write an article together, meaning I will write, she will comment. Also, with the help of some of my research contacts, she and I set up a three-day seminar on one of the northern Norwegian islands. The seminar, which locally was regarded as a very big event, covered fisheries, fish farming, access and ownership of natural resources, internationalization, new restrictions and possibilities for working with the EEC, and so forth. All the themes resulted from discussions between the researchers and local people.

Although the seminar was traditional in structure, with lectures followed by discussions in work groups, the process of organizing the event entailed a strong participatory element. It was truly a collaborative effort that linked my contacts in academic circles and my informants' contacts locally and regionally. The locals see it as good that researchers, planners, and politicians, for once, came out to meet them. The whole event, from the first planning to the publication of a book (Meland *et al.* 1993), occurred because of my longtime research involvement in the Helgeland area.

The action orientation of my project did not occur because of a moral imperative. On the contrary, I gradually got to know my informants and their local community better, after evenings spent drinking beer and coffee with them, and became part of their lives, just as they became more important parts of mine.

This involvement generated a new kind of contract between us, based on moral engagement. As we shall see in the next section, this participation is not always easy to handle.

Research Strategies

My project has moved from "pure" research focused on organizational models to applied research and now involves aspects of participatory action research. The researched gradually came to participate in defining the research questions, in conducting the analysis, and in shaping the final report. The research questions, however, still very much depend on analytical models. The difference is that I am now in a position to analyze local development and change from "the bottom up."

The rights and obligations I have as a researcher and the fish farmers have as the researched are different from those of participants in common applied research. Questions like the following arise: How can I secure my own integrity as a researcher? How can I avoid being controlled by the informants' special interests? How can I avoid going native, getting stuck in the field and falling into the trap of delegating the analysis to the informants? These are important questions, and they raise the crucial question of what is research.

Greenwood and González (1992) report that the professional action researcher operates in various roles: consultant, teacher, researcher, and team member. I would add that the action researcher also operates as a partner in conversation and as a critic and aid in clarifying the actors' opportunity situations. In Selander's reflection on action research, he states that "the presence of a researcher within a process could be a good basis for new knowledge for all of the agents — the researcher could be of great help to give perspectives and tools for reflections-in-action" (1987: 7). Later on, Selander states that the researcher has the capability of reflection-on-action. To enable this reflection-on-action to take place, it is necessary to have elements of both participation and distance — participation, to get as close as possible to opportunity situations; distance, to be able to describe and analyze them.

In the future, my project will involve a few key informants with whom I will try to maintain an informal co-researcher relationship. This is possible because of our shared interests. Some of these co-researchers are interested in what I am doing and in my views and perspectives. They in turn provide the local knowledge and information that I need to conduct my research. This relationship does not necessarily include any planned change, although change or a participatory project may result. It is not always possible to know this in advance; it may not even be an aim. According to Greenwood, Whyte, and Harkavy, one cannot "mandate in advance that a particular research process will become a fully developed participatory action research project" (1993: 76). This review of my own process of participation in my research has shown that there are varieties of action research and degrees of participation over the life of a project.

Verstehen and Causality

My aim now is to develop an analysis of fish farming that is as close to "the actors' points of views" as possible. By this I mean I hope to explain the development of fish farming in Helgeland in a way that makes local choices understandable.

It is not enough merely to describe local actors' views. We must also explain their views, their actions, and how these views and actions generate a system (cf. Berger and Luckmann 1983). The concept of *Verstehen* (Weber 1947), which resembles the concept of grounded theory, is useful here. According to Anselm Strauss and Juliet Corbin, the goal when trying to achieve grounded theory is "to build theory that is faithful to and illuminates the area under study" (1990: 24; see also Glaser and Strauss 1967).

Further, it is not enough to cite the cause (Elster 1989; see also Barth 1981) of an event or situation. The research task is not primarily to suggest an analysis in which the local actors can recognize themselves but to suggest an analysis in which local actors' actions are understandable and rational.[7]

The search for mechanisms that enable us to analyze change as the result of a combination of individual actions and larger causes represents the research component of a project. Studies on "operating systems in action," to use van Beinum's words, need explanatory elements in addition to descriptions to be called research. Kalleberg (1992) points out that the most important intellectual movement in a scientific work is the line of argumentation from the creation of important scientific questions, through many-sided and clear-cut discussions on the material, to the grounded answers to the formulated questions. Kalleberg states that such answers must be valuated within the scientific community and may be approved or rejected there. Kalleberg (1989) also makes the important point that the sociologist is engaged in a dialogue with his field, with sociology itself — with existing literature and colleagues.

Creative Surprises

According to Whyte (1991), participatory action research is likely to depend more on "creative surprises" than on preformed hypotheses. It is probably also fair to say that many action researchers give the action itself primary status, especially by focusing on implementation, and they therefore tend to be pragmatic and to search for solutions to solve the actors' problems.

Elden states that participatory research is characterized by the absence of "predefined categories" (1983), a notion he probably suggested in opposition to the more popular notion of "creativity." If he means one should enter the field without fixed answers, then I agree with him. If he means one should enter the field without theoretical glasses and hypotheses ("tabula rasa"), I would argue that this is impossible. Put simply, theory arranges or orders facts.

In popular explanations, theory is normally implicit, while in scientific explanations, there is at least an attempt to clarify the theoretical perspective.[8] To avoid seeing only trivialities, a creative basis for good research is to enter the field with "predefined categories," based on substantial knowledge of the field in question. If one does not have substantial knowledge, it is of course fair to start with some explorative preproject activities. As Strauss and Corbin state, "One does not start with a theory and then prove it. Rather, one begins with an area of study and what is relevant to that area is allowed to emerge" (1990: 23).

In explorative research, the researcher also tests assumptions. The process of working out a research question to the building of theory implies moving between inductive and deductive thinking, as there is "a constant interplay between proposing and checking" (Strauss and Corbin 1990: 11).[9]

When a strategy of workability replaces a strategy based on testing assumptions,[10] research aimed at a knowledge of social science will tend to be replaced by a search for practical solutions. In search conferences (Brokhaug 1985; Ebeltoft 1991), dialogue conferences (Engelstad 1993; Gustavsen 1992), and round table discussions (Greenwood and González 1992) — all tools for gaining both practical and theoretical knowledge — more effort is put into the pragmatic aspects of workability than into the scientific question-answer logic. In fact, there is nothing wrong with this, and morally it might even be appropriate. Action researchers simply have to be more clear about their research questions, about the kinds of knowledge and theories they are building upon, and about the answers they actually produce and how they produce them.

Thus, an applied research question should be important both for practical and scientific reasons and should be linked to earlier research contributions. Likewise, other researchers should be able to use and build upon the findings action researchers contribute. Since action researchers engage in research of an idiographic character, reliability and replication may not be possible, but that should not prevent us from living up to scientific principles as best we can. As the fight against positivism in social sciences has taught us, we do not arrive at any final truth, so that the status of our theories and generalizations are always at a preliminary stage.

Yin suggests that the general way of approaching the problem of reliability in case study research "is to make as many steps as possible as operational as possible, and to conduct research as if someone were always looking over your shoulder" (1989: 45). The two most important steps are (1) the documentation, so that our suggested experiences can be valuated by others; and (2) the line of argumentation, which must be related convincingly to the documented material and to alternative ways of interpreting the material and reality (see also Kalleberg 1992).

As Brox (1990) has pointed out, the limitations and ambiguities of weberian ideals are not an argument for rejecting them.[11] Instead, they are an argument for defining and operationalizing those ideals more precisely. It is obvious that action research must be more than pure data collecting and a search for practical solutions. In an effort to clarify the research component in our projects, Brox's simplified version of the research process is useful:

1. Research question
2. Developing hypothesis
3. Collecting data
4. Treatment
5. Explanation
6. Practical conclusions
7. Feedback

Although a research project will not necessarily follow this model exactly, any research project will feature at least the first five phases, while applied research must also feature phases 6 and 7. To be called action research, an action research project must also feature some sort of participation during some or all of the phases of the process.

The difference between the applied research model and the action research model is that participation with the actors in the field is an important part of action research. Phases 1 to 5 of Brox's model represent the phases of a basic research project, while the two last phases constitute the beginning not only of applied research but of action research as well.

Although the applied research model is very general, it is no different epistemologically from an action research model.[12] Action research is simply one of several possible ways to conduct applied research, part of "the tool kit of the social sciences" (Whyte, Greenwood, and Lazes 1991: 19). It follows from this that combinations of strategies are possible and in many respects are fruitful. Both Whyte (1991) and van Beinum (1993) state that all possible methods may be used in an action research project. Thus, action research is a method that can be fruitfully combined with other methods (questionnaires, interviews, observations, whatever), and in this respect it does not require specific epistemological commitments.

Conclusion

The project reported on here used both applied research and action research methodologies in an effort to fit the methodologies to the research tasks in question. When participation is not necessary to answer the research question, participation should not be considered. In that respect, I do not agree with Greenwood, Whyte, and Harkavy (1993), who argue that developing participatory action research is both a scientific and a moral goal.

Van Beinum insists that action research is not necessarily better research but different. Rather, I would say that because action research *is* better, the choice to use it should be made on practical or pragmatic grounds. When we choose action research, we should choose it because it produces better scientific results than other tools in the toolbox of possibilities.

The moral dimension in research is much more linked to the question of whether to do applied research or not. Values count, first of all, when it comes to deciding whether a project, program, or change process is worth research support. In the rat race of getting funding, this is an important consideration to take into account, especially for action researchers who believe that a critical goal of action research is to underpin the democratic values in society. Is helping Norsk Hydro gain larger shares of the world market underpinning democratic values? What about helping a manufacturing industry implement more efficient technology? What about engaging in industrializing fish farming? When we choose action research methods, we should at least see to it that our research aims are supporting participatory-based processes of development.

If we use action research methods, we must be aware of the commitments involved. Participation in a development process means working in close collaboration with the researched. One should, however, be aware that there are degrees of research involvement and coparticipation. It is important, therefore, always to remember that features of action research can be integrated with more common applied research strategies.

The aim of applied social science is to find variables one can manipulate (see Brox 1990). To learn or to act on the basis of scientific knowledge requires the knowledge that can help actors find better ways of realizing their values within the framework of what is possible. Whatever we do to produce this knowledge is method.

Acknowledgments

Many people have given me valuable comments on drafts of this article. In particular, I would like to thank Olav Eikeland, Davydd J. Greenwood, Kari Marie Helle, Ragnvald Kalleberg, Morten Levin, and Robert Salomon.

Notes

1. In orthodox basic research, the notion of respondents suggests an even more passive appre-
    hension and distance.

2. The concept of "peasant" as used in my analysis is somewhat equivalent to small-scale
    production by the household members; much less emphasis is placed on the subsistence
    consumption aspects than in Alexander V. Chayanov's model (Sahlins 1972; Shanin, ed.
    1987; Thorner *et al.* 1986). The distinguishing feature of this type of adaptation is that the
    household bases its strategies for viability on several income possibilities in addition to fish
    farming.
        The concept of "industry" here indicates the reduced importance of the household in the
    production system and the growing importance of the capitalist relationship between owner
    and externally recruited workers. On another level, there is a change of focus from fish
    farming as a possibility for local self-employment to fish farming as a possibility for gaining
    a share in a worldwide market (Spjelkavik 1990, 1992).

3. Occupational pluralism is crucial in north Norway. Characteristically, jobs on the coast are
    seasonal, and the traditional economy has been based on subsistence agriculture and fishing.
    Because of the increased circulation of money, animal husbandry is very much reduced
    nowadays (*cf.* Brox 1966; Seierstad *et al.* 1985; Spjelkavik 1990).

4. Pure researchers are, of course, part of the official policy debate, but they often obscure the
    political implications of their research under the cloak of "objectivism" and natural develop-
    ment, instead of treating economic categories as social constructions. Or they analyze
    enterprises in isolation and not as a part of populated local communities (see, for instance,
    Hannesson 1991 and Munkejord 1985). The notion of natural development in fish farming is
    treated more closely in Spjelkavik 1993.

5. According to James D. Spradley (1979), key informants must be as typical as possible of the
    cultural group under study and have participated in the culture for a long time.

6. The problem of developing locally controlled resource regimes is tied to the fact that control
    over natural resources such as land, waterfalls, fish, recreation, and so on is being delocalized
    and made negotiable on international markets (*cf.* Brox 1992). The main issue then is whether
    resource-based businesses can be secured by institutional frameworks that support local
    resource administration (Spjelkavik 1994).

7. It is therefore misleading to say that "for our research to be valid, we must be able to say that
    what we describe is recognized by the research participants as so," as Sandra Kirby and Kate
    McKenna (1989: 36) suggest. *Verstehen* consists of placing oneself in a position that enables
    one to see the meaning or purposes other people give to their actions. It is important to notice
    that the first-order explanation is the situational explanation of the people who carry out the
    actions, while the second-order explanation is the explanation suggested by the researcher (*cf.*
    Berger and Kellner 1981).

8. The purpose of concepts like *Verstehen*, grounded theory, local theory, and so on is to clarify
    popular theory or assumptions — that is, to transform popular theory into scientific theory. In
    fact, setting out to describe a local theory in itself implies a theory. As Cato Wadel points out,
    "Description implies both generalizations and abstractions. . . . We could say that by
    classifying we are already violating reality" (1988: 19; my translation).

9. "While creativity is necessary to develop an effective theory, of course, the researcher must
    always validate any categories and statements of relationships arrived at creatively through
    the total process" (Strauss and Corbin 1990: 28). Clearly, this notion of creativity does not
    imply the absence of clarifying and testing assumptions, as Elden seems to claim.

10. In grounded theory, as presented by Strauss and Corbin (1990), verification is the ideal. This is problematic, since in idiographic sciences we can never prove what is true — at best, we can only falsify assumptions that are not true according to our empirical data (*cf*. Popper 1963).

11. A very simplified version of Weber's solution to the problem of striking a balance between engagement and objectivity is to tell the truth and not hide facts that are not supportive of one's own political views (see Brox 1990; Fivelsdal 1971). Strauss and Corbin (1990) argue along the same lines when they claim that the requisite skills for doing qualitative research are analytical distance and the ability to recognize and avoid bias, to obtain valid and reliable data, and to think abstractly.

12. Olav Eikeland (1990) insists that by focusing on the "methodology of methods," action research ought to be something other than the prevailing applied research, as well as the prevailing action research. His point is linked to the different status of knowledge produced in the research process, while my point is linked to the roles and commitments involved in the research process. I have no difficulty seeing that choice of method influences the knowledge produced. My argument is simply that we have to be explicit in why we chose a certain method, what questions we set out to answer, and what knowledge we produce by doing so.

Chapter 8

Linking Social Science Working Life Research and Work Reform

A Role for Universities

Kjell Eriksson

This chapter discusses the potential for universities to function as agents in regional working life development. One motive behind my analysis is that in Sweden research and development on working life has until now largely taken place outside universities, by individual institutes and consultants (AMFO 1991: 15-17). The institutional basis for working life research is thereby split between the university system and several autonomous institutes.

Another motive behind my analysis is that regional systems appear to be of increasingly greater interest to researchers engaged in working life action research than single organizations (Levin 1993; Engelstad and Gustavsen 1993). This is certainly the case with my own institute at Halmstad University, where the role of the university in regional development is very much on the agenda. More generally, the role of universities as supporters or even generators of national and regional growth, innovation, and development has for a long time been discussed both in Sweden and elsewhere (see, for example, Piore and Sabel 1984 and Stankiewicz 1986).

I base my analysis and arguments mainly on my participation in the LOM program, through which I became engaged in regionally based, action-oriented social science research being conducted through the young and newly established Halmstad University in southwest Sweden in the late 1980s and early 1990s. This research eventually led to the formation of an institute, where I have been acting as the director and a research team member, and subsequently was developed further. My intentions in discussing this process are to identify some of the problems that arise during the development and institution building of a research program at a new university as well as to point to examples of practical solutions to such problems.

Institutional Background

In the postwar period, Sweden, like other industrial countries, has been providing large amounts of money to universities to support social science research and development on such working life issues as work organization and industrial democracy, technological change and productivity, psychosocial problems, and health. Most of the time, these issues have been considered virtually unanimously in the public debate as the mutual responsibilities of Sweden's highly organized labor market parties (the collective bargaining organizations) and the political system. These partners have also been critics of such research, however, saying that although much research money has been spent, the research has contributed little to producing a healthier, more effective, democratic, and humane working life (Gustavsen and Sandberg 1984).

The respective roles of the partners in these programs have occasionally come under discussion. The mix of research and social change roles expected of researchers has been troublesome, too. For example, the researchers sometimes lost respect from their academic colleagues for doing action research in collaboration with collective bargaining organizations because the assumption was that such values as "objectivity" and "disinterestedness" had been sacrificed.

In an evaluation initiated by the Swedish Work Environment Fund, Naschold looks into three major nationally supported broad working life development programs that have been conducted in Sweden since about 1970 — the URAF Program (1969-1973), named after a joint council established to address issues of collaboration identified by the main labor parties in Sweden; the Development Program (1982-1986); and the "Leadership, Organization, and Codetermination" (LOM) Program (1985-1990) — all supervised by university researchers, as opposed to private consultants (Nashold *et al.* 1993: 25). The programs have engaged about one hundred researchers and several hundred workplaces in either applied social science or action research and have cost U.S.$30 million in 1996 dollars, according to AMFO annual reports. The results, however, in terms of the connections developed between the national university system and working life reform programs have been weak, to say the least. Sustainable infrastructures for future work reform research were not created (Naschold *et al.* 1993: 95-96).

The URAF Program and the Development Program focused on a limited number of firms in which direct changes in work and organizational design were occurring. The URAF Program demonstrated the possibility of organizational choice (as opposed to, for example, technological determinism), whereas the Development Program made "the connection between work organization and economic and technical progress explicit, public and legitimate" (Rankin 1989: 66). The goal of both programs was to make the results of a small number of "star projects" available to a large number of firms eager to apply the experiences of successful projects.

In the LOM Program, which took place in 148 organizations in the private and public sector and involved 72 projects, the aim was to create the largest possible number of links between and within the 148 organizations so as to provide the greatest possible support for change activities. University researchers were not supposed to engage primarily in designing new work organizations, new workplaces, and so on but, rather, to facilitate ways for organizations to collaborate with each other around working life development issues so as to guarantee widespread effects from their efforts to change. The focus of the LOM Program was on communication and network-creating activities (Gustavsen 1990: 3-4).

On the whole, none of the institutional infrastructures for Sweden's major work reform programs was very stable. In each case, a national *ad hoc* program committee was created by the national labor market parties and the national funding agency for projects addressing the "working environment — the Swedish Work Environment Fund (AMFO). Then single researchers or small groups of researchers from the university system were recruited to the programs. The most important sources of research support were the central national program committees and two research institutes that operated independently of the university system, the FA-Council and the Swedish Center for Working Life, both located in Stockholm. The national university system was not supportive to any great extent, with the possible exception of during the later stages of the LOM Program, when a new social science working life research facility was established at Halmstad University and a facility strengthened at Karlstad University.

Naschold *et al.* (1993: 95-96) has commented on the relation between the academic system and the work reform research being conducted in Sweden and has concluded that the extremely unattractive working conditions for the researchers make the academic system incompatible with the structure of work reform research programs. The short duration of many of the programs made them hard for individual researchers to combine with normal academic careers. As a consequence, it has been "difficult or even impossible to build up an experienced scientific personnel potential of the required size and quality for work with development programs" (Naschold *et al.* 1993: 96).

But this is only one part of the problem. Deeper problems exist at the interface of university research and working life.

Shipbuilding Program

Goals and Organization

Occasionally, concrete, practical problems become the focus of both people from workplaces and social science researchers. For example, in the late 1970s, thousands of blue- and white-collar shipyard workers were put out of work in Sweden as the shipbuilding industry, with Gothenburg at center stage, entered a phase of stagnation and ultimately collapse. In a span of only a few years, more than ten thousand work opportunities were lost because of the crisis. The University of Gothenburg was called upon to do research, cast light on, analyze, and dissemi- nate information about these events, with the hope of being of use to those people most affected by this dramatic situation.

The severe crisis within the shipbuilding industry functioned as a continuous motive for research conducted collaboratively by university researchers and local blue- and white-collar unions. Research was carried out not "on" the organizations and their employees but as collaborative efforts aimed at learning how to meet the threats and challenges of a complex situation. Different activities were organized, such as combined (union-researchers) groups for research and analysis and a regular multidisciplinary university course based on problems and questions that had been developed in collaboration. The program was very effective from a research point of view. It produced nineteen research reports from the field, part of a dissertation, and several contributions in scientific publications.[1] Some reports were written by researchers, some by union representatives, and some collaboratively. This mutual involvement in the writing process was, and probably still is, unique or at least rare.[2] (Table 1 provides an overview of the program.)

During the period of the shipbuilding program, similar activities were set in motion in other regions in Sweden. I and Jan Holmer mapped out these activities in a survey (Eriksson and Holmer 1982) and, with two exceptions,[3] they took place mainly in the regions where the newer universities and colleges were located and involved organized intervention, that is, participation from the researchers in actions aimed at solving practical problems.

Problematic Issues

Although the shipbuilding program was in many respects successful, it nowhere near reached its potential. First, the resources the University of Gothenburg had at its disposal to contribute to the program were limited because of the institutional organization of the university. The more than three-year-long period of collabora- tion was possible only because the national Work Environment Fund provided extra money to the university. Second, faculty and researchers in different disci- plines were not used to cooperating with one another on comprehensive tasks. Third, individual work situations made the participation of most researchers fragmented and temporary.

The traditional disciplinary organization of the University of Gothenburg was not complemented by multidisciplinary institutions, and the technology institutes were even organized in a university of their own. Furthermore, and maybe more important, during the program university staff were not supposed to cooperate with people from the practical trades in the shipbuilding industry. On several occasions other senior university researchers criticized the collaborative activities and the mix of research with "teaching and consultancy." Their criticisms revealed differences between the rather pragmatic and utility-directed values of most of the research staff in the shipbuilding program and those more orthodox academic values held by several researchers in positions outside the program.

One important conclusion of the program was that Swedish universities were less ready for collaborative research and educational activities than they might have been, since such research currently depended too much on only a few enthusiasts and the tools and experiences for such an endeavor generally did not exist within the universities' regular activities. For example, working life problems often demand multidisciplinary approaches. The practical prerequisites for multidisciplinary research programs, however, are still not very well developed. The work units of the universities are still organized mainly along disciplinary lines. Further, knowledge of relevance to local action and local problem solving is held in rather low esteem among significant numbers of social scientists. Even more serious, critics suggested that the primary goal of university social science research — the enrichment of social science — was difficult or even impossible to combine with the advancement of practical affairs important to local labor organizations. (Table 2 outlines criticisms of the program.)

One could easily conclude from these criticisms that the social sciences have been isolated in Swedish academies, which is not correct as a general statement. The shipbuilding program may serve as an example, however, of how university social science research — which at the time of its introduction in Swedish academies was directed toward improving social conditions — had idealized the goal of seeking abstractions removed from both local and unique experiences. To restore (or establish) its connections with ongoing societal reform and change processes, university social science research needed to develop a new range of tools or models as well as organizations to meet the important demands put forward to the university not only, as in the above case, from blue- and white-collar labor unions but from other groups of employees and from employers (Sandberg 1981).

Since the early 1970s, most social science research carried out at Swedish universities has not been concerned primarily with understanding the practical consequences of scientific explanations or with developing methods of intervention or with inventing new solutions to practical problems. Rather, most social scientists are content with scientific explanations and interpretations.

I think it is an issue of significant importance that large numbers of social scientists keep avoiding the experience of taking part in practical problem solving. If the aim of social science research is to contribute to the development of knowledge that is useful to people facing difficult practical situations, it would be a good tactic for social scientists to learn how to construct and implement practical solutions to address these situations. Knowledge that leads to "applications" and "innovation and social renewal" must be considered a more important part of our knowledge of social problems (see, for example, Kalleberg 1993).

Finally, the central criticism from orthodox university researchers regarding the shipbuilding program concerned the alleged impossibility of promoting the mutual enrichment of social science and the important affairs of man at the same time (what Emery in 1960 defined to be the primary task of the Tavistock Institute of Human Research, or what later was defined as the central epistemological question of action research [van Beinum 1993: 190-98]).[4]

Center for Working Life Development

The question we are left with then is, How can the research capacity of universities be developed to support working life reform? Something can be learned perhaps from the case of a research institute at a new university in southwest Sweden. It may be possible, using its examples of collaboration and action research projects, to develop a research plan that will be of general interest to other newly established universities as well as to those older ones developing an interface with their surrounding regions.

The Center for Working Life Development (CAU) is a work unit at Halmstad University, which as of 1996 had more than four thousand students and a staff of more than 250. Expansion plans indicate those figures will increase. The major programs of study are education, economics, the social sciences, engineering, the health sciences, and the humanities.[5]

Working life research and development were initiated at Halmstad University in 1985. Initially, they were locally and regionally financed. Beginning in 1986, however, a research project was connected with the Work Environment Fund (AMFO) program LOM, and an important part of the research since has been financed by AMFO.

In 1988, CAU was given the status of a research institute at the university. Formally, the institute is headed by the university board, which has appointed a director. During the startup period of four years, there was also an advisory group of representatives from the labor market parties, from some regional authorities, and from within the university.

CAU has three strategic goals: conducting research, making constructive contributions to the working life of the region ("innovation and social renewal"), and providing education. The research goal is the basic one. It means making contributions of general value to national and international working life research, that is, the enrichment of social science. The innovation and social renewal goal means CAU strives to be a regional resource in working life innovation and development, applied research, training, information, and so on. Finally, the educational goal means that CAU will train students and new working life researchers/staff members, contribute to the research base for the educational programs of the university, initiate and assist in developing relevant courses and programs for the students, and provide support to university faculty.

Research Capacity

CAU has managed in a relatively short time to define and develop what seems to be sustainable social science research in the field of working life. This has been achieved by following four main strategies. First, the institute has adhered to the ideals, as Williams (1991) reminds us, that were once central to the American land grant movement — namely, innovation and social renewal and practical problem solving. Second, the institute has emphasized the unity of goals and activities that in most university contexts are clearly separated — that is, education, research, and the improvement of practical affairs. Third, the institute has encouraged its researchers to engage in action research or participatory AR when possible. Fourth, the institute has supported the creation of multidisciplinary educational forums, such as seminars, work groups, courses, and programs.

How Did We Get Here?

CAU staff and associates are a multidisciplinary mix of people with backgrounds in the social and behavioral sciences, economics, technology, and agronomy, although those in the social sciences are in the majority. Of the ten staff members, two are senior researchers, one is an administrator, and the rest are students in Ph.D. programs. About half the staff have commitments at other research institutes in Sweden or are also teaching.

Organizationally, CAU is clearly part of Halmstad University, but it can also be described as a program directed at intervening in working life reform processes in a regional context. Since 1986, CAU staff have been involved in at least fourteen major projects. An overview of the general orientations of these projects and the kinds and numbers of organizations involved are presented in Table 3.

While several CAU projects or interventions have developed in ways that could be characterized as action research activities, others have developed in more conventional nonparticipatory directions. But all of these projects demonstrate that what starts as conventional research, for example, a survey, may in a later stage develop into a truly participatory collaboration if both parties take an interest in it. This has been of special importance to CAU since it is aiming to establish long-term relations with firms in the surrounding region.

In a broad university setting, there need to be means by which to encourage the university and other organizations to maintain dialogues over long periods. This is one of the reasons CAU produces and distributes a monthly newsletter that is sent to every organization with which it has ever been involved. Monthly lectures/seminars also are held on work reform issues. Finally, recent ongoing projects explicitly encourage network building in the region.

Issues Covered in CAU Projects

The various projects or interventions in which CAU has been involved have been motivated by different events and situations, but a pervading interest among the firms as well as the researchers has been, in a broad sense, "high participative work organizations" and "high participative change processes." This is partly because of the interest in participatory aspects of work shown by mainstream Scandinavian working life researchers, as well as by managers and the major labor market parties. For a long time Swedish social science research has evidenced an interest in participation as a determinant of healthful work (Gardell 1980; Karasek and Theorell 1990). There has also been growing interest at the national political level and among managers in human economic competitiveness at national, regional, and specific company levels through the development of more participative work organizations (Produktivitetsdelegationen 1991). In the projects listed in table 3, participation frequently was defined as a central variable for action and in the analyses of the projects (and sometimes also conceived of as an independent variable in a causal relation), often in combination with other variables such as productivity, organization/management, technology implementation, product innovation, or market or customer/client relations.

All CAU projects have a process focus — that is, research expertise on process and participation is asked for — but a large number of specific content areas are also addressed. According to CAU annual reports and activity plans (1986-1995), the issues have tended to grow in number and to reflect more variety over time, covering a broad spectrum from technology implementation to gender issues.

CAU experiences indicate that researchers need to have a "mix" of local knowledge and general science knowledge. When this is the case, communication is easier between the general practitioners and the researchers. Cooperation also becomes easier. Since practical problems seldom follow the parameters of academic disciplines, researchers who can organize themselves into multidisciplinary teams are at a significant advantage.

Creating and Sustaining Institutional Support

Research, teaching, and renewal should not be defined as separate activities. CAU emphasizes that, although research and teaching may be of primary importance, innovation and social renewal is also critical if working life research is to be developed.[6] These three functions must also be looked upon as a unity. CAU staff have reasoned, and found in practice, that connecting their roles to all three institutional activities or functions increases the chances of developing sustainable research resources at Halmstad University. These insights have developed gradually as a result of CAU's experiences in interacting with its environment and were by no means obvious at all in the early years. From the beginning, CAU staff were put under constant pressure by the university board to get approval and economic support for its activities from at least three sources, namely, the national research councils, the educational programs within Halmstad University (especially the technology programs), and the regional working life community, including both its private and public organizations and institutions.

Over time, educational activities, such as discussing the problems of AR projects in classes and taking the students to the field, have become linked with research and social renewal activities. Today, comprehensive student projects of five to fifteen weeks' duration enable students to conduct fieldwork in organizations already running, or interested in starting, working life development programs. Universities are frequently called upon to provide training that is at one and the same time connected to scientific research and of practical usefulness. CAU's experiences should be of general interest in the discussions on national education policies going on in many countries today that focus on the practical effects of higher education on the social welfare and economic growth of nations and regions.

The R&D going on at CAU has, to a large extent, grown out of regional needs and possibilities, in the agricultural sector and among small and medium-sized industrial enterprises, for example. Agriculture has been undergoing heavy restructuring in line with the integration of the European market, and small and medium-sized enterprises have been defined regionally as problematic with respect to the relatively low level of competence in new technology. CAU has also been asked to provide consultancy directly to workplace organizations in the private and public sectors.

A recurring problem has been how best to utilize and combine the innovation and social renewal and research functions. This has often been hard to manage, since taking an advisory role with a single or a few organizations easily overstrains the resources available for such "research work" as writing articles.

Using and Developing Collaborative Tools

In the evaluative report on the LOM program (Naschold *et al.* 1993), one of the conclusions was that it was important to create processes to facilitate broad and sustained collaboration, as well as tools for controlling these processes. One of the functions of the interventions taken by CAU is to help invent and test something like a large participatory action research toolbox, with tools suited to initiating processes, diagnosing problems, developing process control, and evaluating the results. This function might be seen as furthering the action research capacity by helping others to use PAR tools.

A preliminary list of such tools, all of which have been used in CAU projects, might include the following:

- *Study circles or development circles* are held mostly during working hours for people in the same company who already know each other and who work at the same location and can meet easily. The formal educational content of study circles is selected on the basis of an identified common interest. The subjects studied are not only read about but dealt with in shared discussions (Eriksson and Holmer 1992: 72). Study circles meet on a regular basis usually for three to six months but may meet longer (Eriksson and Holmer 1992: 124-26).
- *Conferences* (group training, search, startup conferences) have been used frequently and functioned best in cooperation with larger and medium-sized organizations. Group training and search conferences as work-reform tools were first developed at the Tavistock Institute (M. Emery 1982). Startup conferences were developed somewhat independently in the Norwegian Industrial Democracy Program and were used later in the LOM Program. They have been fully described by Engelstad (1993) and Gustavsen (1992: 41-46), for example.
- *Social/community gatherings,* which serve as an alternative to conferences, have been conducted in twenty-four rural and other settings with farmers and others in very small enterprises. This method was developed by CAU staff in the Network Halland project (Svala *et al.*, 1993).
- *Project groups* have their roots in conferences and are the most common tool for getting things done in a development project. They have been used in most CAU projects.
- The *information network* includes newsletters, published monthly by CAU and addressed to all organizations that have ever been in contact with CAU.
- The *Working Life Forum* is a seminar/lecture series, held regularly and monthly at CAU, in which a working life researcher meets and discusses the practical implications of his work with a group made up primarily of nonacademics. The audience is invited through advertisements in daily newspapers.
- *Student projects* contribute to both research and innovation and social renewal projects. Students work in the field and have feedback seminars with representatives of regional enterprises (Organization and Leadership for Innovation 1993).
- The *work redesign game* is a language-picture tool workers and middle managers in small and medium-sized companies can use to conduct a work process analysis on site. This tool was developed by CAU staff in the NordNet project.

- *Participative design workshops* engage shop-floor employees in socio-technical analysis and design of their workplaces. The method was developed in the Norwegian Industrial Democracy Program and is described by Emery and Thorsrud (1976). It has been used in some CAU projects.
- *Study visits* have been conducted when small enterprises had a good example/good experience to relate. Representatives of six to ten other small enterprises may be invited. Visits have been made when companies have been especially successful at developing new ways to organize work, introducing new technology, or reducing work-related injuries or illnesses. Those firms that are invited normally are in the same geographical area and from a variety of industries. During the study visit, the host company describes itself and its project and there is a guided tour of the firm. An important part of the visit is a discussion in which representatives of the visiting companies challenge and ask for clarification of what has been done.

Case Summary

What is the research capacity that is being developed at CAU and Halmstad University? CAU staff agree that partly it is the ability to mobilize resources so as to create institutional bases or networks of organizations involved in working life research and reform. CAU has tried systematically to connect itself to national and international action research networks, to private and public regional institutions and companies, and to university departments and programs. CAU has thus chosen to define working life research capacity in part as sustainability in upholding the three important functions of research, innovation/social renewal, and education.

This is not enough, however. Research must also take into consideration the external relevance of the activities and their results. The external relevance of social science research may reasonably be considered to be greater if the local knowledge of those concerned with a social problem is utilized at all times in the research process, that is, if there is genuine cooperation throughout a project, not only when the results are fed back.

AR is clearly considered a necessary criterion for working life research at CAU. Thus, social science research capacity is defined as sustainable resources to conduct action research. This does not mean, however, that every project must be highly participative. The specific context of a project also has to be considered. In some situations traditional research designs are judged to be relevant to the long-term promotion of both democratic values and good research capacity but lead to AR later. For example, as a result of one survey investigation, participatory action research was conducted on worker skill development in four metal workshops (Eriksson *et al.* 1993).

The research capacity of CAU is sustained by maintaining a comparatively large volume of projects, initiated successively in an effort to keep staff together over many years. This is done to enable a creative culture to develop and to ensure the generation of results. Clustering projects and clustering organizations as well as clustering researchers may raise the level of efficiency by facilitating communication of practical and research results. This may also be facilitated if researchers divide their time between several projects. At CAU, researchers sometimes work in "double pairs" — two front stage and two back stage according to the so-called Karlstad model (Engelstad 1993). Creating working life development project networks and combining third- or fourth-year student educational programs with working life development projects and research may also enhance the use of the resources available for action research.

Research capacity might be achieved more easily if research projects, educational programs, and regional renewal and innovation activities supported each other rather than competed for university resources. The emphasis should be on developing AR projects that integrate the elements of research, education, and regional renewal and innovation.

Value of Universities to Working Life Research

In developing resources of their own for research, Sweden's young universities may end up contributing to the institutional renewal of working life research and the promotion of action research. One reason for this is that compared with the old universities, these young universities, as a rule, interface more with regional working life organizations and their practitioners. Another reason is that the establishment of the young universities in the 1970s-1980s led without exception to intraregional mobilization and interregional competition, which helped create broad interfaces between the young universities and their political, economic, and industrial surroundings. Finally, since they are also young and flexible as organizations and are still expanding in terms of staff, students, and activities, these universities also have the prerequisites for encouraging interdisciplinary collaboration between researchers. Bureaucratic patterns are not yet established.

The young universities may also advance working life action research in other ways:

- They may systematize local action knowledge, such as information gained in regional working life contexts.
- They may function as repositories of action research information and training.
- They may integrate action research into continuing educational programs, project work conducted by students may be integrated into research work, and both may enhance the innovation and social renewal role of the university in its regional context.

- They may direct educational programs or special extension programs toward the goal of emancipation by stimulating people to search for knowledge about their current situations during turbulent organizational changes or industrial crises, for example. This was in fact the effect of the study circles and educational activities on the labor union representatives during the shipbuilding crisis program.
- They may organize larger empirical studies (national studies, for example) by sampling plus replicating across systems. Comparative research may be combined with action research case studies through networking with other universities. CAU, for example, collaborates in this way with Karlstad, another new university.
- They may speed up cultural change processes in working life by building innovative support structures, by training consultants and entrepreneurs-practitioners, for example.

Conclusions

The case study reported on in this chapter is shedding light on ways the Swedish university system could develop more supportive infrastructures for social science research on work reform. To do so will take several specific changes:

- The working conditions for researchers, resulting from the short duration and discontinuous nature of the research programs, will have to be improved.
- Young researchers in the field will have to be made aware of career paths available to them and experienced scientists encouraged to pursue research on working life reform.
- The structure of universities has to be put under a microscope and maybe changed so that the functional divisions between research, teaching/training, and the practical use of knowledge do not lead to a reification of scientific knowledge and to a growing gap between science and working life.
- Links between enterprises are important to regional (and national) economic and social development. Regional networks need support, however. Universities may eventually fulfill this function. As CAU's experience shows, however, this probably cannot occur unless they first reorganize their research in relation to national working life reform programs.
- Collaborative programs between researchers and working life practitioners may be effective in producing both scientific and practical results of great value.

Only if there is an openness to investigate and try new approaches to the advancement of science — that is, for example, a willingness to attempt to generate scientific knowledge based on local knowledge from workplaces — can new roles for universities develop. The splitting up of important university functions is inimical to such progress. Common resources will continue to be underutilized if departmental constraints put limits on interdisciplinary cooperation and if people from different departments do not engage in cooperative undertakings. Such splits also create fragmented work situations and lead to multidisciplinary research being held in low esteem compared with intradisciplinary research. The goals of enriching social science while at the same time improving the practical affairs of man will also often be seen as incompatible. As the experiences at CAU indicate, however, there are certainly opportunities available for the newer universities in Sweden to establish new roles for themselves as a result of the growth of regional working life research and reform.

Acknowledgments

The process of writing this chapter was part of a CAU project financed by the Swedish Work Environment Fund. I was given many valuable comments by Henrik Dons Finsrud, Preben Lindoe, Anneli Pulkkis, Øystein Spjelkavik, and, in particular, Davydd Greenwood. Others who gave me valuable comments were Agneta Hansson, Jan Holmer, Morten Levin, Ingrid Ljungberg van Beinum, Hans van Beinum, Martyn Dyer-Smith, Claude Faucheux, Ann Martin, Bertil Olsson, John L. Puckett, Derek Raffaelli, Rob van Eybergen, and René van der Vlist.

Notes

1. A complete list of reports, most in Swedish, may be found in Boglind *et al.* 1981 and in Eriksson and Holmer 1982.

2. Greenwood *et al.* 1992 reports on a similar example.

3. The exceptions were the universities of Lund and Gothenburg. Both were supported with extra budget means from, among other sources, the Swedish Work Environment Fund.

4. It should be noted that the experiences from the shipbuilding program at Gothenburg University were brought into the new working life research program that was developed at Halmstad University.

5. According to Y. Hayrynen and J. Hautamaki (1976), polytechnic education aimed to build a bridge between "pure theory" and "pure practice," so as to increase the contacts between science and practice.

6. This argument is in accordance with Kalleberg (1993), although he defines social science research as having a "constructivist" function. I do not find it necessary to define innovation and social renewal as part of the research process even if its meaning is similar to Kalleberg's term "constructivism."

Table 1. Overview of Project Conducted by University Researchers amd Blue- and White-Collar Unions in Midst of Crisis in the Shipbuilding Industry

Background, practical concern	– acute regional industrial crisis
Collaborative activities	– conferences
	– round-table seminars
	– steering group
	– study circles
	– investigations
	– regular university study courses
	– interviews, questionnaires, and documentary analyses
Practical results	– well-informed union leadership
	– larger number of active leaders
	– better information to rank-and-file union members
	– new networks between unions and university
	– reorganization of union executive committee
	– study materials on the shipbuilding crisis produced by the unions and applied in study circles with several hundred union members in many workplaces
	– investigations on alternative production
	– AR as model for union collaboration with research (evaluation report made by the national white- and blue-collar unions — TCO, LO)
	– written report from the union participants of the program forwarded to the Social Democratic Party MPs
	– university/union committee for planning and supervising university courses directed at blue- and white-collar workers
Social science results	– academic dissertation
	– development of tools for collaboration
	– testing methods: study circle, study courses development circle
	– insights into processes of industrial restructuring
	– insights into PA functions when closing down an industry — AR experiences

Sources: Boglind *et al.* 1981; Eriksson and Holmer 1991; Metal Unions reports 1978, 1980.

Table 2 Problematical Positions in Shipbuilding Crisis Action Research Program

Problematical positions	Criticisms
Neutrality of knowledge	– Lack of distance between researchers and unions
	– Risk of going native; getting blind to the point of view of others besides the unions
Knowledge for action	– Unscientific approach to search action knowledge as opposed to knowledge for the enrichment of social science
Local knowledge	– Not of general interest
Case study	– Limited possibilities to generalize from this kind of study

Sources: Boglind *et al.* 1981; Eriksson and Holmer 1991; Metal Unions reports 1978, 1980.

Table 3 Characteristics of CAU Projects

	Number of organizations
Group-organized production work, metal industry	1
Customer-driven production, engineering enterprise constructing special trucks	1
Introduction of computers in community departments, departments in municipal administration	2
University reorganization project, university college	1
Participative redesign in mass-production company, engineering industry	1
Employee skill development in metal workshops, Two metal industries, two engineering enterprises	4
Rural development in network project, farming enterprises, farmer cooperatives, small rural enterprises, preparatory school	>10 (active phase)
Redesign of cleaning organization in a school district, municipal school administration	1
Participative redesign, laundry company	2
Investigating and developing management organizational change strategies, 34 diverse private and public enterprises and administrations	35 (active phase)
Developing a district organization for care of the elderly and handicapped, organization for community elderly care	1 (active phase)
Developing gender relations in organizations, municipal school district, nuclear power plant, regional organization of national mail	3 (active phase)
Regional networks — tools in a work reform program, > 15 small to medium-sized industrial enterprises	>15 (early phase)
Regional evaluation of a major national working life reform program, "many and diverse"	"many" (early phase)

Sources: CAU Annual Reports and Activity Plans 1986-93,

Chapter 9

The Action Research Tradition
in the United States

Toward a Strategy for Revitalizing the Social Sciences, the University, and the American City

John Puckett and Ira Harkavy

As we near the end of the 1990s, the core problem for the social sciences may be stated as follows: What can the social sciences do to help solve the complex, deep, pervasive, interdependent problems affecting our society and our world?

Thoughtful critics have posed this question with increasing frequency in recent years, along with questioning the role of the university in society. This recurrent questioning is indicative of the failure of American social science and universities to fulfill their stated mission of advancing and transmitting knowledge to improve human welfare. As Kurt Lewin ascertained, if we were doing our job well, the questions would be answered by our practice — by what we clearly contribute to society (Marrow 1969: 153–59).

After approximately two decades of mounting criticism of the social science system, dissent is now emerging from the very core of the disciplines themselves. In 1988, for example, Richard A. Berk sketched the rise of the "insider critique" in sociology in an article that noted that eminent sociologists Peter Rossi, William Foote Whyte, Otis Dudley Duncan, and Stanley Lieberson had all voiced criticisms. Berk writes that these criticisms provide "a prima facie case ... that mainstream sociology is in serious, and perhaps unprecedented, trouble" (57–58).

The critique of the university has followed a similar pattern. Since 1981 and the publication of Ernest Boyer and Fred Hechinger's *Learning in the Nation's Service*, there has been a growing reproach that "higher education in America is suffering from a loss of overall direction, a nagging feeling that it is no longer at the vital center of the nation's work" (3).

With the publication of Derek Bok's 1990 book, *Universities and the Future of America*, that criticism reached a new level of urgency and significance. Harvard's president concluded that "most universities continue to do their least impressive work on the very subjects where society's need for greater knowledge and better education is most acute" (122). Bok's conclusion, reached at the end of his presidency at Harvard, necessarily leads to the further conclusion that the American university has failed to do what it is supposed to do. In short, esoterica has triumphed over public philosophy, narrow scholasticism over humane scholarship.

What accounts for the rise of insider critiques of the social sciences, the professions, and, indeed, the university in general? Stated directly, the crisis in American society has highlighted the crisis in and the failures of the American academy. The pervasive societal problems exemplified by the interrelated plagues of crack, crime, AIDS, and homelessness require a fundamental change in the stance and dominant culture of the university. On moral-pragmatic grounds, the unremitting poverty and deprivation that affect a scandalously large number of Americans cannot help but lead to a "Boklike" conclusion that universities need to do much better, for society's sake. As a matter of self-interest, urban universities in particular ignore at their peril the safety and attractiveness of their physical settings and immediate geographic community — factors that contribute mightily to a general campus ambience and to the recruitment and retention of faculty and students. Less directly, universities are being subjected to what University of Pennsylvania president Sheldon Hackney described in 1992 as a "new age of scrutiny," involving both the costs (financial, public relations, and political) that result when an institution retreats from the community and the benefits (public, private, and foundation support) that accrue from active, effective engagement (also see Harkavy and Puckett 1994).

How can universities and the social sciences in particular move from where they are now to where they should be? A first step is to understand the roots of late twentieth-century American social science. Thus, our analysis begins with an overview of the rise and decline of applied social science in the Progressive Era (1890 to World War I), particularly the contributions of Jane Addams and the residents of Chicago's Hull House. We then trace the development of participatory action research from its origins in the 1930s to the present. In the final section, we outline a PAR-based strategy directed toward revitalizing American social science and improving American society.

Reformist Social Science in the Progressive Era

Modeled after Toynbee Hall, the first English settlement house, Hull House was founded by Jane Addams and Ellen Gates Starr in 1889 on Chicago's West Side. In addition to its numerous social services, Hull House provided a residential base and a perennial support group for such activist women as Florence Kelley, Julia Lathrop, Edith Abbott, and Sophonisba Breckinridge, who went on to become national leaders in social work.

In her autobiography, *Twenty Years at Hull-House*, Addams (1910) emphasized the benefits the activist social worker realized from engagement with the community and its problems. She wrote of "a fast-growing number of cultivated young people who have no recognized outlet for their active faculties ... Their uselessness hangs upon them heavily ... There is nothing after disease, indigence and guilt so fatal to life itself as the want of a proper outlet for active faculties" (118–20).

Settlement work provided a satisfactory outlet for women that was not incommensurate with established Victorian gender roles and practices, particularly the idea of the "woman's sphere." Addams acknowledged this when she remarked that "many women today are failing properly to discharge their duties to their own families and households simply because they fail to see that as society grows more complicated, it is necessary that woman shall extend her sense of responsibility to many things outside of her home, if only in order to preserve the home in its entirety" (qtd. in Ehrenreich 1985: 35; also see Sklar 1985).

In 1895, Addams and the residents of Hull House — notably, Florence Kelley, Agnes Holbrook, and Julia Lathrop — published *Hull-House Maps and Papers* (Residents of Hull House 1895) whose central focus was the social conditions of the Nineteenth Ward, the neighborhood immediately to the east of Hull House. Inspired by Charles Booth's *Life and Labour of the People in London* (1891), the Hull House residents compiled detailed maps of demographic and social characteristics and produced richly descriptive accounts of life and work in an immigrant neighborhood.[1]

The methodological orientation of *Hull-House Maps and Papers* was markedly different from the disciplinary conceptualization of social science that would dominate the academy after 1918. Recognizing the interrelatedness of environmental factors, Addams and her colleagues approached social problems holistically; they "did not separate what would later be seen as the economic aspects of a problem like unemployment from sociological or psychological or even political aspects" (Lagemann 1989: 67). Their approach, however, was largely descriptive, not theoretical.

Although they engaged in action as advocates for social legislation, the Hull House residents ultimately separated action from research. Their methodological approach is perhaps best described as "descriptive empiricism." They believed that a full disclosure of the facts would, on moral grounds, impel action by others.[2]

Closely associated with Hull House in its early years were the male sociologists at the University of Chicago. Indeed, *Hull-House Maps and Papers* oriented the Chicago school of sociology to urban studies and strongly influenced its direction for the next forty years (Deegan 1988: 24).

The changing relationship of Addams and her Hull House colleagues with the Chicago sociologists from the 1890s to the late teens mirrored the American university's transition from an outwardly directed, service-centered institution to an inwardly directed, discipline-centered institution. By the end of the Progressive Era, the change also signified the separation of *knowledge production* from *knowledge use*, indeed, of social science from social reform.

In its early years, the University of Chicago demonstrated that by doing good, a research university could do very well. When Chicago's first president, William Rainey Harper, described the mission of his newly minted university as "service for mankind wherever mankind is, whether within scholastic walls or without those walls and in the world at large" (Fitzpatrick 1990: 33), he expressed a pervasive attitude of Progressive Era academics that research, teaching, and service were compatible missions. Harper and his colleagues also realized that the university's funding was contingent on the public's good will.

In the early years, no invidious distinctions were made between the applied sociology pursued by Jane Addams and the Hull House residents and the academic research of the first generation of University of Chicago sociologists. Indeed, the two groups had a close working relationship and shared social philosophy. In the early 1890s, for example, Albion Small, George Vincent, and Edward Bemis worked with Jane Addams, Florence Kelley, and community leaders to help secure legislation to eliminate sweatshops and regulate child labor, and in the winter of 1910, Charles Henderson and George Herbert Mead joined the women of Hull House in support of forty thousand striking garment industry workers.

Social research, Chicago-style, encompassed scholarly documentation of a social problem and the lobbying of politicians and local community groups to obtain action.[3] In fact, nearly a quarter of the University of Chicago faculty participated in municipal reform activities at the high-water mark of the city's Progressive movement (Shils 1988).

After 1915, Chicago sociology, under Robert Park and Ernest W. Burgess, increasingly distanced itself from social reform, notwithstanding the continued focus on the form, structure, and problems of city living. More and more, that focus was circumscribed by a natural science model and an underlying commitment to "the detached and objective study of society," which "allowed no room for an ameliorative approach" (Bulmer 1984: 64) and emphasized "urban studies ... within a scientific framework" (89; see also Fitzpatrick 1990: 200; cf. Shils 1988 and Ward 1989: 151-79).

The Retreat from Reformist Social Science

Applied social science largely vanished from the academy after 1918. The brutality and horror of World War I ended the buoyant optimism and faith in human progress and societal improvement that had marked the Progressive Era. American academics were not immune to the general disillusionment.

Despair led many social scientists to retreat into a narrow scientistic approach. One economist wrote that "they began to talk of the need for a harder science, a science of facts and numbers that could moderate or dispel the pervasive irrational conflicts of political life" (qtd. in Ross 1991: 322). Scholarly inquiry directed toward creating a better society was increasingly deemed inappropriate. While faith in the expert and in expert knowledge still dominated, it was now divorced from its reformist roots. The new conception of science was clear and simple: it was what physical scientists and engineers did (see Bender 1993: 30-46, 46-77, 127-39; Hackney 1986; Ross 1984; Bulmer and Bulmer 1981).[4]

Between the wars, the reform impulse was further weakened by the fact that every major university formed similar and increasingly specialized departments. A faculty member's primary source of identification and allegiance became his or her discipline, not the university.

Since World War II, a steady infusion of federal funds allocated to individual researchers working under departmental auspices has accelerated the growth of a disciplinary-based reward system (Alpert 1985; Jencks and Riesman 1968: 523–31). These departmental and disciplinary divisions have served to increase further the isolation of universities from society.

A 1982 Organization for Economic Cooperation and Development report entitled *The University and the Community* noted, "Communities have problems, universities have departments" (Center for Educational Research and Innovation 1982: 127; also see Bok 1982; Hackney 1986; Kerr 1982; Szanton 1981). Beyond being a criticism of universities, that statement neatly indicates why universities have not contributed to society as they should. Quite simply, their unintegrated structures work against understanding and helping to solve highly complex human and societal problems. This has resulted in less effective research, teaching, and service. Indeed, all three missions have been impoverished by what might be termed a false trichotomization, which has contributed to an enormous imbalance in the production of knowledge.

Dazzling advances have occurred in university-based research in science and technology. But although designed to improve human welfare, the application of scientific advances too frequently results in new and more forbidding problems. The wondrous possibilities of new medical technologies, for example, have become distorted, helping to create a health care "system" unresponsive to the "low-tech" preventive needs of the vast majority of citizens.[5]

How to make rational use of science and technology should be a primary consideration of university research because it is a primary problem facing human beings at the end of the twentieth century. If universities had an integrated mission — the creative, dynamic, and systemic integration of research, teaching, and service — intellectual resources would be significantly devoted to developing humane applications of scientific knowledge to help those living in conditions of profound poverty and neglect.

Such integration will be particularly difficult because of a fundamental contradiction in the structure of the American research university itself — that is, its very creation as a combination of the German research university and the American college. In fact, Daniel Coit Gilman, the founder of Johns Hopkins University and the central architect of the late nineteenth-century research university, claimed that one of his proudest accomplishments was "a school of science [Sheffield Scientific School] grafted on one of the oldest and most conservative classical colleges [Yale College]" (1898/1969: iii).

Gilman did not make reference to the contradiction that necessarily derived from such a merger. The research university, on the one hand, was dedicated to specialized scholarship; for the American college, on the other hand, general education, character building, and civic education were the central purposes. The research university has, of course, dominated this merger, creating an ethos and culture that rewards specialized study rather than more general scholarship and the education of the next generation for moral, civic, and intellectual leadership.

Given the structural contradictions built into the American university and the increasing specialization, fragmentation of knowledge, and separation of scholarship from direct service to society, it will not be easy for higher educational institutions more effectively to integrate research, teaching, and service and to increase substantively their contributions to knowledge and human welfare. New directions will have to be forged. But will they be the right directions, directions that enhance the university's ability to integrate research, teaching, and service?

Participatory action research is one approach that shows particular promise. Until recently, action research and its PAR variant have been lumped into the category of "applied science" and consigned to a marginal status in the academy. Yet, as the following analysis indicates, participatory action research has strong potential for advancing both theoretical knowledge and social reconstruction.

Kurt Lewin and the Rise of Participatory Action Research

Writing in the mid-1970s, Paul Lazarsfeld and Jeffrey Reitz described the phase of sociology from 1940 to the present as marked by a "search for a new synthesis between practical work and sociological knowledge" (1975: 8-9). The exigencies of waging war had compelled sociologists to shift from engaging in an "autonomous sociology" to applying their knowledge to help win the war at home and abroad. "When the war was over, it was clearly impossible to revert to the separation of sociology as an academic pursuit from the problems of governmental and private organizations," said Lazarsfeld and Reitz (1975: 7). Lazarsfeld's own work on mass communications policy during the war is a case in point. Under his direction, the Bureau of Applied Social Research at Columbia University "concentrated on the testing of films and radio programs devised to maintain the morale of various sectors of the civilian and military operations" (1982: 66), a project Lazarsfeld (1975) described as "empirical action studies."

Kurt Lewin, the eminent social psychologist, field theorist, and founder of topological and vector psychology, provided a segue into the current phase of sociology, leading the way to the development of "action research," a term he apparently coined in the 1940s while heading a series of action research experiments. Lewin's particular genius lay in mapping the complexities and multiple interdependencies of human behavior and devising practical strategies for behavioral change. During his nine-year tenure at the Iowa Child Welfare Research Station (1935–1944), Lewin increasingly focused on problems in group dynamics, the seed bed of action research, and especially, says Gustavsen, on *how to create a better working life through processes of change to which research makes significant contributions*" (1992: 12; emphasis in original).

As Lazarsfeld and Reitz note, Lewin's German background, particularly his work at the Berlin Psychological Institute from 1921 to 1933, heavily influenced his later research methodology:

"In Germany, the notion of human action (*Handlung*) had been central to all of the social sciences. Lewin wanted psychology to make its special contribution by conducting experiments in realistic situations. ... What Lewin did was to add the role of small groups as an influence in the *Handlungen* of their members" (1975: 7).

Lewin's action research on problems of industrial democracy was preceded, if not directly influenced, by the Hawthorne studies on productivity conducted at the Western Electric Company's Hawthorne Works in Chicago from 1927 to 1932. Subsequently, from 1939 to 1947, the year of his untimely death, Lewin and two of his proteges, Alex Bavelas and John R. P. French, conducted research on group behavioral problems related to industrial management and productivity within the Harwood Manufacturing Corporation of Virginia (Marrow 1969: 141–59; also see Lewin 1951: 214–22 and Maier 1946/1955: 160–62).

Bavelas's research on overcoming resistance to change involved participatory decision making, prefiguring industrial democracy action research studies of the 1970s and 1980s. Responding to the frustration and "very low level of aspiration" felt by workers being transferred to new jobs, Bavelas conducted small-group research in the Harwood plant to "discover if it were possible to transfer workers more smoothly from old jobs to new ones, and if technological changes in job methods could be introduced without the usual manifestations of hostility and falloff in production" (Marrow 1969: 149–50). Bavelas observed the effects of organizing workers in three different modes of decision making in relation to the change: managerial-autocratic, democratic-representative, and participatory. Whereas average production in the nondemocratic group fell precipitously and never reached the prechange level, productivity increased in the two democratic groups, most notably in the participatory group, which "regained the prechange output after only two days and then climbed steadily until it reached a level about 14 per cent above the earlier average" (Marrow 1969: 151).

Bavelas's study had several noteworthy methodological traits. First, "research played an *active* role." Second, it was guided by the Lewinian hypothesis "about the need for, and positive functions of, participation," grounded in a theory derived from social research. Third, the research was organized as a field experiment. It took place in the immediate context of a "real-world" problem, the research was embedded in action, and it stimulated "a real change for those involved" (Gustavsen 1992: 12–13).

In 1944, Lewin was invited to MIT to create the Research Center for Group Dynamics with the goal, in his words, of developing "scientific methods of studying and changing group life and . . . concepts and theories in group dynamics" (qtd. in Marrow 1969: 172). When the center opened in 1945, Lewin linked its work to the Commission on Community Interrelations (CCI) of the American Jewish Congress. The CCI conducted action research on community affairs, focusing on minority problems, ethnocultural conflict, and discriminatory attitudes and behaviors. (For a discussion of these developments and action research more generally, see Lewin 1948: 201–16).

"The Commission means action, and action now," Lewin said. "If we speak of research, we mean 'action research,' action that is always followed by self-critical objective reconnaissance and evaluation of results. ... We aim at 'no action without research; no research without action'" (qtd. in Marrow 1969: 193).

CCI staff members coined the term *participant* action research to describe the involvement of community members in the research process from the beginning. The major example of PAR developed by the CCI was the Community Self-Survey on Discriminatory Practices.[6] Margot Hass Wormser of the CCI directed this project in a small American city she called Northtown, whose population was approximately forty thousand, 12 percent of whom were black, 9 percent Jewish.

During the winter of 1947, Wormser organized a sponsoring committee for the self-survey composed of representatives of thirteen community organizations, including the Council of Social Agencies, the Council of Jewish Organizations, and the NAACP. At the committee's first meeting, she "explained that the Northtown survey was to form the basis for a blueprint for other communities anxious to study their intergroup relations problems. The survey was to be concerned with discriminatory practices, not attitudes, and deal with the most vital areas of community life. After some group discussion, it was decided that the Northtown survey would focus on practices affecting Negroes and Jews in employment, housing, education, public facilities and services, and community organizations" (Wormser 1949: 8).

At the outset, Wormser noted, some delegates questioned the real motives behind CCI's involvement: "Was this a program of fact-finding or really a program of action? What were we going to do with the findings? My answer was that any program of action based on whatever might be learned from the survey would be entirely up to the local group; CCI's interest in the survey was that of developing a blueprint of community self-survey methods. This answer seemed to be satisfactory" (1949: 9).

The Community Relations Committee of the Employers Association provided more serious opposition, "directed against the fact that *outsiders* were running the survey" (Wormser 1949: 11), but Wormser and the committee were able to overcome the resistance. Such episodes reveal the CCI group's continuous interaction with the Northtown community.

In the summer of 1947, seventy-three volunteer interviewers provided by the sponsoring organizations were trained to carry out the survey. They conducted interviews with 409 respondents randomly selected from four areas of community life: employment, housing, education, and public facilities and services (community organizations was dropped as a category). In drafting the final report, Wormser worked closely with four subcommittees appointed by the sponsoring committee. "Experience with these area subcommittees convinced me that such committees should have been appointed at the very outset," she said. "Each committee should have been given key responsibility for all work in its area from reviewing the questionnaires to preparing the final report" (1949: 17). The "fact-finding" component of the survey concluded in February 1948, when the sponsoring committee officially received the survey findings.

The final report exposed discrimination in employment, housing, and public facilities in Northtown. For example, whites earned considerably more than blacks with the same educational background; blacks and Jews were excluded from 95 percent and 15 percent of Northtown's residential areas, respectively; and blacks were excluded from hotels, commercial recreation facilities, and certain restaurants. Only the area of public education seemed to be free of exclusionary or differential treatment of minority groups.

Wormser and the CCI concluded their involvement in Northtown with the release of these findings, declining an invitation to work on a proposed follow-up survey. Wormser reminded the sponsoring committee that "CCI's concern was with developing self-survey methods and that any action program to change such discriminatory practices as were found would be entirely up to the local organizations" (1949: 18). The contrast between Hull House's ongoing, locally focused engagement and CCI's contract-researcher approach is worth noting.

The Northtown study reflected Lewin's interest in the contingencies of behavioral change, particularly the effects of small groups on decision making and the way those decisions can be manipulated to change behavior and practice (cf. Lazarsfeld and Reitz 1975: 8). The multiyear Harwood study also fit this category, as did Lewin's well-known "Food Habits Study" for the National Research Council, which tested how housewives might be persuaded to increase their use of beef hearts, sweetbreads, and kidneys (1947). As a field experiment in group dynamics, the "Food Habits Study" captured the major emphasis of Lewin's work as an action researcher and had a strong influence on the development of action research in Western Europe in the 1950s and 1960s.

Lewin's premature death from a heart attack in 1947 dealt a severe blow to action research in the United States and particularly to the CCI, where Lewin had overseen or planned at least eight major action research projects in just two years. (For descriptions of these projects, see Marrow 1969: 201-18.) After 1950, the center of gravity for action research shifted to Great Britain and later to Norway and Sweden. It was not until the 1980s that action research made a resurgence in the United States, where Lewin's influence endures.

Lewin's Legacy: The Action Research Tradition, 1950–1994

Without a scholar-leader of Lewin's stature, action research rapidly declined in the United States after 1950. "What has happened to action research?" Nevitt Sanford mused nearly twenty years later. "I would say now that, contrary to the impression I had in the late 1940s, it never really got off the ground, it never was widely influential in psychology or social science. By the time the federal funding agencies were set up after World War II, action research was already condemned to a sort of orphan's role in social science" (1970: 323). As Sanford further noted, orthodox social scientists insisted on the separation of science and practice, even in the arena of applied social science: "The emphasis is most certainly not only the study of actions as a means for advancing science but rather on the application to problems of what is already known" (6-7).

Over the past twenty years several new varieties of action research have emerged to challenge the domination of establishment social science, and each group has claimed the mantle of participatory democracy. American action researchers prefer the term *participatory action research* to distinguish their approach from action social science that is nonparticipatory.[7] Scandinavian participatory action researchers insist on the term *action research*, arguing that the term PAR creates a tautology, although some writers compromise by using the designation P(AR). As Hans van Beinum put it during a conversation on March 11, 1992, at one of the ACRES sessions, "The participation is in the action; you cannot separate the two."

Since the 1970s, "a very heterogeneous group" of participatory action researchers has been working in such areas as education, community, Third World, and urban community development, as well as industrial development (Greenwood and González 1992: 172, 180–84). There is often heated disagreement within the PAR community about the aims of such research. For example, researchers in the Swedish LOM program have targeted as joint goals of PAR: (1) increased industrial productivity, to be achieved through a "vertical-slice" process of democratic dialogue and collaborative decision making, and (2) the improvement of the social science system (Gustavsen 1992). By contrast, a group that includes Orlando Fals-Borda (1987), Paolo Freire (1970), and activists at the Highlander Research and Education Center in central Appalachia (Gaventa 1980; Appalachian Alliance Task Force 1983) view PAR as an emancipatory process to help achieve social justice for poor, dispossessed peoples and, by implication, the transformation of advanced capitalist society.

Brown and Tandon have labeled these two contrasting traditions "Northern" (action research) and "Southern" (participatory research), respectively, viewing the former tradition as work *with* "the system," the latter as work *against* it. "Participatory researchers seek to transform the existing order and its oppressive consequences, while action researchers believe in basic consensus and incremental reform. So action researchers can be expected to avoid or minimize the revolutionary aspects of participatory research" (1983: 291).

Brown and Tandon indicate that the two perspectives, while fundamentally different, are not necessarily mutually exclusive: "Consensus and conflict intervention strategies are both relevant to promoting constructive social change. ... Action research is appropriate when parties have common interests and accept present power and resource distributions as legitimate. Participatory research is appropriate when party interests conflict and parties disagree about the legitimacy of power and resource distributions" (1983: 292). (Also see Cohen, Greenwood, and Harkavy 1992.)

Kurt Lewin's influence may be traced lineally from the Center for Research on Group Dynamics and the Commission on Community Interrelationships to developments in Western Europe from the 1950s to the 1980s. Lewin's research on group dynamics helped shape sociotechnical design thinking at the Tavistock Institute for Human Relations, where in the early 1950s, Eric Trist and other Tavistock pioneers applied Lewinian principles in field experiments on industrial relations.

A famous example is Trist and Bamforth's 1951 study of a British coal mine operation, discussed elsewhere in this volume. Although the study helped catalyze "real experiments" at Tavistock, as van Eijnatten points out, "The co-influencing researcher's role of action research was found minimal: the deviant form of work organization was already implemented by the miners themselves" (1993: 26).

Whyte and Whyte assess Trist's influence as follows:

> Trist developed the sociotechnical systems framework, which has guided much of
> the work in subsequent years. The basic idea is that organizational changes can be
> most effectively brought about through an integrated strategy, in which changes
> in technology and in human relations are worked out at the same time by the same
> groups of people. While this notion may now seem obvious, in earlier years social
> researchers tended to concentrate almost exclusively on human relations. We
> gave lip service to the importance of technology but tended to treat it as a constant
> instead of as a variable, which could be changed along with changes in human
> relations (1984: 168).[8]

In the 1960s, the pattern of field experiments pioneered by Lewin and his
associates was adapted to the framework of the Industrial Democracy (ID)
Program in Norway, where the sociotechnical perspective of the Tavistock Institute was salient. As Gustavsen points out, in one important respect the Industrial
Democracy Program transcended Lewin and Tavistock: "Even though Lewin and
associates as well as the Tavistock researchers had the aim of contributing to
change in working life as a whole, the ID Program was the first effort where this
was an explicit consideration. The experiments were done not only for their own
sake but for the purpose of providing points of departure for natural change"
(1992: 16).

Parallel developments occurred in Sweden with the URAF Industrial Research Program in the 1970s (see van Eijnatten 1993: 34-36) and the LOM
("Leadership, Organization and Co-Determination") Program in the 1980s. Increasingly, Scandinavian action researchers abandoned Lewin's experimental
requirements for action research, insisting on the participation of the research
subjects in the design of the research.

Since the early 1980s, William Foote Whyte and his associates at Cornell
University have carried out PAR agendas at industrial sites in New York State
and in Mondragón, Spain. The research in Mondragón, a complex of worker
cooperatives in Spain's Basque Country, has been in progress for more than a
decade. Cornell-related PAR is currently networked with the Scandinavian programs, joined by a similar philosophy of action research, a commitment to
industrial democracy, and a common pool of concepts, strategies, and techniques.[9] Like the Scandinavian programs, this work has focused on "industrial
democracy, labor-managed systems and participation in the workplace" (Greenwood and González 1992: 37).

Cornell research in the Xerox-Amalgamated Job Preservation Program in
New York demonstrates how PAR can be used effectively for social problem
solving. In the early 1980s, Xerox management learned that the company could
save $3.2 million by purchasing from vendors components currently manufactured
in one Xerox department; the company immediately announced that it would
purchase the components and lay off 180 workers. Assisted by Peter Lazes, one of
Whyte's associates, the Amalgamated Clothing and Textile Workers' Union

organized a joint study team representing labor and management to effect a job-saving alternative. With Lazes serving as the facilitator, the team worked for six months and produced a successful cost-cutting plan that saved the 180 jobs. Specifically, the Quality of Working Life (QWL) plan reduced company overhead costs, eliminated unnecessary services, and "opened up a re-examination of relations and functions within the management organization far above the departmental level. ... solutions that were both technically and financially adequate and that were socially acceptable" (Whyte and Whyte 1984: 185–89).

The recent PAR activity being undertaken by Davydd Greenwood and José Luis González with others in the labor-managed industrial cooperatives of Mondragón, Spain, provides a detailed case study of PAR methodology — and exemplifies the interaction of theory, empirical analysis, and social action in high-quality PAR studies. Located in the Spanish Basque province of Guipúzcoa, the Mondragón cooperatives have manufactured a diversity of products for several decades, ranging from heavy household appliances to electronic components to automated manufacturing systems. Collectively, the 173 Mondragón cooperatives employ more than 19,500 workers, more than half the employed labor force in the Mondragón area; in 1985, when the Basque country had a 27 percent unemployment rate, the rate for the town of Mondragón was only 6 percent.

Intrigued by Mondragón's success in the midst of a deep economic recession in Spain, William Foote Whyte and his wife, Kathleen, arrived in the Basque Country in the fall of 1983. Fagor, one of the groups of cooperatives, invited Whyte to help organize a research program in organizational behavior. When Whyte returned to Cornell, he and Davydd Greenwood, director of Cornell's Einaudi Center for International Studies, obtained a grant for "an inter-institutional relationship for research and educational collaboration between Mondragón and Cornell." Whyte and Greenwood envisioned the collaboration as a way of "getting members of the Mondragón cooperatives involved in doing their own research." In April 1985, Greenwood, an anthropologist, began an intensive seminar in Fagor that included a study of Ulgor, Mondragón's first worker cooperative. Following a second seminar in July 1985, Fagor appropriated funds for organizational behavior research in its 1986 personnel department budget (Whyte and Whyte 1991, 302-6).

The intent of the research was to "illuminate generic problems of advanced organizational organizations" (Greenwood and González 1992: 7). Specifically, the PAR team focused on the problem of apathy and alienation within Fagor. The study that resulted has been described as one of the world's most successful experiments in industrial democracy. The authors note:

> Our study of this problem revealed institutional dynamics in Fagor that separate the mechanisms of governance from the operations of the work place. In governance, Fagor members are fully equal and have elaborate process guarantees to assure that this equality suffers no abridgement. The processes of governance also highlight the values of democratic process.

In the work place, the dynamics are different. Though they have developed some participatory work forms, ... social relations and production systems in the work place in Fagor are still quite similar to those found in any business environment. Hierarchical systems of command and control operate, albeit in a muted form (Greenwood and González 1992:).

Combining data from documentary study, surveys, face-to-face interviews, and round table discussions, Greenwood and his colleagues used an anthropological-structuralist perspective — creating a dialectical process focusing on social structures and cultural values — to help interpret the problems in Fagor. As they noted, they "only broached theoretical perspectives and methodological issues when directly necessary to examine a particular set of problems in the cooperatives. The test of a theory or a method was its contribution to the problem at hand, not the contribution of the problem at hand to the enhancement of social science per se" (Greenwood and González 1992: 45). On the strength of a pilot archival and statistical study, the researchers rejected the dichotomies used in the literature on Mondragón to distinguish the cooperatives from private firms, based, for example, on their equality and hierarchy, cooperation and conflict. Instead, they developed a cultural model of Fagor that helped reveal "dimensions of the cooperative experience that were otherwise not easily perceived and that had been missed in many previous analyses" (Greenwood and González 1992: 49).

The model supported a view of Fagor as a "system in dynamic equilibrium"; significantly, one of the main equilibrating factors of cooperative working life is *conflict*, focused on "institutional commitments so important that they generate continual debate and tension within the system" (Greenwood and González 1992: 65–66). The anthropological orientation allowed the researchers to reconstruct "the ways the [cooperative] members experience these organizational realties" (68) or, theoretically stated, "the processes of attempting to reconcile social experience and cultural meaning into coherent personal and group living" (92).

The PAR process unfolded in three phases. First, the PAR team administered a pilot survey to seventy members of different cooperatives, "with different levels of responsibility, professional backgrounds, and personal situations." The generally positive tone of the answers contradicted the researchers' own insider knowledge of the cooperatives, leading to the identification of defects in the survey and to the decision to diversify the sample and to probe extensively for "conflicts, divergent positions, and contradictory perceptions" (Greenwood and González 1992: 99).

The researchers then designed interview schedules around five broad themes: participation and power; relations between management and membership; employment security and transfers; concentration and autonomy in the cooperatives; and compensation. For each theme, three cooperatives were selected for interviews: a cooperative that had experienced strong conflict over the problem, another that was deemed "the most remote from the problem" (Greenwood and González 1992: 102), and a *control* cooperative that was deemed "normal" or standard.

Third, the researchers facilitated a series of round table dialogues "to deepen the analysis of themes" and to stimulate "realistic plans of action" (Greenwood and González 1992: 122–23). The decision to reject the results of the pilot survey reveals one of the epistemological strengths of PAR. Ordinarily, outsider-researchers take responses at face value. In the Mondragón case, the data did not square with what the researchers tacitly knew to be the reality of the cooperatives: that there was a growing sense of disillusionment and diminishing commitment to collective goals.

In their study, Greenwood and his colleagues rejected the parametric logic of Gaussian curves and "the tendency within the social sciences to portray human realities as average values or ideal types that homogenize the diversity of behavior into a single model (Greenwood and González 1992: 36). Applying different criteria for validity, they adopted a nonparametric approach to study the heterogeneity of the Fagor cultural and social system. "We examine general themes and structures to seek out the range of diversity and variability each contains. We characterize social and cultural systems by the amount of diversity they embrace, not mean values" (37; *cf.* Lewin 1935).

Conceptualization of a Communal PAR Project

At the University of Pennsylvania, participatory action research is a key element in an institutional strategy directed toward the reinvention of the American research university and, ultimately, the revitalization of the American city. Our approach has been to advance academically based community service rooted in and intrinsically tied to research and teaching, while also encouraging intellectual integration *across disciplines.*

We have found that the very nature of concrete, real-world problems, particularly those of the university's immediate community of West Philadelphia, encourage interschool and interdisciplinary collaboration. No single component of the university can significantly help explain and reduce the complex, myriad, interrelated problems of the urban poor. Significant advances can be made, however, when public schools, businesses, unions, community organizations, government groups, and voluntary associations join forces and work together.

Our project builds on Dewey's proposition that knowledge and learning is advanced most effectively by working to solve major societal problems. For Dewey, "Thinking begins ... in a *forked-road* situation, a situation which is ambiguous, which presents a dilemma, which proposes alternatives" (1910: 11). To a significant extent, our work can be viewed as testing the validity of Dewey's proposition about how we learn and think.

Even more fundamentally, our project tests the validity of Francis Bacon's central proposition that knowledge advances most effectively when the "relief of man's estate" is made the true end of knowledge. According to Bacon, knowledge should be sought not "for pleasure of the mind, or for contention, or for superiority to others, or for profit, or fame, or power, or for any of these inferior things; but for the benefit and use of life" (qtd. in Benson and Harkavy 1991: 46).[10]

Since 1985, Penn has been involved in a broadly based community project to help improve the quality of life in West Philadelphia. The project has two main organizational components: the West Philadelphia Improvement Corps (WEPIC), representing university faculty, staff, and students (undergraduate and graduate), which has staff offices in West Philadelphia, and a coalition composed of West Philadelphia teachers, students, and school administrators. The year-round program currently involves more than two thousand children, their parents, and community members in educational and cultural programs, recreation, job training, community improvement, and service activities.

WEPIC is coordinated by the West Philadelphia Partnership, a nonprofit, community-based organization composed of major institutions, including the university, and community groups, in conjunction with the Greater Philadelphia Urban Affairs Coalition and the Philadelphia School District (see Harkavy and Puckett 1991). The Center for Community Partnerships coordinates and provides opportunities for PAR projects conducted under the aegis of WEPIC.

WEPIC has reinvented and updated an old notion: the neighborhood school can effectively serve as the core neighborhood institution, providing multiple, comprehensive, and diverse services while also sparking, galvanizing, and energizing other community institutions and groups. Since the early 1900s, this idea has motivated social reconstructionists, who recognized the centrality of the neighborhood school in community life and its potential as the catalytic site for community stabilization and improvement (see Dewey 1902; Clapp 1939; Everett 1938; Henry 1953; Totten and Manley 1969). As Benson and Harkavy have argued (1991: 23-27), although Dewey did not make the explicit case, it follows logically from his general theory that the community-centered school would help catalyze the development of a "cosmopolitan local community." For the neighborhood school to function as a community center, it needs additional human resources and support, however.

In 1930, near the end of her extraordinary career, Jane Addams wrote that the social settlement served the same function as the university but encompassed a broader and needier population:

> It was the function of the settlements to bring into the circle of knowledge and full life, men and women who might otherwise be left outside. Some of these men and women were outside simply because of their ignorance, some of them because they led lives of hard work that narrowed their interests, and others because they were unaware of the possibilities of life and needed a friendly touch to awaken

them. The colleges and universities had made a little inner circle of illuminated space beyond which there stretched a region of darkness, and it was the duty of the settlements to draw into the light those who were out of it (40–45).

The key challenge today is not to have social settlements that function as universities but to have universities that function as perennial, deeply rooted settlements, providing illuminated space for their communities as they produce and transmit knowledge to advance human welfare and develop theories that have broad utility and application. As comprehensive institutions, universities are uniquely qualified to provide broadly based, sustained, comprehensive support, which is a sine qua non of effective community schools. The community school project itself becomes the organizing catalyst enabling the university to function as a social settlement, one innovative, humanistic strategy to better perform its traditional mission, as well as to better perform its role as a cosmopolitan civic university.

If it is to be an effective partner in the revitalization of collapsing urban centers, the university must institutionalize a strategy that engages academic resources in ways that integrate and strengthen its missions of teaching, research, and service. The strategy we have chosen at the University of Pennsylvania is to develop a permanent natural laboratory in West Philadelphia. To avoid misunderstanding, let us emphasize that we neither conceptualize nor treat West Philadelphia as a laboratory for experimentation on poor people, that is, as a site for study rather than assistance. We believe that West Philadelphia, and the community school in particular, should serve as a natural social and cultural laboratory in which communal participatory action research functions as a humanistic strategy for the advancement of knowledge and human welfare (Benson and Harkavy 1991; Harkavy 1992).

Distinguishing between PAR and communal PAR is important here. Both research processes are directed toward problems in the real world, are concerned with application, and are obviously participatory. They differ in the degree to which they are continuous, comprehensive and beneficial, and necessary to the organization or community studied and to the university.

The PAR process is exemplified in the efforts of William Foote Whyte and his associates at Cornell to advance industrial democracy in the worker cooperatives of Mondragón, Spain, but the research at Mondragón is not an institutional necessity for Cornell. By contrast, the success of the University of Pennsylvania's research efforts in West Philadelphia is in its enlightened self-interest, hence its emphasis on communal participatory action research. In short, proximity and a focus on problems that are institutionally significant to the university encourage sustained, continuous research involvement. A crucial issue, of course, is the degree to which these locally based research projects result in general knowledge. We would argue that local does not mean parochial, and solving local problems necessarily requires an understanding of national and global issues, as well as an effective use and development of theory.

Two research projects exemplify these propositions and the multidisciplinary nature of the Penn approach. The first such undertaking is the Turner Nutritional Awareness Project (TNAP), a joint community/university-sponsored PAR program at the John P. Turner Middle School. Headed by Francis Johnston, chair of Penn's anthropology department, the project is designed to improve the nutritional status of the community. TNAP is "comprehensive in scope, with components dealing with nutritional assessment, with instruction in concepts of nutrition, and with the collection of a broad range of related information, including such areas as knowledge, preferences, and attitudes concerning food, food streams within the neighborhood, and other sources of information (merchants, media, etc.)" (Johnston and Hallock 1994: 742). Turner School teachers participate in the design of the intervention, its packaging, and the way it is presented. Sixth-grade Turner students participate in the nutrition education program; then, as seventh-graders, they teach elementary school students about basic nutrition and healthful habits.

In a recent study, Johnston and his students in an undergraduate anthropology course entitled "Biomedical Science and Human Adaptability" collected data on the physical growth status and dietary intakes of eleven- to fifteen-year-old African Americans. Data for the former were collected on 136 individuals; for both sets of indicators, data were collected on 113. A software package was used to calculate the nutrient values of students' dietary intakes, and individual records were merged into a single data set for statistical analysis. The tabulations indicated the population had a very high prevalence of obesity and that their diets were high in saturated fat and low in polyunsaturated fat and low in zinc and high in sodium, suggesting the need for "the development of programs designed to improve diets and enhance health in general" (Johnston and Hallock 1994: 741).

Johnston's work with undergraduates further distinguishes the Penn approach: communal PAR extends to creating or restructuring academic courses to include an explicit community focus and action component. The assumption is that embedding community service into courses, research, and general intellectual discourse will lead to positive changes in the institutional climate, providing a link between service, morality, and education.

A dissertation study in the Annenberg School for Communication provides the second illustration of Penn's involvement in communal PAR. For two years, Eleanor Novek, a former professional journalist and editor, was involved at West Philadelphia High School, a WEPIC site, as a co-teacher and researcher in "an educational demonstration project, an urban high school English/journalism class which uses production of a community-focused newspaper as a strategy for the self-determination of young African Americans" (Novek 1993: 1). Each component of the newspaper, *Q-West*, was adjudicated and carried out by students.

Novek's research on self-determination and student empowerment built on Jürgen Habermas's theory of communicative action, elements of reference group theory (for example, Robert Merton), and superordinate goal theory (Muzafer Sherif and Caroline Sherif) not only during the process of interpreting and theorizing from ethnographic data about the students but also, simultaneously, in shaping the intervention strategies, thereby effecting an ebb and flow of theory and action. In a report on her study, Novek constructed several criteria of self-determination, such as "providing experiences of mastery, strengthening group bonds and increasing [the students'] influence in social systems" (1993: 21). Her description of risk taking and the crossing of social boundaries is a case in point for the progress she cites:

> A shy young woman who never spoke up in class not only obtained an interview with Ramona Africa, the lone survivor of the world-infamous MOVE bombing in May 1985, but also brought her to the school to address the whole class. A taciturn young man interested in rap music visited one of the largest African American radio stations in the city and interviewed a popular disc jockey on the air. Another student took it upon himself to develop and distribute an attitude survey about the *Q-West* project to class members. Two students applied for and won admission to a minority workshop for high school journalists — the first time any students from their school had participated. Another began freelancing sports reports for a community newspaper (15).

As these examples suggest, genuine thinking has occurred as a result of the Penn project, engendering new ideas, concepts, and approaches to school and community development. We believe we have made a good start. The interaction of faculty, staff, and students attempting to solve immediate, concrete, real-world problems has fostered an unprecedented degree of academic integration at Penn and has spurred the development of new organizational structures and mechanisms to encourage, support, and coordinate academically based community service. We want to emphasize, however, that changing the university and its community is extraordinarily difficult. Even after nearly twelve years, our work is still in an early, developing phase.

Historical analysis indicates not only that progressive change can occur but that such analysis can be useful in revealing and clarifying deeply embedded impediments to change. To locate WPIC historically, we have traced the development of PAR from the work of Kurt Lewin in the 1930s to Cornell's studies in Mondragón in the 1990s to academically based community service projects being developed at the University of Pennsylvania.

American social science should be about the "relief of man's estate." More precisely, it should be about overcoming the urban crisis and preventing urban chaos. The problem of the city is the strategic problem of our time. As such, it is a problem most likely to advance the social sciences.

In his studies of creativity, psychologist Howard E. Gruber emphasized the connection between individual creativity and a desire to solve real-world problems, a concept he called creative altruism: "Creative altruism, when it goes the limit, strives to eliminate the cause of suffering, to change the world, to change the fate of the earth" (1989: 285).

Creative altruism imbued the work of Jane Addams and the women of Hull House at the turn of this century. Their humanistic, real-world, problem-solving approach to social science has strong potential to produce better teaching, better research, and better service than conventional social science. We believe the explicit problem-orientation and theory-driven approach of Lewin and his colleagues are necessary components of a genuinely scientific and socially useful social science. If the American university is to fulfill its promise and help create a fair, decent, and just society, it must give full-hearted and full-minded attention to solving our complex, interrelated problems, building on the legacies of both Addams and Lewin.

Acknowledgments

John Puckett's work on this chapter was sponsored by a Spencer Foundation postdoctoral fellowship. We are also indebted to Lee Benson for his superb advice and encouragement.

Notes

1. *Hull-House Maps and Papers* helped inaugurate the Social Survey Movement, of which the Pittsburgh Survey (1907–1909), was the largest and most prominent example. Carried out by a combination of academics and nonacademics, including Florence Kelley, the survey was conceptually unified around the seminal role of the steel industry in shaping Pittsburgh's urban environment and growth. See Cohen 1991.

2. Gordon has astutely written, "The notion that policy should rest on accurate data did not make the early social work researchers aspire to objectivity in the sense of disinterest or political neutrality. . . . They believed that scholarship could be truthful and moral *and* partisan" (1992: 41–42).

3. The most important study from the early Chicago school was *The Polish Peasant in Europe and America,* a 2,232-page study coauthored by Thomas amd Florian Znaniecki in 1918 (see Bulmer 1984: 45–63, 238).

4. Turner (1991) traces the origin of this viewpoint to Karl Pearson's *The Grammar of Science,* as refracted through Franklin H. Giddings, the first chair (1894) of sociology at Columbia University. Formerly associated with the reformist (nonacademic) American Social Science Association, Giddings advanced community studies as a legitimate field of sociological research at Columbia but emphasized the development of scientific theory over social action; in fact, he intensely disliked Chicago sociology. "Giddings men" dominated American sociology after 1918; six Columbia-trained sociologists were presidents of the American Sociological Association in the interwar era. For a discussion of Columbia University's broader disengagement from civic affairs after 1901, see Bender 1987.

5.   For a discussion of the environmental threats posed by science divorced from social, moral, and ethical concerns in quantum mechanics and molecular biology, see Bernstein 1987: 37-68.

6.   CCI members Isidor Chein, Stuart W. Cook, and John Harding identified four varieties of action research: diagnostic, or "research designed to *lead to* action" (1948: 45; emphasis in original), limited to making recommendations; empirical action research, which entailed doing something and keeping a record of what happened; and experimental. The authors, who believed participant action research yielded "primarily facts about a particular community rather than general principles which can guide action in other communities as well" (47), clearly preferred experimental action research, in which "the research program is planned from the beginning in collaboration with an operating agency which takes responsibility for seeing to it that the necessary action is carried out" (48).

7.   Lee Benson has contributed the following typology of American social science: (1) scholastic social science, which is nonparticipatory, nonapplied, directed almost exclusively to the internal debates of the discipline, and virtually always conducted by professional social scientists; and (2) action social science, which can be subdivided into (a) professional expert, (b) participatory, and (c) communal participatory action social science, and which is concerned with application and focused on solving problems in society.
      There are important differences among the three subtypes of action social science. Professional-expert action social science is nonparticipatory in design and research practice, as exemplfied by James S. Coleman *et al.*'s *Equality of Educational Opportunity* (1966) (See Benson and Harkavy 1991, esp. 14–15.)

8.   For Tavistock, see Trist and Murray 1990b: 133, 811; Marrow 1969: 222–24; and van Eijnatten 1993: 22–32. For a history of sociotechnical design thinking and action research, see Trist and Murray 1990b. Hans van Beinum (1993) notes that three "action-oriented research projects" independent of sociotechnical systems analysis were under way at the Tavistock during World War II. These projects concerned the transformation of officer selection procedures (using Bion's leaderless group method); the discovery of the therapeutic community, originally designed to reduce the outflow of soldiers experiencing psychological illness; and the innovation of transitional communities, designed to help resettle repatriated prisoners of war and later, as a general concept, to socially reconnect individuals "outside or alienated from main society" (Trist and Murray 1990c: 41–43). For details, see Murray 1990; Bridger 1990; and Wilson, Trist, and Curle 1990.

9.   For Sweden, see Gustavsen 1992; for Norway, Elden and Levin 1991; for Cornell and Mondragón, Greenwood and González 1992, esp. 121-45. For an excellent summary, see van Eijnatten 1993: 68–76.

10.   Ian Box suggests that Bacon prefigured the democratizing component of action research by expressing "a fundamental conviction that the advancement of learning could only be the result of a collective endeavour in which even those of meanest capacities could participate. The project did not depend on the unique genius of a Plato or Aristotle but was open to every man's industry. Everyone could contribute in some way" (Box 1989: 3).

Chapter 10

Bottom-up Organizational Change

The Segerström Case

Bertil Olsson

At the heart of Swedish workplace reform strategies is the desire to develop individual workers' and employees' opportunities to make decisions and have a real influence on working conditions. But in spite of comprehensive labor legislation and agreements on codetermination, attempts to change and democratize industrial organizations have had only meager results. Nevertheless, the internationalization of industrial competition has once again fueled discussions of alternative models and principles of work organization. The participation and emancipation of workers and shop-floor employees are now associated with the economic development and competitiveness of industrial organizations.

In practice, however, workers and shop-floor employees continuously indulge in processes of change, as a result of developments in technology, market preferences, trade conditions, and so forth. Researchers with the goal of reconstructing work organizations try to influence these processes and give them a desirable direction. If this strategy is successful, it may lead to innovative collaboration between researchers and practitioners, which could eventually result in a better understanding of organizational change and of the role of organizational research.

The Segerström case was a five-year collaborative project undertaken between a manufacturer of pressed and welded sheet-steel components and a research team from Dalarna and Linköping universities. The project started after a conflict erupted between management and the unions concerning a management proposal to sell off one production line. Formal negotiations were entered into, a time for consideration was agreed on, and eventually two union consultants, who subsequently formed part of the research team, were engaged. In their report, the consultants emphasized the need to restructure the work organization, and before long what had started as the union consultants' assignment had turned into an action research project, financed partly by the LOM Program.

At the time this project was initiated, conditions in the auto supply business were tough. At Segerström, the economic margins were tight, and the customers were making new demands concerning production quality and the need for on-time deliveries. Furthermore, the loss of a major product, steel wheel covers, representing one-third of the company's output, emphasized even more the need to develop the company's competitiveness. The rising mistrust and frustration among workers and shop-floor employees made the situation appear even less hopeful.

Aims and Theoretical Perspective

One of the aims of the LOM program was to initiate and support local development efforts by private companies and public organizations that could be characterized as having harmonious and stable industrial relations. Following the strong emphasis on collaboration, a key characteristic of the program was its focus on communication and language and the concept of democratic dialogue. According to Björn Gustavsen (1992), the way to develop organizations is to ensure that communication is open and democratic. Consequently, the LOM program focused on how such dialogue should be carried out, not on its content or actual purpose. Enabling democratic dialogue to take place became both the goal and the strategy of the LOM program, both theory and practice.

The concept and practice of democratic dialogue was never developed into an efficient tool for solving real interest-based conflicts, however. Deeply rooted in an idealistic and regulatory tradition, the LOM program concentrated on mobilizing for broad participation, expecting that innovative processes would emerge, while not even considering the risk that local development projects could reinforce the prevailing social dominance and inhibit radical initiatives (Burrell and Morgan 1979). The LOM program took no position regarding management-controlled rationalization schemes or the centralization of decision making and the intrinsic conflict between management control and the autonomy of workers and employees.

Symbolic Aspect

The Segerström project was grounded in a conception of organizations as social constructions (Czarniawska-Joerges 1993). From this perspective, work organizations, like social reality at large, are not conceived as objective in a realist sense. Instead, they are viewed as ongoing processes that are constantly confirmed and maintained by those who are active in the organizations. Certainly, an objective structure, which is normally designed by specialists, can readily be observed that consists of instructions, routines, methods, wage systems, and so on. Without the compliance and collaboration of the participants in the organization, however, these objective features become no more than pieces of paper, software, or management intentions. Consequently, work organizations are understood as intersubjective and existing principally as extensions of the participants' collective consciousness. According to this view, work organizations can be changed, and improved, as a result of workers' and employees' growing awareness and understanding of their role in maintaining unsatisfactory working conditions.

At Segerström, a bottom-up strategy was outlined so as to give the workers a central position in testing out new ways of organizing work. The core strategy was to mobilize the innovative capacity of the workers — a fundamental resource seldom recognized in hierarchical organizations (Fricke 1983). The approach aimed to identify variances in the manufacturing process and then to develop the collective ability of the workers to correct these variances (Pasmore 1988). This mapping of the work process was not treated as objective fact but recognized as an expression and articulation of shop-floor experiences. The purpose was to provide material for meaningful dialogues to take place between different tiers in the hierarchy and between employees with different work experiences.

Political Aspect

Social conflicts, concentration of power, and authority distort communication and thus the creation of meaning and understanding. The research team had experienced how workers perceived shop-floor reality as the manifestation of a dominating social order that impeded any radical change. Generally, workers on the shop floor went about their business silently, suspiciously, waiting for orders and information. In this respect, a top-down perspective pervaded the workdays and the minds of workers.

Once the workdays have been routinized, the constitutive processes that construct and sustain this reality are hidden and protected from critical reflection and alternative ways of organizing the workdays appear increasingly unrealistic (Deetz and Kersten 1983). Efforts to develop efficient work organizations should therefore include actions that promote personal growth, reflection, and autonomy, with the aim of freeing workers from the taken-for-granted conditions that limit their potential for innovative action. As objectified and routinized as the workdays might seem, they are, nevertheless, created by individuals and might therefore also be changed by organized action (Höglund 1991). In a bottom-up process, workers and shop-floor employees are given the opportunity to reflect and reason and to develop their skills so they may play an active role in the reorganization of the workplace. Dialogues with different members of the organization support a learning process that enriches their reasoning and argumentation and that might clear the way for daring proposals and radical change.

Research Aspect

The research team intervened in the work process and organized meetings that were meant to be important elements in an innovative process. The goal was that workers and shop-floor employees would gradually take over the meetings and eventually find good arguments for taking action. In this way, the research team tried to bring together different frames of reference and to contribute to a change in practice and the production of new insights.

One basic (research) assumption was that alternative solutions emerge out of impressions from the outside and from enlightened participation within (Elden and Levin 1991). From experience, the research team knew that outsiders can uncover myths at the workplace and expose insiders to unsatisfactory conditions to which insiders usually shut their eyes.

To cope with a combined theoretical and practical aim, researchers have to get out of the workplace situation and reflect on their personal experiences and impressions of crucial situations, supported by notes, documents, and interviews, in short, to contribute to the understanding of the nature of social change. For practical and political reasons, action research results in researchers having less control over the research process in favor of the participation of insiders. The researchers do not claim authority over truth but recognize that the situation is best described and problems best identified by insiders. In the process, researchers and practitioners do something together and develop mutual goals grounded in a shared conception of the situation and what solutions are attainable. The creation of a common language and an enriched frame of reference clear the way for new understanding and new solutions to practical problems (Dahlgren 1993).

Segerström Factory

The action research project took place in a family-owned company, established on a small scale in 1906 to manufacture and sell ornamental objects and gift trays in silver and gold plating. After the acquisition of the considerably larger Albeca Ltd., a manufacturer of loudspeakers and miscellaneous metal components, Segerström expanded.

In the 1980s, Segerström's emerged as one of the biggest Swedish suppliers of pressed and welded metal parts for the car-manufacturing industry, and by mid-decade, it had a 20 percent market share. In 1986, there were about three hundred employees and an annual turnover of U.S. $25 million.

Small economic margins had forced Segerström's to keep all of its manufacturing costs down. Nevertheless, and although the car market was growing, Segerström's profits were falling. The ongoing expansion had caused a delivery lag that the company had been fighting for many years and had put a strain both on the economy, caused by delayed invoicing, and on the organization, caused by replanning and extensive overtime and work during weekends. Maintenance routines had been neglected, and machine breakdowns and unexpected disturbances had become frequent. By the autumn of 1986, Segerström's faced an acute liquidity crisis that resulted in a financial reorganization of the company and the hiring of a new managing director.

Concurrently, the Swedish automobile industry was creating a hierarchy of suppliers in an effort to cut its administrative costs. Under this plan, only the most competent suppliers — those taking total-quality responsibility for more complex components or whole systems like the rear axle or transmission system — would deal directly with the automobile makers.

The car manufacturers also intended to intensify their capital rationalization schemes, so new demands were made on the suppliers to cut their inventories and prepare for just-in-time delivery. Concurrently, the car makers' quality-control organizations were preparing a new procedure for quality audits, which would result in all suppliers being ranked, with a likely result that only the best would survive.

The new CEO at Segerström's expected these changes to lead to even tougher competition and even smaller economic margins. Yet he chose to concentrate the company's operations on the car-supply business and to intensify relations with the car industry. His goal was to turn an entrepreneurial business into a manufacturing organization with stable and bureaucratic management routines. A production manager, a quality control manager, a personnel manager, and an economic controller were hired to play decisive roles in this new strategy.

Considering the financial reorganization, the new business strategy, and the new demands from customers, by now workers were speculating whether the new CEO really had the situation under control. How many jobs would disappear? Feelings of insecurity and worries about the future development of the company ran deep. It was amid this growing confusion that the local leader of the Metal Workers' Union demanded help from external consultants.

Premises

Visitors to Segerström's are normally shown upstairs, where, in addition to a reception area, the offices of about twenty managers and administrators are located. The offices are small, and most of the inner walls are of glass, which makes any intruder very conspicuous. At the far end of the second floor is a metal door that opens onto a spiral staircase from which one has a complete view of the large press shop, which is dominated by an eight hundred-ton hydraulic press. At the far end of the press shop is a specially designed group that manufactures details for microwave ovens.

To the right as one stands on the staircase are two more production groups: a welding shop with spot welding machines, excenter presses, and three automatic punching machines and, farther down, a surface-conditioning shop for chromating, zincification, and nickel plating. Underneath the top floor is a tool room where chucking fixtures are manufactured and tools are adjusted and a small office for the engineers. To the left as one stands on the staircase are doors to the warehouses and office barracks for the technicians. Though the shops are full of activity, not many machines are actually working. Dominating the scene is the movement of materials. Thirty-five to forty tons of plate are brought in every day, and 150 loading stools of manufactured parts are delivered and loaded on trucks.

Working Conditions

Although the manufacturing process at Segerström's may seem technically advanced, many operations are performed within a gray zone where, for a variety of reasons, tolerance and quality standards cannot be established. Tolerances may be extremely difficult to measure, operations may be insufficiently documented, the capabilities of the process or tools may not be stable enough, and so forth. Nevertheless, the workers have to maintain a high work pace and therefore have no time to be cautious or to identify problems; the task is simply to produce. On the shop floor, supervisors and technicians, maintenance men, controllers, fitters, and truck drivers swarm to keep workers in direct production busy.

In the mid-1980s, most of the jobs at Segerstöm's were characterized as boring; workers sat waiting for the time to pass, moving parts out of one box and into the next. Jobs were routinized and adapted to a machine logic, and workers were isolated and felt deprived of human dignity. As one supervisor put it: "You have to admire workers that stick at it. There is no social life. There used to be hell if anyone earned a penny extra. Today nobody cares. Everyone is working for himself. What could motivate people here? There is no contact, no understanding of what's going on." Management had some general ideas about how to make the workers' situation more agreeable: renovate the dressing room, put in new lockers, showers, and a sauna, buy new furniture for the lunchroom, and so forth. But there were no programs that addressed working conditions. Moreover, a number of workers and shop-floor employees had developed a kind of delivery know-how, trying out quick solutions as new and unforeseen problems popped up, and they were reluctant to change a work situation that provided opportunities for extra earnings and problem-solving activities for more regulations and routines.

Bottom-up Strategy

After failing the first quality audit, conducted by the most important customer, Segerstöm's management faced a major problem. As the front page of one corporate newspaper, *Double-SS*, said in 1987, no less than 90 percent of the faults in production could be spotted without using any instruments, with just the eye: "In other words, the operative can find almost all faults by looking at each part that he or she is machining before letting it pass on." The solution was for management to make the workers take a more active interest in the work output.

Once it defined production quality as the key criterion for success, management was caught between two organizational design principles, described by Fred E. Emery as the principles of redundancy-of-parts and redundancy-of-functions (1977). Management began looking for ways to utilize the workers' qualifications and to increase their involvement in whatever jobs they were performing. The problem with this new approach, as Emery points out, was that the workers needed to be willing to put their unused capabilities into action, and without considerable sharing of values and objectives between the workers and management, the potential of this design might never be realized. With top-down measures, management would run the risk that changes would stop at output demands and disciplinary measures (Kelly 1982). Eventually, management recognized the benefits of a bottom-up strategy that aimed to achieve broad participation by the workers and shop-floor employees and that had as its ultimate goal shared understanding of the problems and the conditions that would lead to an improvement in quality.

Meetings and Regular Proceedings

The idea to organize production groups that would meet regularly started from the assumption that an understanding of the practical actions of workers and shop-floor employees is the basis for organizational developments at work. To make the meetings meaningful, however, the workers and shop-floor employees had to feel confident that management was treating their suggestions and criticism seriously and that the result would be practical actions and measures. Consequently, the production groups needed support both from within the formal hierarchy of authority and in the formal agreements between the local unions and management.

Addressing the problem of inequality also was important. Study circles, conducted by the local Metal Workers' Union, aimed to strengthen the workers' belief in their own abilities and to let them experience an increase in self-esteem (Holmer 1993).

The actual forming of production groups was done by the leader of the local Metal Workers' Union and plant supervisors. The idea was to create better connections between informal groups, such as workers who sat together at coffee breaks or whose work areas were close to one another. A series of meetings was proposed that was supported by formal authority and the bargaining and codetermination processes. In addition, a group to coordinate the meetings and union-managed study circles was introduced.

Results

The research team planned to start the process of changing routines and working procedures — to make things happen — and to leave future responsibility for the project with the participants. A decisive step in the project was therefore the point when most of the production groups were formed. One researcher chaired the meetings, which were usually held between shifts in the lunch room. Just outside were the three big automatic punching machines, running on a different shift, which meant they could not be turned off during meetings. Because of the noise, the participants could barely hear each other talk.

Moreover, it was almost impossible to plan group meetings in advance. Sudden changes in the delivery schemes, machine breakdowns, delays, and other problems meant that meetings often had to be canceled at the last minute. Complicating the situation, supervisors continuously had to shift workers between different operations and departments because of the high labor turnover and absenteeism. The planning of meetings also was made difficult because of various development projects and continuous changes at the organizational level. For these reasons, only groups with a high degree of internal stability — namely, the press-welding and assembly groups — actually conducted a series of meetings. The participants in these groups liked the project, however, and were prepared to continue the meetings as the project was coming to an end.

The resistance and obstacles to accomplishing even minor changes were greatly underestimated at the beginning of the project. During the project period the company had four different production managers and three different quality control systems. A new inventory system was installed, the shop-floor layout was changed, and new products and new machines were brought in. For these reasons, even very concrete and simple suggestions from the production groups, such as one to keep access open to water fountains, did not lead to immediate actions.

The production manager argued that there was no time or resources to deal with anything but immediate delivery problems. Support from staff and administration also was difficult to achieve. For example, to many white-collar employees, organizing group meetings to address problems in the manufacturing process was a challenging and provocative idea. Middle managers and technicians feared that the project might lead to cuts in such traditional white-collar work as surveillance, planning, and control. They further feared that a direct dialogue between the shop floor and management might reduce their authority. It was therefore argued that the production group should not develop alternatives to the formal line of authority. In short, many white-collar employees tried to position the meetings as peripheral activities without strategic importance (Cole, Bacdayan, and White 1993).

Business negotiations also significantly restricted any radical change. Tools, drawings, and products were owned by the customers, and production methods were part of the business agreement. To redesign jobs based on the supplier's initiative would require renegotiating the whole business agreement. Further, the supplier had to cover any extra costs for new tooling and redesign. This seemed out of the question.

There were those who supported the meetings, however. The leader of the local Metal Workers' Union, for instance, saw the meetings as a way to develop a team-based work organization and thus get rid of the piece-rate system and degrading work situations. And the new quality control manager saw the meetings as a way to mobilize a broad interest in quality and improved understanding of customers' demands. Both these individuals participated regularly in the meetings and consequently discussions focused on the urgent need for improvements in quality control and in workers' rights to participate in the decision-making process.

Learning by Change

Another serious impediment to conducting the meetings was that Segerström's had a large immigrant population, so that no fewer than seventeen different languages were spoken on the shop floor. Many of these immigrants had a very poor command of Swedish. Furthermore, many of the old-timers did not want to participate in production group meetings. Mr. S., a very experienced and respected worker, expressed this opinion: "To hell with this project. If someone could just find a way to make management pay me more, I'd give them whatever quality or commitment they want."

The workers who could handle the piece-rate system and get their work done at top speed were viewed negatively. Ms. E., who handled an astonishing seven hundred details of sheet metal an hour, argued that she would lose money if conditions were changed. Many workers had also lived through other projects that had deteriorated to blunt rationalization schemes. Many of them expressed mistrust: "This project is just another way to cheat us, and to make us work harder."

The managers had a frustrating time reading the reports from the meetings, which were filled with grievances about how gloomy and greasy the workplace was. They were distressed by these reports and, feeling bad, realized that the conditions on the shop floor were really unforeseen consequences of their own actions — or lack of action.

As a result of the production group meetings, new opportunities opened up for the workers to take part in problem solving. This was especially true of "upstream" problems, most of which it was possible to detect with just the eye — press marks from the press sections, particles of dust or splashes from the surface-conditioning process, and so forth. When workers from the previous process areas were invited to meetings, discussions centered on what defects looked like in input materials downstream, which helped workers upstream to identify the problems that had caused the defects. Engineers were invited to discuss improvements in tools and equipment and to plan new devices that could ease the assembly work.

Once some of the technicians left their offices and became visible on the shop floor, many small improvements were made. One press/welding machine was raised a few inches, making room for workers' legs; new chairs were tested; and lift boards, lifting devices, and hand cranes appeared. Approved standard pieces from all operations were made available to workers, who then could use them to check a process. Tooling manufacturers and engineers were invited to meetings to document mistakes and learn about production conditions, which could help them to improve the construction of new tools. Eventually, the production manager considered forming groups composed of shop-floor workers, fitters, supervisors, and technicians to work on new products and production methods.

As the project continued, three technicians formed a coordinating group with the assignment of coordinating operations across the shop-floor department as well as the meetings of production groups. Under this new coordinating group, a more project-like organizational thinking was introduced. It opened the way for a new take on the analysis of problems and disturbances and ways to improve control of the manufacturing process.

Conclusion

The bottom-up project was introduced at Segerström's during a time when it was unclear whether the company would stay in business. Measures that would lead to increased production quality and cost reductions were urgent. The short-term objectives were reached. Performance was improved, and the number of customer complaints decreased substantially, as did internal complaints and rejections.

In September 1989, the company passed the quality audit and was approved of as an A supplier. The quality audit report specifically mentioned that Segerström's was pursuing a quality-development program based on broad shop-floor participation.

These results showed that the project had provided crucial support for obtaining better control over the manufacturing process. The fears among managers that the production group meetings would get out of control and eventually lead to anarchy were proven unfounded. Although workers certainly had expressed grievances and demands for improved working conditions, they had also shown that they were able and had an interest in improving the general level of performance on the shop floor. Workers and shop-floor employees had taken a constructive position and revealed they were interested in analyzing and developing new routines and work procedures and in engaging in constructive discussions with their supervisors.

The lack of response and management's hesitant attitude could have turned the bottom-up process into a series of meaningless discussions the sole purpose of which was to make workers and shop-floor employees feel more appreciated and attended to. Through the participation of the quality manager and the union leader, however, the meetings gained strategic importance and issues of workers' autonomy and control became management considerations.

As a result of the bottom-up process, workers and shop-floor employees were mobilized as an important potential for the development of the work organization. They were given time and space to reflect on working conditions and to develop an understanding of how routines and different operations coordinated with the whole working process. To do this, they had to get out of their roles and prescribed work situations and participate in dialogues and discussions.

The Segerström case shows that a bottom-up strategy opens up possibilities for dealing successfully with the important need to find ways out of the continuous routinization of industrial work and to explore new patterns of communication. The result was improved control of the work process and increased autonomy for workers and shop-floor employees.

Chapter 11

Setting the Scene for Effective Dialogue Between Men and Women at Work

Ingrid Ljungberg van Beinum

> *"We were going to repaint a room. Some think it should be painted yellow, others that it should be blue. Most women want the yellow, but still quite a few want it blue. . . . Then I say, 'Yes, we will paint it yellow.' And in my stupidity I think they will all be satisfied with what I do. But you are damned whatever you do, because now I see the women are dissatisfied because not everyone wanted it yellow. [He laughs.] I understand we should have discussed it further and perhaps we would have come to the conclusion that it should be green. So, after all, I have made a compromise that no one was satisfied with. This is not the way of thinking that men use; they notice that now it is yellow and it's okay. . . . But the women notice that not all are satisfied with the choice of yellow. . . . These are the kinds of things you have to accept as a male manager and it's not very rewarding."*

This vignette, provided by a male manager, who noted a year later that the room was still not painted, describes a situation that occurs frequently in workplaces. It illustrates in a nutshell the interdependency between gender relations and organizational practice.

This chapter focuses on a critical episode in a large interorganizational action research project that concerns gender relations in the workplace. The analysis presented here is based on discussions between men and women talking about men and women. The project was financed by KOM, a five-year program set up by the Swedish Work Environment Fund that focused on collaboration between men and women in the workplace.

It is not my intention here to describe the whole project but, rather, to focus on a specific part of the start-up phase. Nor is it my intention to discuss at length what action research is, although the project is an action research project. Action research is sufficiently explained in the introductory chapter of this book (see also van Beinum, Faucheux, and van der Vlist 1996; van Beinum and Pålshaugen 1996; Greenwood and González 1992). A short description of the participating organizations and the development and organization of the project will be necessary, however, to put the project in context.

Participating Organizations

The project involves three organizations: (1) a nuclear power station, which has 1,200 employees; (2) a school district, consisting of a secondary school, primary schools, and day-care centers, which together have 300 employees; and (3) a postal district, consisting of more than a dozen post offices and a distribution center, with a total of 650 employees. The nuclear power station is totally male dominated; about 200 women are employed in administrative functions, but of the 1,000 persons in the production area, only about 80 are women. In the school district, the distribution of men and women is about equal in the organization as a whole, although most of the women work in the day-care centers and the primary schools and the men in the secondary school. In the postal district, the mail sorting, letter carrying, and other transport functions are performed primarily by men, while cashier work, postal order, and banking services are done predominantly by women.

Objectives of the Project

The three organizations are all concerned about improving the quality of male-female relations at their workplaces. In particular, they want their male and female employees to be more equal in daily organizational life,[1] to improve the status of women in their organizations, and to develop a more even vertical and horizontal distribution of men and women in their various work areas. To achieve these broad objectives, the organizations have formulated specific objectives of their own.

The nuclear power station is clearly different from the other two organizations in that it is a very specialized, high-technology workplace. Traditionally, it has not employed women, partly because of the risks of contamination from the radiation but also because few women have had the necessary technical qualifications. Finding women with the required technical training is still a problem. Further, some women find it difficult to work alone in a group of men, and many find the shift work inconvenient. Also, many of the men are not used to having women in the workplace, and in some work areas there is clear resistance to facilitating the employment of women. Thus, one specific goal is to change the attitudes of the male workforce toward the idea of women performing the power station's particular kind of work.

The youth and school district has defined its problem not in terms of the structural features of its organization but with respect to the unequal ways in which staff treat the boys and girls at the schools and at the day-care centers. The ultimate objective is to develop a new policy aimed at achieving equality in the education of children.

The specific, long-term objective of the postal district is to achieve a more even horizontal gender distribution in the organization as a whole, as well as to change the attitudes of both the men and women in the workforce.

Reasons for Pursuing the Research

Various concerns motivated me to pursue this research. First, progress with regard to the integration of men and women in the labor market has been rather slow. Second, legislation concerning equality in organizational and family life has had only a limited effect and has sometimes even led to maladaptation on the part of women (*e.g.*, women often try to live up to the male culture in organizational life instead of identifying and developing a niche of their own). Third, in spite of new policies and legislation in the fields of equality, the attitudes and values of men and women are changing very slowly because of the dominant influence of the traditional process of socialization with its stereotypical gender orientations. Fourth, very little research has been concerned with male-female relations in general and with the connection between these relations and organizational theory and practice in particular. The few researchers who have addressed the subject of women in the "world of business" (*e.g.*, Kanter 1977; Ferguson 1984; Ressner 1987; Sørensen 1982; Acker 1988) have been preoccupied with problematizing the issue from a woman's point of view. Hanne Haavind (1992) and Elin Kvande and Bente Rassmussen (1991, 1993) focused more directly and comprehensively on the practice of male-female relations. Fifth, and finally, the obvious way to influence the awareness of men and women with regard to gender relations is through communication.

I was aware that men and women communicating about men and women would unleash deeply ingrained social imagery and expose complex, individual, internal worlds. It seemed to me, however, that the only realistic and promising way to address the sometimes overwhelming issue of gender relations was for men and women to communicate with each other about men and women.

Through this project, ordinary women and men, in talking about gender in the workplace, address in their way — and that is the only way there is — one of the most pressing and problematic issues we face today, which is how to understand and meet "the other." In this chapter I try to address this issue and at the same time to describe the way my own understanding developed.

Organization and Development of the Project

The project consisted of four phases: (1) preparation and planning for action by each of the organizations (November 1992-February 1993); (2) a planning conference, in which the three organizations, in interaction with each other, developed their action plans, using search conference methodology (M. Emery 1989a) (March 1993); (3) a period in which each of the organizations put their plans into practice (April 1993-November 1993); during this period four "theme" days were organized on which members of the three organizations met with each other to discuss their experiences; (4) an evaluation conference, at which members of the three organizations discussed and reflected on their experiences and engaged in joint planning of further action (December 1993).

A steering group was established, as well as a work group for each organization participating in the project. The steering group provided overall guidance for the project and was responsible for identifying policy implications of the research. This group consisted of two senior representatives from each of the organizations and the researcher. Each work group consisted of its two representatives to the steering group and six to eight men and women who represented a vertical slice of the organization. The three work groups were responsible for the research and development process.

As part of the research process, I held discussions with each of the participants in the three work groups. I use the word *discussion*s here and not *interview*s because these were open dialogues aimed at mutual understanding. Members of the work group also held discussions with women and men volunteers at each organization: three at the nuclear power station, two in the school district, and three in the post district. In addition, each work group met regularly for discussions about its own project. Finally, interorganizational discussions took place at the search conference and on the four theme days, when the work groups came together to learn about and discuss specific issues pertinent to their developmental activities. The evaluation conference, held in December 1993, was also organized as an interorganizational discussion.

Analysis

The analysis presented in this chapter is based on individual discussions I conducted with the twenty-seven members of the work groups. The discussions were recorded and then transcribed.

The objectives of these discussions were, first, to begin a dialogue about the experiences of each participant with men-women relationships in the workplace and thus to begin to develop an impression and understanding of the nature of these relationships and, second, to give each participant a feel for a discussion of this kind, to prepare him or her to moderate group discussions with colleagues. The discussions were open and loosely structured, in that I had identified beforehand some areas I wanted us to cover.

I approached the material in a dialogical manner. Initially, I listened to the tapes (in Swedish) and read transcripts of the discussions (translated into English). Thus began a process of listening, reading, listening again, and rereading, in which I paid particular attention to the tone of the spoken language behind the written text.

At this stage, my interpretation was framed by four lines of questioning: (1) what were the women saying about women, (2) what were they saying about men, (3) what were the men saying about men, and (4) what they were saying about women. I thought that in this way I would be able to see the nature of the relationship between men and women as the "figure" and the work situation as the back "ground." While reading and listening, however, other patterns started to emerge. My framework did not fit; it was too structured. I had been using my so-called expert knowledge and had tried to force the material into a framework with which I was familiar.

I then experienced a figure-ground reversal as I started to realize that the content of what the various individual men and women were saying did not reflect "components" along my four dimensions but "clusters" of positions of a different kind, cutting across organizations; a different logic was needed. The whole was obviously more than the sum of the parts. At this point, I started to see the similarities between the three organizations and therefore cross-organizational patterns. An important trigger mechanism was the sudden awareness that the behavior of the young boys and girls in the day-care centers was somewhat similar to the behavior of the men and women at the nuclear power station and in the postal district. The interorganizational structure added an unexpected richness to my understanding.

When one is engaged in an analysis of this kind — that is, interpreting discussions and examining the meaning of statements and interactions — one is using oneself as a tool. I was my own method, conducting a reflective inquiry. I thus became involved in two dialogues: one with the participants by means of the transcriptions and tapes and the other one with myself. This is of course what happens when one reads any text, but in this case, probably in view of the topic, I felt the latter very strongly.

Having done the analysis, I realized that the process I had gone through while engaging with the material had been very similar to the process I go through in an action research project. It is like going through an epigenetic landscape (van Beinum, Faucheux, and van der Vlist 1996). One is simultaneously involved in discovery and creation.

I have tried to organize the material and the comments that follow in a dialogical fashion. They reflect in a way the actual discussions I had with the participants.

Four main patterns concerning male-female relations in the workplace emerged from my interpretations of the discussions: (1) the socialization process strongly reinforces some relatively "innocent" biological differences; (2) the early socialization process strongly affects whether one's orientation is community-based or individuality-based; (3) there are significant differences in the degree of awareness of the meaning of the male-female relationship; (4) men and women have different strategies for dealing with male-female relations. The statements that follow have been grouped accordingly.

As I grouped the statements according to these patterns, however, I started to realize that I was doing more than just presenting clusters; I was writing a story. The question is, who's story? A story consists of a theme and a plot. The plot, in this case, is formed by the way the clusters have been arranged. They seem to have organized "themselves" from open to more focused. It looks like a story about actual and potential developments, about fixed and static as well as dynamic and creative ways of looking at the world. The theme, which in this case is the "world of gender," consists of a struggle to focus on a shared horizon of men-women relationships.

I have divided the four clusters into subclusters. For each subcluster, I have included the quotations associated with it. In this way the voices of the participants come through. The total number of quotations that were extracted from the discussions was about three hundred. Because of space limitations and reasons of confidentiality and/or to avoid repetition, many quotations have been excluded in this chapter. Each quotation is marked with "(w)" or "(m)," indicating whether it was said by a woman or a man.

Are There Differences between Men and Women — Really?

General Observations

"I'm sure that we are already imprinted from early childhood; it is not something which suddenly comes about, but I have no clear understanding of what's biological and what's social." (w)

"You start to see the difference when boys and girls are about two years old. Boys move about more; they are louder and more physically active. The girls sit and paint and play games, while the boys run around and shoot and so on, . . . although there are boys who are a bit calmer and girls who are wilder. Boys demand more time; you have to tell them to calm down and activate them. They often have problems . . . with their movements: they can't sit still without falling; they can just stand up and fall down. Later they go to school and their teachers become irritated because they can't sit still on a chair and concentrate. But it's because they can't. They have so much energy." (m)

"I have noticed that when a boy falls and hurts himself and starts crying, I tell him that this wasn't so bad, go and play again, while with girls you take them up and say, hush, hush, hush, and where did you hurt yourself and shall I blow on it. And then you realize what you are doing and that there is really no reason for doing it this way. You just support and underpin the behavior of many six-year-old [girls] to moan and cry. But as long as you realize it yourself, you can change it." (m)

"There is a hidden norm staying alive from old times when [girls] were supposed to sit still and write neatly and everything should be clean and proper everywhere, and the boys still need more attention and the girls adjust easier." (w)

"We see the difference with regard to working with computers. The girls don't grab things for themselves but sit beside while the boys use the keyboard." (w)

"There are some clearly separated areas dominated by women in the school, where none of the pupils want to do their 'practice,'[2] such as cleaning and working in the kitchen. These areas have a very low status." (m)

"I think it's more interesting to try to recruit girls for areas like designing, new technology, or natural sciences, as these jobs fulfill the women's demands for a clean and beautiful environment, coziness, that the work shouldn't be too heavy, and that you can wear beautiful clothes and not have to wear an overall, which makes you look clumsy, but rather one should look nice and fresh and womanly in a technical job." (m)

"To work within the salary administration was no job for any of the three men who tried it. . . . It is too detailed and precise. . . . You have to sit on your chair for eight hours a day and not run around in the corridors. That's the reason men don't stay." (w)

"We speak a different language, of course, as we have different ways and objectives already from childhood. We play differently, and [girls] play more two and two, and boys play more tough in groups, so we become different and come across differently. I think it is very important that we both know that this is how it is and that we accept it and that we in that way understand better, when we present a problem. . . . Of course, we as women have learned a lot, but it would be good if men learned a bit about how women function." (w)

Self-Confidence, Risk Taking, and Responsibility

"Women are much more precise. . . . I check everything five to six times. Some men do, too, but women do it more. Then, when they move to a higher level, they are normally better than their male colleagues because the whole time they have had to show that they are good." (w)

"The men find new things easier and find it easier to take on projects. The women are more cautious, they don't think they will manage, try to find other explanations, and are satisfied with things as they are. At the same time, a moment later they can complain about the situation." (m)

"Women perhaps have a mentality that makes them think that, no, I won't manage that. But there is nothing saying that women can't manage as well as men do." (m)

"[When you apply for a job], of course, you look the whole time at what it is you can't do, and if there is one thing I don't know how to do, I won't apply." (w)

"Sometimes if a man doesn't know a special task, he will at least talk about it and sound as if he knows it." (m)

Subordination

"In my work I don't experience any difference. Rather, I'm the stronger, [and] the man takes the position of waiting for what I will say and do. This I experience as very frustrating, because how will I get him to say what he thinks and wants and show that he is doing well. I think most of the time that I must not dominate him; we have similar tasks. It worries me and at the same time I can't be totally straight with him because then I might cut him off because of that. I'm also ten years older, . . . I don't know why he subordinates himself, but there has become some kind of hierarchy in our roles. . . . With older men I have always talked about this with good results and they have been surprised that I have experienced it in that way." (w)

"Older men often take on a father role." (w)

"It is easier for a man to be in command; he doesn't have to argue as much as a woman to get a decision. He gets questioned less than a woman." (w)

"Sometimes I think the women agree too easily; after all, there are the three of them, and I am alone." (m)

This cluster can be broken down into statements reflecting two levels of significance — a general and a specific — both of which relate to the complex issue of socialization. In the various statements at the general level, women and men recognize and discuss the differences between them. But although they talk about it, they seem puzzled and question it. They recognize biological differences between boys and girls, men and women. The question is how much emphasis they should put on these differences and to what extent they are being reinforced through what we are taught by "significant others"[3] at a very early age.

In the statements at the specific level, men and women express their differences from the point of view of their being active versus nonactive, a difference that is manifest from a very early age. As the above quotes indicate, from the age of two, boys are more physically active and girls are more likely to sit still, painting and playing games.

Later, when they are in school, girls adhere to the norm of "old times, when they were supposed to sit still and write neatly and everything should be clean and proper." Male-female differences are reinforced by teachers, who give more attention to the boys because of their demanding behavior. They do not sit still, they ask questions, and they disrupt the teacher's plan (Einarsson and Hultman 1984). The girls are not really inactive, however. They are working hard and getting good marks.

What is considered good behavior at school is mostly not appreciated later in working life. By that time "sitting still" is perceived as evidence of passivity, low risk taking, and a lack of confidence and assertiveness. In school, one also learns one's first lessons about the divided labor market by noticing that "there are some clearly separated areas dominated by women, . . . such as cleaning and working in the kitchen" and that "these areas have a very low status."

The traditional image of womanhood is probably one of the more devastating influences on young women. It is only indirectly spelled out in the following quote: "Women's demands . . . that you can wear beautiful clothes and not have to wear an overall, which makes you look clumsy, but rather one should look nice and fresh and womanly." This statement, like similar statements in advertisements, fairy tales, soap operas, women's magazines, and so on, perpetuates the problem women have in finding their own, authentic identities.

One of the men questions the differences in his behavior toward little boys and girls who have hurt themselves. He is asking himself if he should treat the girls the same way he treats the boys, by saying "don't cry, be strong." In his case similar treatment means treating the girls like boys and not the other way around. Thus, the male way is the norm.

The comments in this cluster show quite clearly the message boys and girls receive from an early age. The first signs of hesitation and uncertainty are starting to emerge in these comments, the first signs of thinking in stereotypes related to power and competence. At the same time, one senses that both the men and women desire better understanding of their relationship as it manifests itself in the context of organizational hierarchies.

In general, these comments demonstrate ambivalent feelings about gender. At this point in the discussion, gender orientations have not yet been totally frozen into stereotypes. There is an opening.

"Real" Differences

Degrees of Directness

"Something which is good with men is that you can reason and then you can shut the door and . . . if we have decided something, that's it." (m)

"Women are not as direct. If something is wrong, they don't tell you directly but complain to others first. This may be women's way of not fighting, as men do. Men are more straightforward." (w)

"[Men] are more just; they don't talk behind your back, they tell you straight if they think something is stupid." (w)

"In difficult [emotional] situations, men get more unsure and don't dare to say either yes or no." (w)

"I don't know if there is a difference. I think women talk a bit more women's talk, are a bit more gossipy. . . . I think it's fine to work together with men when something happens that isn't so good. Then they say that this is totally wrong, then they become sour, and then it is okay. With girls . . . they are sour such a long time. With men it is done and over with." (w)

"I have never met a man who has been interested in how I experience him and what I might be thinking. I wonder much about this. But if you try to talk about it, it's alright." (w)

"Some years ago I asked them [the men in her group, where she is the only woman] what they thought about [having] me as a female colleague. . . . Some said that they hadn't thought very much about it, but they had seen that it worked out well, although they had been wondering in the beginning as they had never worked with women. Some said they didn't know what to do but thought: I do it the usual way, come what may." (w)

Differences in the Way Men and Women Talk

"There can be a bit too much 'cackling.' . . . One of the men hit his fist on the table and told us to stop. . . . He thought we were just speculating, without any facts, only irrelevant things." (w)

"You can joke with the group, but the jargon is rude and I don't think all women would be able to stand it, but if it goes too far I say so. [The men] know I have an awful temperament and can get very angry." (w)

"This cunningness that you sometimes notice with women, that they say one thing and mean another and perhaps point to a third, is something I have great difficulty in grasping. But I know women who say that that's how it is in reality." (m)

"I'm working only with men, but we have young girls coming from school and doing their practice here.[4] The work doesn't change, but the coffee breaks do. You chat differently, calmer, the jargon and the jokes become different with girls around. It is positive." (m)

Differences in the Need to Belong

"I was lucky [in the beginning that] there was a girl in another shift team who I had seen at school [and] with whom I could sit and talk typical women's talk that the men would not have understood." (w)

"What I miss, especially now when I'm back after having had a child, is other women. The other women work so far away from me, so we don't have so much contact." (w)

"It is much easier to phone a woman, like when I couldn't come to the last meeting [because her child was sick]. It was very easy to talk to my female manager. If it would have been a man, he wouldn't have understood, but, of course, I don't know if she did either, but you take for granted she does." (w)

"Women are more inclined to look for similarity. Men look more from the outside, both at themselves and at the team." (m)

"Women sometimes suffocate themselves and protect each other in the group. Men look more at themselves and think it's nice if someone succeeds and think that perhaps I can do the same. Women say: what is she doing, we usually don't do that and she shouldn't do it now either." (m)

"Women in day care create a kind of girlfriend relationship instead of a professional relationship, which is no good either for work or for themselves. They get into difficulties later if they advance into a managerial position." (m)

"I haven't sat down and consciously thought about this, but what's important to me is that you don't . . . try to turn everything into a women's issue. I'd rather weave it into the total work, . . . and if something looks very wrong when it comes to men and women, I don't want it marked as an equality issue; rather, it is important, via discussions in the daily work situation, to try to solve things. It's important to handle [problems] like that, because there is a certain 'oversatisfaction' with equality, and then it's difficult to have an impact." (w)

The Whole versus the Part

"To develop a group means to me that everybody likes what they are doing, perhaps developing their ideas and advancing a bit further, while the women see development as liking one's group and having security at work, being satisfied with it. Development happens somewhere else, perhaps at home, then." (m)

"We look at organizations in different ways. Men just decide that now you do this. . . . But I want to know what there is he wants to have done, what the content should look like, before you start to look at who does what. . . . It probably takes the same time whatever way you do it, but you do it in different ways." (w)

Dealing with Emotions

"I always think it's hard to tell someone he is wrong because you get so emotionally involved. For instance, one can start crying although you're angry. . . . A man never does that; he wouldn't cry because he is angry. You don't want to show yourself as being weaker than you are and also you are so different as a woman, so you cry when you are angry and when you are sad and you show more what you think and feel." (w)

"We are more caring and that may be good. . . . We are better at taking care of people and being leaders from that point of view, talking to people, not forgetting them, thinking of details and such, while men just run past and go for the technical aspects, . . . forgetting that the human being sometimes needs a pat on the shoulder [and to be told], 'You did this well and we can help each other.'" (w)

"[Men] see when I'm happy or sad [because] I've got a different facial expression I think, and a guy can be a bit sour and irritated and no one really thinks about it, apart from me, who sometimes can say, 'What is it with you?' The guys don't think about it or they don't care . . . or they see it but don't want to interfere and it's more legitimate if I ask. . . . I can go and ask if there is a special problem and discuss a bit. . . . You have your eyes open a little more for emotional nuances because I think girls are a bit more emotional themselves." (w)

"We have really tried to take care of [our male colleagues] and to help them." (w)

This cluster reveals different observations from the first one, insofar as the views are more decisively expressed. Clear differences are emerging about the behavior of men and women. More specifically, the influence of the socialization process seems evident in the firm beliefs and behaviors the participants describe. Both men and women express the belief that men are more direct when talking to others and that if something is wrong, they hear it from a man, not from a woman, who prefers to "talk behind your back."

One can also see in these statements the reemergence of the theme that men and boys are "active" whereas women and girls "sit still," although this idea is expressed less directly in these statements. Here, both men and women express positive feelings about men's directness and negative feelings about women's tendency to not say what they think. The tendency men have to be direct and to say what they think straightforwardly seems to be most apparent in situations in which no emotions or conflicts are involved. In more conflictual or emotional situations, women are the ones who take the initiative in an effort to find solutions. Under these circumstances, they are far from passive.

The women also express a greater need, both literally and figuratively, to belong. Both Carol Gilligan (1982, 1988), in her research on boys' and girls' moral judgments, and Bjørg Åse Sørensen (1982), in her study of men's and women's different rationalities/reasons for making decisions, have concluded that women's relations with others play a decisive role in the way they handle situations. Men, by contrast, handle situations more according to "the rules of the game" (Gilligan 1982, 1993) or by means of a "technical/logical rationality" (Sørensen 1982). These empirical findings, especially Gilligan's, are probably some of the most cited in feminist research on male-female differences. That women are relational and men are not has almost taken on the weight of biological fact, at least in popular literature, rather than being an expression of socialization.

From the above statements it seems that men are less comfortable than women dealing with emotions and are also more individualistic and that women are more concerned about relations and caring. According to Stephen J. Bergman (1993), this is a characteristic of Western culture, where in men the development of the self is taken as the point of departure, not the self in relation to others. The development of boys is viewed as fundamentally different from that of girls' because boys, at an early age, become aware of the difference between themselves and the mother as part of the process of developing a male identity. In various Freudian theories, the development of a boy's identity is seen to take place through identification with the father, a process that involves competition, fear, and denial, which are also important ingredients in the formation of bureaucratic hierarchies.

It is worth noting that in 1937 Karen Horney had already taken a different position and pointed to the basic influence of cultural factors in the development of men and women. Others who placed the relationship between self and other at the center of their developmental theories include Eric Fromm, Harry Stack Sullivan, W.R.B. Fairbairn, and H. Winnicott.

Gilligan *et al.*, referring to Hanna Arendt, says: "To see self-sufficiency as the hallmark of maturity conveys a view of adult life . . . that cannot sustain the kinds of long-term commitments and involvements with other people that are necessary for raising and educating a child or for citizenship in a democratic society" (1988: xii). Other feminist psychologists have criticized developmental theories on the grounds that they are reductionistic, because they make no distinction between the developmental process in boys and girls. Consequently, a female developmental psychology has evolved in which relations to others play an important role in the development of a female identity.

A striking difference in boys' and girls' upbringing is that while little girls start defining themselves positively, as "like" someone (*i.e.*, the mother), little boys start defining themselves negatively, as "unlike" the mother. If the boy grows up in circumstances in which men are less visible, if the father is seldom home or the mother is single, for instance, he has to learn about masculinity from peers, teachers, grandfathers, and others (Phillips 1993). The need for both female and male role models during children's development is clearly demonstrated in the statements about male day-care providers in both the first and second clusters.

Implications of Male-Female Differences in the Workplace

Awareness and Understanding

"Yes, [younger women] are [different from older women]. It feels like [younger women] don't question their being, while I always thought that I had to maintain my rights and also had to be very cautious in how I maintained those rights, because with the slightest exaggeration you were seen as a radical and then my colleagues reacted aggressively." (w)

"The women working here are colleagues; it is not something you think about. I don't think the girls think of it either." (m)

"One thinks there is equality in the school, because there are so many women working there and we have the same salary." (w)

"I must say it's not often you feel you get special treatment. But it is very clear . . . that the men are in the lead, but at the same time many women speak up, too. But the men in my organization translate this into some kind of general opinion and say that in our organization we don't have to talk about equality." (w)

"If you look at averages, I think men are better in mathematics than women [and] women are better in languages. One can probably never come to a fifty-fifty situation, because women haven't got that talent. It's possible that this is a prejudice, but that's how I think it is." (m)

"What you can learn from each other is above all to listen, something men don't do as well as women. At the same time, . . . it must not lead to that you listen and listen and then nothing happens. " (m)

"There [was a] guy who always used to carry my bags and open the doors. He was very polite, but that is suitable for outside work. He didn't know how to behave so I had to tell him that I'm one of the team and don't look at me as a woman. This is important to talk about. I don't think [the men] would have started talking about this themselves or talked among themselves about this. . . . There is a difference with the younger guys because they have experience with women from their education." (w)

"Sometimes you don't care, but sometimes you get very angry when they say that women should have a chain between the bed and the stove. You get so tired of it and you see red every time you hear it." (w)

Sex and Work

"Men often see women as sex objects and women don't see themselves as such; they don't think in those terms. . . . It is something the men think more of and in that way they get the wrong picture." (w)

"You talk about sexual harassment in training courses, but the discussion easily ends up that if she is too provocatively dressed, then she is willing and it is her fault. But no one really wants to talk about it; there is a lot hidden; it's difficult." (w)

"Pornography, it's like a red rag to a bull for me. . . . We sometimes put up half-naked men, but [the men] take [the pictures] down. . . . {She laughs.) We don't take down theirs. They can have pictures of good-looking girls, but they don't have to be naked. . . . I guess their wives don't allow them that, so they have them at work instead." (w)

"There was a meeting . . . with dinner and a dance afterward, and the manager of my manager touched me during the dance on a place that I didn't, eh . . . . Nothing had happened before. It just came out of the blue. I replaced his hand. I don't know if he got angry. . . . I didn't think such things could happen." (w)

"Female role models are lacking within the nontraditional areas." (m)

"Perhaps the women are a little more motherly, but no, that isn't right either, it's more a matter of personality." (m)

Views about Equality

"I'm the only woman on the executive team. I'm no threat to [the men] because I'm not a technician, but if I also were a technician, then I would be a threat, and then they would perhaps not be as nice, because then I, too, would be one of the alternatives for the next level." (w)

"I'm responsible for the equality policy, and the man in personnel was happy to 'duck' this job. It is cumbersome and boring, not totally seen as serious, a lot of work and no status." (w)

"We have a guy and a girl who are married who have children and they share the parental leave. Then it's the same for both; it's no drawback for the woman. But of course that doesn't happen often." (m)

"In the technical office there are only men, no women, bad." (m)

"Women are a bit different in some respects. I can think of [having] women in the control room. . . . I notice it myself; I have difficulties in doing more than one thing at a time. . . . In the control room, you have to do many things at the same time, and I think women would be very suitable for that. It will take a long time to get there, because [control room work requires] a long training and you have to wait for space, but I think it will be very successful with a large number of women there." (m)

"It is positive . . . to have women on a work team. We have a female personnel manager and that is good. I don't think we treat her differently." (m)

"If I have an office manager who doesn't want to put pressure on women, it is a bit difficult to force the issue; you have to show some consideration." (m)

"Perhaps [the men] are afraid of the power of women." (m)

"In this organization they give great advantages to women who go for it and had I been a woman, things would have been much simpler. I have even heard that from women managers. Women can have a disadvantage in general but they have more advantages." (m)

"Mixed [groups] are best." (m)

"I think perhaps a bit differently, but I don't think male cashiers are real men (laughing). All men and women have, of course, male and female parts in them, but those male cashiers I've met are men in a womanly way. They have female interests and a soft manner and you need that in this job. It is not possible to put a very 'male' letter carrier in a job as a cashier, but the other way around is okay." (w)

"We have come far with equality in Sweden; we have the greatest number of women working . . . but on men's terms." (w)

"They say that it isn't so good to have only one woman on a team, because then she becomes a kind of mascot and that's no good. But two is no good either because then they compete. It should be three. The expert has said two is no good, not we; we have gotten advice about that. But with three, then the team engineers say it can be a bit difficult with the work." (m)

"There are many more complaints when you once in a while favor a woman than when all the time you favor men." (m)

"I find that I have the same chances as the guys to get into training programs and it can also be a bit more difficult for my boss to say no to me." (w)

"The girls have detected that . . . choosing a technical profession doesn't have to mean that you get dirt under your nails or that you deny your womanhood." (m)

Awareness of the differences in male and female identities varies from person to person, of course. The less experience one has with the opposite sex in the workplace, the less one seems to be aware of and know about the differences that can affect the work process. Further, awareness and knowledge seem to differ not only between men and women but also between people of different generations. Many men who have spent their working lives mostly with men and whose only contact with the opposite sex has been with their mother, wife, daughter, or sister give the impression that they feel "handicapped" *vis-à-vis* their lack of knowledge about male-female relations in the workplace. They may have some vague awareness of gender issues, but they are unable to articulate them.

Elin Kvande and Bente Rasmussen (1991, 1993), in their work with male and female engineers in Norway, found that the men who had no experience with women at work had the greatest difficulties relating to the female engineers and managers and preferred to avoid them. Men like this constitute a hindrance to women in the workplace, not because of what they are doing but because of what they are failing to do. As Kvande and Rasmussen point out, when such men are in the role of mentor, they also treat men and women differently. Men become sons, and women become daughters. Traditionally, the son — not the daughter — is expected to take over the business.

In contrast, many young people have recently completed their training in mixed groups and gender differences in the workplace are not an issue to them. One of the male participants in my project expressed this feeling: "The women working here are colleagues; [gender] is not something you think about. I don't think the girls think about it either." These men appreciate their female colleagues and working in mixed groups.

According to Kvande and Rasmussen (1993), men who are in competition with women for limited career opportunities feel more ambivalent about their female colleagues. Working with a mix of men and women on the lower organizational levels is considered acceptable to them, but the more they advance up the career ladder, the more they consider the higher positions suitable only for men.

These men are also of the opinion that men and women already have equal opportunities, in a formal sense, and they are skeptical about the need to make special efforts to help women advance.

It is common knowledge that resistance to women still exists in most organizations, and from the participants' statements, it seems that those men who are in favor of real equality have to demonstrate both bravery and caution. At the same time, virtually everyone participating in this project stated that having mixed teams in the workplace was the ideal.

Having both men and women in the workplace means not only that there may be difficulties with regard to competition but also that sexual issues may become a problem. Although hardly talked about, sexual attraction may play a significant role in the workplace. In my work with groups of senior male and female managers in Canada, it was suggested that as long as sexual attraction is a matter between people at the same level, it can be a positive and even a creative component at work. But if there is sexual attraction between employees at different levels of the organization, which mostly is the case, the effects on the whole are negative. This is an issue that needs to be investigated further. If one also takes into account men's more direct way of addressing issues and women's more indirect approach, it is easy to understand the basis for some of the statements the women made about their reluctance to react strongly to pornography in the workplace, for instance, or to sexually explicit jokes.

This cluster illustrates some of the practical ways in which gender issues emerge at work. Some of the participants' comments reflected strong stereotypes, and clearly some knotty problems still need to be solved. The action research approach will make it possible for the process of men and women talking *about* men and women to develop into a process of men and women talking *with* men and women. In other words, change in understanding and behavior will go hand in hand with developing a common language, with engaging in dialogue.

Managing Male-Female Relations

General Statements

"In the beginning [the men] asked, 'Have you got your period now, you're so touchy.' Now I say the same to them, and it has resulted in that someone always has a period, and now . . . anyone is allowed to have a period, even the guys (laughter). . . . We talk a lot and joke, but there is seriousness behind it." (w)

"[The men] told me that they thought I was too tolerant [of sexist language in the group] in the beginning, that they could go too far before I told them off. But I said that I didn't want to be special in any way and you talk the way you want to talk. But now I tell them how I want it and they say that I can decide exactly what I want because they can't stand anything else. So it's clear the girl decides a little what she wants. If I want rude but hearty slang, I can get that, and if I want it more soft, I can get that, too." (w)

"Perhaps it is easier for men to work alone with women. It is worse for women alone with men. It is a tougher environment; the men test her a lot to see how much she can stand. It is not like that for a man working with women. . . . [When I worked in a hospital] I wasn't tested by the women but instead was very well cared for." (m)

"When I have been working together with a colleague and we are going out to meet personnel together, we have between us made up a plan about who does what. The man will perhaps come with the direct facts and decisions and I will take care of the explaining and interpreting. This has been our strategy." (w)

"In the beginning it is difficult because you don't understand a joke is a joke, but as soon as you get accustomed to it, you find it a rather nice joke even if it may sound coarse to an outsider. . . . We joke a lot with each other and then at the same time you haven't got a lot to talk about." (w)

"The next step would be to become a B operator and then I would automatically be moved to another shift. . . . Personally I don't think I would like it; it's tough, it is still work in shifts, and there are still shift teams that have no women and then you have to fight your way in again. But of course we have had women here for six years now; perhaps people are getting used to it, perhaps it is easier now." (w)

"I think you are more sensitive as a girl. If you are going to the toilet, you don't want anyone to know how long you are there, but guys don't care. I have a feeling they can take a newspaper and say, 'Now I'll go to the toilet, I won't be back for a long while.' I can't say that. . . . I don't want them to know what I do the whole time. But that's probably how it is in the beginning; later one adjusts and doesn't care." (w)

"It may be easier for women to work alone in male groups than the other way around, because the women stick together and it isn't easy for a man to get in." (w)

"I think you have to try learning to respect that you're not the same, and that goes for both men and women." (w)

"I have experienced men who almost have done away with their manliness. I find that wrong. They have become kind of 'nothing' persons and instead of thinking 'I'm a man and I have certain characteristics,' they have almost become women. Not that there is anything wrong with women, but I'm a man and I'm proud of it." (m)

"At first it is a bit difficult if [the men] continue to behave as they used to do. They can be a bit strange, fart and so on and be somewhat coarse to each other, and they were afraid, I guess, that they would have to change it all — the slang they had used for ten years — only because a girl started working there. They were testing how much I could stand, when I would put my foot down." (w)

"We share the change room. We are supposed to get our own, but we don't know when. It's one of the details that was difficult in the beginning. How do you [change together with the men]? So we change together, although perhaps not with everyone, but with those who were employed at the same time and are about the same age. With the others it is a bit more difficult . . . and with some easier. I don't know what to say, but you don't exactly go in there and throw off your sweater, but in a way you think of what kind of underwear and bra you've got on, not too much lace, but rather ordinary cotton and so on. . . . One does think of it." (w)

Work and Family

"When we have children, I would like to share the parental leave; you see other colleagues do it . . . but you have to take it when there isn't too much to do at work." (m)

"When you have a child, it is difficult to combine [work life and family life]. I think an unmarried mother could never work the three shifts." (w)

"I only work 70 percent, three days one week and four the other; it feels like bits and pieces — nothing gets finished. It doesn't feel good, but when the children are young that you should be as much at home as away." (w)

"It's important for men to be with their children." (w)

"As women we often take it on ourselves to care for the children, but to take care of children has less worth. . . . You have to push for it . . . find alternatives . . . build organizations and administrative parts that allow women to take care of a child and work." (w)

Working in an area where everyone is of the opposite sex is one way to break new ground with regard to gender issues. There is a difference, though, between being a woman in a male-dominated area and being a man in a female area. Women who start to work in traditionally male areas are usually in for a rough ride. If they want to succeed, not only do they have to show that they are as good as the men at performing the job but they also have to develop a strategy for dealing with the "locker room" culture of the work team. They basically have two options: One is to accept the culture, including the language and behavior of their male colleagues, which from a woman's point of view is a form of maladaptive behavior since that forces her to be like the men. The other option is to be herself, to act like a woman, to refuse to be defined by the men, and in doing so to try to bring about change. According to Gilligan *et al.* (1988), as shown in her research on decision making among young boys and girls, boys and girls use different strategies in assessing their possibilities, as illustrated in the following story: Two four year olds, a girl and a boy, were playing together and wanted to play a different game. The girl said, "Let's play next-door neighbors." "I want to play pirates," the boy replied. "Okay," said the girl, "then you can be the pirate that lives next door." The boy thinks taking turns and playing each game is a fair solution, while the girl sees an opportunity to combine the games and thereby invent a solution that is inclusive.

Later in life these differences in styles manifest themselves in the differences between majority voting and consensus seeking. Women's preference for reaching consensus is clearly demonstrated in most of the statements in this cluster. The vignette at the beginning of this essay demonstrates even more clearly how men's and women's different styles of decision making can cause conflict and reduce organizational effectiveness.

It is worth noting that virtually all the statements in this cluster were made by women. One might conclude that although Sweden is one of the most advanced countries with regard to parental leave, the creation of day-care centers, and so on, when it comes to male-female relations at work and at home, it still has a ways to go.

Conclusions

The way little girls and boys grow up to become the women and men they are, the way in which they experience from their early days on their relationships with significant others and develop a sense of self, and the way in which their internal world, thus formed, plays a role in their understanding as well as in creating their external world represent some of the basic dynamics of communication between men and women. When women and men meet in their similarity as equal, rational beings, in dialogue, they are up against this phenomenon. They are confronted with the way their internal and external worlds interact, with the way they have been socialized. They are trapped in their roles, encapsulated in their differences, and imprisoned by "gender at work."

My comments thus far have focused on the above issue. To reach a better understanding of this process, I would like to draw attention to some notions in the philosophy of Emmanuel Lévinas that are highly pertinent to the question of women and men faced with meeting each "other."

According to Lévinas (1993), it is not autonomy but heteronomy — the dependency of the subject — that is the basis of the human condition. The relationship with the other is the primary relationship, and by responding to the other, by being responsible, one enters into an ethical relationship.

Dependency requires independence, however. Thus, we are characterized by a fundamental ambivalence insofar as we are both autonomous and heteronomous. A genuine human relationship, which requires both dependence and independence, is possible only because of this ambivalence.

In relationships between women and men, we see a double ambivalence — a primary and a secondary one. The primary one is formed as a result of the basic ambivalence we all have as people, because of our need to be both dependent and independent women and men. The secondary ambivalence is actually a frozen ambivalence and occurs as the result of the way our society has used the sexual/biological differences between men and women to construct gender stereotypes. It represents an embodied embeddedness.

The frozen ambivalence appears to be interfering with the primary one and thus making it difficult for men and women to develop mature, genuine relationships. The sociocultural characteristics of our society make it, generally speaking, difficult for a man to be dependent, while being independent is difficult for a woman. He is trapped in his own stereotype. Conversely, women collude with men in their dependence and have difficulty developing a sense of an identity that is based on independence as well as dependence. In other words, as in any genuine human relationship, the challenge is to get beyond the stereotypes. For such a relationship, trust is essential.

It is in our language that the collusive relationship between our primary and secondary ambivalence is acted out. Likewise, it is only through dialogue that men and women can learn to develop a shared understanding of this ambivalence and learn to recognize that women and men may be different but they are equally human.

Three major themes run through all four of the clusters: both men and women have feelings of uncertainty and ambivalence about the nature of male-female relations; men and women think of themselves and the other in stereotypes; and women have a strong relational orientation, whereas men generally have a more individualistic stance. Placing these three issues in the context of the philosophy of Lévinas leads to three primary observations. First, the ambivalence both women and men express with regard to understanding of the other seems to suggest that further dialogue could help improve the quality of male-female relations. Second, the women's relational orientation indicates an ability to respond and be responsible for the other in the sense that Lévinas defines this concept. Third, the individualistic position of many of the men and their resulting inability to interpret the other, as reflected in their descriptions of women in stereotypes, will make it more difficult for the men to engage in an open process of discovery and development concerning gender issues.

In view of the desire for better understanding that emerged in the discussions, and given the feelings of ambivalence expressed by both the men and women as well as the women's relational orientation, one would expect further dialogue and activities to take place, in spite of the independent and individualistic orientation of many of the men. One might also expect that as a result of today's dominant technical and functional rationality, the women will have a more difficult time than the men, at least initially, as they try to improve the quality of male-female relations at work. Because of their relational orientation and more "substantive" rationality, the women may well be seen as less decisive and less effective partners in the workplace. If this assumption is correct, then in the process of improving male-female relations at work, women and men will be confronting one of the most challenging issues of our times.

A major challenge facing these men and women will be to transcend the need to adapt and to move into the realm of discovery so that they may take the risk of meeting the other. On the interpersonal level, this relationship would be defined not in terms of self but by its acceptance of the other as other. In this way we would, in the true sense of the word, learn to manage differences creatively and thus to achieve equality.

Notes

1.   I use the term "equality" in accordance with the way thes participants in the project used the term. From the quotations, it shall become clear that the meaning of the term, according to their understanding, can range from legislative measures to informal rules of behavior. It refers to equal opportunity regardless of whether men and women are similar or dissimilar. It can also mean that, although men and women are different, both should learn to handle the differences (*i.e.*, mutual understanding and corresponding behavior would constitute equality). In short, the term "equality" is used in a very broad sense.

2.   *Practice* is a direct translation of the Swedish word *praktik*. The participant is referring to the "practice" in Sweden whereby students in secondary schools spend two weeks each year gaining real work experience at a workplace.

3.   The term "significant others" comes from object relations theory, which is based on the notion that relations with others constitute the fundamental building blocks of mental life and that people simultaneously live in external and internal worlds. People react to and interact with not only actual others but also internal others. According to Greenberg and Mitchell (1983: 11), "What is generally agreed upon about these internal images is that they constitute a residue within the mind of relationships with important people in the individual's life. In some way crucial exchanges with others leave their mark: they are 'internalized' and so come to shape subsequent attitudes, reactions, perceptions, and so on."

4.   See endnote 2.

Chapter 12

Do We Need a Gender Perspective in Action Research on Work Organizations?

Agneta Hansson

Today numerous signs tell us that the structure of work life organization is moving in a new direction. It seems that decades of searching for optimal forms of work organization are finally resulting in the insight that broad participation in organizational development leads to both higher productivity and better jobs, there being no necessary contradiction between these goals (van Beinum 1993). Thus, we increasingly attempt to identify and meet important psychological job requirements, such as job satisfaction through self management, adequate elbow room, opportunities for learning, variety, respect and meaningfulness in our organizational change efforts.

The new organizational paradigm

Framing this in terms of the modernity/post-modernity debate (Giddens 1990), it appears that the modernist organizational paradigm, characterized by Max Weber as a bureaucratic, mechanistic structure of control, built on processes of differentiation, principles of centralized organization and erected upon a fully rationalized base of divided and de-skilled labor is becoming *passé*. Surviving in a more complex and internationalized world, organizations need to be organically structured, de-differentiated, and characterized by more flexibility and multi-skilled jobs. The era, brought about by the Industrial Revolution with Tayloristic labor organization is now being replaced by new forms of organizations (Clegg 1990).

    This change of principles underlying the design of organizations and the way of looking at human beings is so extensive that it is considered a "new organizational paradigm".[1] Within this paradigm, the employees are involved in a participatory way in the whole organizational process. Their ideas, experience, and knowledge are valued, utilized and considered not only important but essential. The ideal organization within the new paradigm is characterized by democratic structures as well as democratic processes. Table 1 shows, in a dichotomised version, a summary of the old versus the new paradigms.

	Old paradigm	New paradigm
Basic design principle	Redundancy of parts	Redundancy of functions
Unit of analysis	Maximum task breakdown, narrow skills; building block is one person-one task	Multi-skilling, "whole task" grouping; building block is a self managing group
Organizational rules	Technological imperative: people added on. Aim to design people out of the system	Design for "man-machine" complementarity and hence for optimal staffing levels
	Coordination and control decisions located above the workers	Coordination and control l located, as far as possible, with those doing the work
	Aim at total specification of responsibilities and authorities	Aim at minimum critical specification of responsibilities and authorities
Typical outcomes:		
Sociotechnical:	Fragmented sociotechnical system, resistant to rational change	Dynamic process of joint optimization of the socio-technical system
cultural:	Autocratic	Democratic
psychological:	Alienation	Involvement and commitment

Table 1. Characteristics of the Old and New Organizational Paradigm (Emery, 1993, 16B) in van Beinum, 1993.

Hierarchy and bureaucracy, with their organizing principles rooted in the patriarchal structures of the military and the church, are fundamental characteristics of the old paradigm. Bureaucracy is, according to Ferguson, the scientific way of maintaining unequal conditions (Ferguson 1984). From the point of view of the need for flexibility in working life, they are neither an effective nor a productive way of organizing work. They do not recognize the human need for being involved, the capacity of people to be committed to their work, and human need for variety. Hierarchical organizations seek a maximum division of labor with the unskilled workers situated at the lowest level.

Women at work

These organizations are particularly bad for women, who often are, from an organizational point of view, the lowest of the low, *i.e.* the most subordinate in the hierarchy. Within the "new paradigm," seen in the light of Weber's theory of rationality, men are let out of their "imprisonment in the house of bondage — the iron cage of bureaucracy" that has restricted their individuality (Clegg, 1990: 4). But what about women? Will the new organizational paradigm let women out of their "imprisonment" as well? In my opinion this will not be achieved without a specific focus on the gender issue in work organization. Hence the question in the title of this paper is a rhetorical one.

Action research in industrial settings

Even though there is a politically agreed-on movement from the old to the new paradigm and the idea of democracy in working life is on the agenda, there is still a gap between the new paradigm and the everyday conditions of work. Change does not occur by itself. The process that takes us from insight to action is often long and encounters a great deal of resistance in work organizations. Action research is a way of developing and implementing effective organizational change. It is a process in which external researchers are actively involved and able contribute to the conditions for organizational change and its development process. The central feature of action research is to improve a situation through joint action between researchers and "researched," *i.e.* the organization. Action research is thus a process of joint learning based on developing relations between researchers and practitioners characterized by joint involvement and shared responsibility when they address problems that require new knowledge (van Beinum 1998).

This paper narrates and analyzes a single organizational intervention in a large industrial laundry, showing how action research approaches were used to contribute to the transformation of the laundry into a workplace that embodies more of the conditions of the new organizational paradigm. But the paper also shows that this transformation was only possible because the intervention re-tained a strong focus on restructuring gender relations in this work place. My contention is to show a gender perspective is essential to action research in work organization change and how action research interventions can be enriched by a greater knowledge of current feminist thinking.

The Laundry — an action research project

I build my discussion on an action research project where, together with three colleagues from the Centre for Worklife Development (CAU) at Halmstad University, I was involved in an organizational change process from 1991 to 1994. The project centered on a participatory redesign process in a laundry — a female-dominated workplace with men in management and middle management positions and women constituting the shop floor labor force.[2]

This public regional laundry is situated in the country in a small village 45 kilometers outside Halmstad. It has about 80 employees, of which 78% are women, most of them middle-aged or elderly part-time workers. Most of the workers, many of whom are related, were born in the village and have lived there all their life. Since the laundry was founded twenty years ago, its customers were hospitals and health care centers all over the county. However, as a result of new political decisions, hospital and other healthcare units, after 1990, were free to buy their services wherever they wanted. As a result, to keep its customers, the laundry had to become competitive with other laundries. The products handled are sheets, towels, nightshirts, etc — the kind of laundry everyone is familiar with. The production process is also close to the women's traditional world — the endless process of washing, ironing, mangling and patching. In work content, this is a female workplace.

Even though there seemed to be an open and friendly atmosphere at the laundry, it was still a typical hierarchical organization when we began the project. Every morning, the foremen assigned the workers their tasks and told them what to do. The gendered division of labor was clear-cut: men handled the dirty laundry and women the clean. Handling the washing machines was also the men's job. This carried higher status and a higher salary. Handling the mangling and the sewing machines, however, was women's work and did not provide a salary supplement. Sorting out dirty laundry was a work station open to both men and women. This work was considered harder and riskier than other work and therefore received a salary supplement. However, most of the women found this work sickening and repulsive and preferred to work with the "finishing treatment" of clean laundry. The foremen and all four employees in the repair shop were men.

A Gendered Workplace

Already in the early phases of the project, the gendered subculture of the company came clearly to the fore. At a first glance, it looked like it that the women's norms and traditions were a guiding force. For example, efforts were made to create an attractive lunchroom, curtains were changed often and the room was decorated to correspond with the season. The informal talk in the lunchroom was about cooking, knitting etc. However we soon realized that the male workers never visited the official lunchroom. They had their own places where they spent their breaks. For lunch they often left the premises. We also noticed that, in the lunchroom, the women had their permanent chairs, they always talked to the same people and never moved to another table. From interviews, we also found out that there was an atmosphere among the women that made some of them feel harassed by other women. There were *cliques*. It was common knowledge, all over the company, that some women would never work together or talk to each other, either in the lunchroom or during the production process. Later in the project, when the work organization was redesigned and everyone had experienced working with other colleagues, these barriers were overcome. Among the men we did not notice similar patterns, or at least they did not show them.

During the project, an attempt was made to assign to some of the women the role of assistant foreman. Some women wanted to apply for this job, but gave up because they did not want to differ from their work mates. In the beginning, those who accepted the offer felt that the other women were envious of them. However, once they were installed in the new role, the other women considered them to be better foremen than the two male foremen. The assistant foremen knew the production process from the inside out and worked very well together with the others.

We also noticed how mean women could be to the male foremen. As these men had no experience in doing the after-treatment laundry work, they were not, in view of the women, competent supervisors. To demonstrate this, the women often did not show initiative themselves; they did not show what they in fact were capable of, but waited for the foremen to tell them what to do. On the one hand they were not allowed to make the decisions, but on the other, their behavior was also a form of protest. The foremen, for their part, protected their territory and did not let the women take full responsibility for their own jobs.

This, as well as other forms of poor communication between men and women, often became visible. For example, the women blamed both the manager and the foremen for not listening to them. We could also see how both the women and the men often misinterpreted each other when they tried to communicate. And, from the women's point of view, we saw that the men were not sensitive enough with regard to the women's needs and demands and this often led to misunderstandings.

The foremen also often put their instructions about production on a piece of paper, which they placed at the mangle or similar location for the women to read. While the men found this very rational, the women's reaction was quite different. They got upset because not to talk directly to those involved and to use a piece of paper instead was, in their opinion, a misuse of power. During the project, as the communication between the employees became more open and the foremen became more confident in their new roles (and the women became responsible for the daily planning), this also changed for the better.

It often seemed that the men overreacted to the women's customary way of gossiping and teasing but, in our opinion, they also did not react strongly enough when their intervention was really needed as, for example, when someone didn't want to work with someone else or didn't want to work at certain stations. The more we got to know the people in the organization, the more we became aware of various subtle phenomena visible in the lack in communication, distance, protection of roles, etc. The need for social contact and to be able to feel confident about their relations with their work mates was of great significance for the women, especially for the older women. They often felt unhappy (or afraid) when they had to work with someone they did not know (or like). This problem had a long history in the organization and we worked a lot on it within the project.

Early in the process it was obvious that the organization was too hierarchically structured to get the best out of the workers' skills and capacities. Over the history of the company, the messages had been mixed. The workers were told to take on responsibilities, but, in reality, they were not allowed to take them on by the foremen. Even after two years, the manager still considered it too radical to hand over the responsibility for planning the daily work process to the workers themselves. Only when we were able to show him, from the follow-up interviews, that the project had generated frustration among the workers about their inability to handle the planning was he able to change his mind and take appropriate action.

The organization changed accordingly and the foremen were assigned different roles. When the new organization finally was introduced, within two years after the initiation of the action research project, there had been an enormous positive change in commitment among the workers, who generated many creative ideas and solutions about how to make the company both more productive and effective.

The intervention process

As described earlier, researchers from the Centre for Worklife Development were contacted in late 1990 by the laundry management and asked to help with a reorganization of the entire production process. The manager wanted the laundry to become more competitive and understood that it was necessary to increase the workers' skills and interest in work by operating in a more flexible and customer-oriented way. The explicit goal for the new organization was to achieve a more flexible and competitive, as well as a more democratic and self-managing work organization. We become involved as action researchers and remained closely connected to the laundry until 1994, that is, for over three years. During this process, we have used a mix of different methods and tools, such as reading historical documents, questionnaires, structured and unstructured individual and group interviews, discussions, observations, project groups, steering group meetings and search conferences. During the whole process, the researchers avoided acting like traditional consultants who take on an expert role (which was what the company expected at the outset). Instead, we emphasized our role as facilitators and partners in the change process. We stressed that the project "belonged" to the company and that the company itself was responsible for the management and continuation of the process. Other important conditions for our involvement in the project were the need for a broad acceptance at all levels of the company (by top management, unions and the ordinary workers), and an agreements that would make it possible for us as action researchers to visit the company at any time and to involve ourselves in all processes. We had excellent cooperation and have been full participants in the process. The doors have always been, and are still, open to us.

We began the process by creating an overview and analysis of the enterprise through discussions and interviews with management, unions, and all the employees. We also talked to representatives of the most important customers. After that we organized a search conference (Emery, 1989) with all the employees to create a common point of reference for the project and to get the employees involved in the reorganizing process from the very beginning (Emery 1989, 1999). When the conference idea was first introduced to the manager, he was skeptical and didn't think that this concept would function with his staff because they were poorly educated, middle-aged or elderly women. By the end, he was positively surprised by the involvement and creativity showed by all the participants.

At the search conference, several themes emerged that the members agreed on should be worked through before a new organizational form could be introduced. These themes were:

- ❑ production and production management
- ❑ information and communication
- ❑ job rotation and plans for learning
- ❑ marketing and service to the customers
- ❑ physical health, hygiene and well-being
- ❑ orientation program for newly recruited and substitute personnel
- ❑ technical improvements

It was decided that an intensive redesign project involving all the laundry employees should be started. Seven project groups were set up around the identified themes. All the staff members were involved. One person was chosen as the contact person by the project groups. With the laundry manager and the researchers, these contact people formed the steering group.

Throughout the process, the discussions were based on the following six psychological job requirements (Emery and Thorsrud 1976):

- ❑ adequate elbow room
- ❑ chance of learning on the job
- ❑ optimal level of variety
- ❑ help and respect from work mates
- ❑ sense of meaningful work
- ❑ desirable future

However, these psychological job requirements, formulated originally by Emery and Thorsrud and later used as key elements in the participatory redesign method (Emery 1989), were not used in this project as design principles or criteria for job design, but as 'tools' for triggering discussions.

The project groups met regularly for six months. During this period the steering group met once a week and were continually updated on the process. The researchers visited the company at least once a week and were available to the groups throughout the whole process. Every month the manager called all the employees to a workplace meeting. At these meetings, information and reports about how the project was going were provided.

During the first phase of the project, the groups were very active. Even if some of the workers were a bit skeptical in the beginning, they became interested and seemed to look forward to the future developments in the project. After about half a year, when the project groups seemed to have reached a point of diminishing returns, the group work was ended and the groups reported their results to the whole organization. At a meeting in the workplace, with all the staff in attendance, each group presented a list of problems that they had taken care of themselves, another list of problems that would require help from management or from other groups, and a few, more complex questions that would need to be addressed by new project groups.

For example, the technical improvement group had taken care of about thirty different problems, from providing advanced ergonomic support to portable telephones and communication systems, such as whiteboards, for short messages. The marketing group made study visits to customers and found out more about their needs; the job rotation group had introduced a new and more advanced system for rotation that had enabled the employees to try new tasks and to work with new people, etc. So, in a short time, many of the suggestions made by the workers had been accepted as new routines and introduced into the ordinary work process.

At this point, there was a pause in the overall project activities and the ongoing process slowed down. Still, two new groups were created by volunteers to work on production flow and product quality. The steering group continued to meet every second week and, after half a year, reduced the number of meetings to once a month. Our role became less active. We now operated more as discussion partners while we continued to follow the process.

Addressing gender

When the project began, the manager of the laundry expressed no ambition to work to create more equal opportunities for men and women in the reorganization process. The gendered labor division was more or less accepted in the organization. However, as the organization needed to gain more competitiveness and flexibility and most of the workers were women, the focus of change was necessarily on the women in any case. When we were introduced at the laundry and were given the background for the change process, many characteristics of the women workers were viewed as problems. For example, most women worked part time and were not willing to change working hours. Women were said to be more committed to their homes and families than to their work. Women complained about workload and got occupational injuries from their repetitive work. Women also were said to have problems in cooperating with each other because they formed closed groups that kept others out. Thus the initial overall problem of the laundry was formulated as how to adapt women to the needed organizational changes.

When we started the change process, we realized that most of what had been ascribed to the women was descriptively accurate, but that the cause was not the women but the way the work was organized and that most of the women were subordinated to the men in the organization. Both in the interviews and the search conference the women were the most active. They had lots of good suggestions and ideas of how to change and improve, but they were also suspicious of the process as they were used to being ignored. They were quite right to be suspicious in the beginning, as there was a double message built into the project. On one hand, they were required to use their creativity and capacity to improve the organization and, on the other, the hierarchical structure in which the foremen decided how the workers should be assigned to production tasks was still in operation.

During the process, however, as the hierarchical structure was slowly broken down and changes came, the women changed. For example, they used their free, unpaid, time to come to the work planning meetings; they voluntarily broke the gendered work barriers by working in the men's dirty laundry departments; and they were much more open to job rotation than the men. By the end of our involvement in the change process, all the women worked or could work together and there were no longer any coteries.

From the laundry project we learned that:

❑ there exists a gendered division of labor in which the women get the lowest paid jobs
❑ even in a woman-dominated workplace, men get the higher positions, even when women are better qualified
❑ men do not adapt themselves to the female subculture, creating their own instead
❑ women are afraid to differ from other women
❑ this fear leads to women holding themselves back in their careers
❑ those women who want to break this pattern may be isolated by other women and from the female subculture

❏   when women do not get enough challenges from their work, they focus their
    attention on their private lives
❏   men and women have different ways of communicating, which often leads to
    misunderstandings
❏   it is more important for women than for men to be able to see the overall
    work process
❏   women want to take responsibility for completing tasks and that they get
    frustrated when they have to leave work before it is finished
❏   social contacts are very important to women to make them feel confident
❏   an attractive, clean environment is important to women

Summary of the laundry project

In the half year since our involvement in the action research project at the laundry
ended, we cannot precisely say how the organization has become more flexible
and competitive. However, we can see that a change process has taken place that
involves everyone in the organization. There is a broad consensus between
management and labor and the manager has developed an open attitude toward
testing new ways of working and new solutions to problems. Most of the workers
have changed their attitude towards organizational change during this process,
becoming more involved when they experienced that real efforts have been made
to improve their work situation. At the beginning of the change process, the male
foremen seemed to be insecure about their changed role and thus reacted by
slowing down the process. However, since they received support about these
concerns, they have now refocused their work from detailed supervising of the
workers to making improvements and innovations in the production flow process.
    Even if the gender balance is still typical within the organization and men
still have more power and better salaries, the organization is moving in a democratic direction. The awareness of men's and women's different conditions has
been raised throughout the project and women get now support from management
to take on new roles and responsibility. The laundry has become a learning
environment, embracing new organizational values. While doors have been
opened, whether this will lead eventually to a balanced equality between men and
women within the new paradigm still remains to be seen.

Action research and gender perspectives

From this point on, I link the laundry case more broadly to the action research
literature and to the frameworks emerging from contemporary feminist work. The
underlying contention here is simple. Without action research, the intervention at

the laundry would not have been successful and without the benefit of under-standings of gender relations derived from feminist thought, the action research effort would not have been successful.

Action research

Participating in organizational changes where hierarchical structures in work life are replaced by democratic processes gives work life action researchers unique opportunities to be involved in processes of change at both the micro- and the macro-level. Van Beinum refers to action research as a way of "understanding and managing a relationship" and describes it as the "study of operating systems in action" (van Beinum 1993). In action research, the researcher and the practitio-ner ("the empirical object") share responsibility for the process and the quality of the communication between them determines the quality of the action research. An action researcher has to be empathic and also has to be aware of her or his own cognitive style. Action research is, by definition, democratizing and, as action researchers, we have an explicit responsibility to work for democracy in work life (van Beinum 1993).

When we were asked by the manager of the laundry to assist with the implementation of a new form of work organization, we responded by suggesting we do this by means of an action research approach. We tried to convince the management that the hope for a long-lasting organizational development process with a broad and active involvement of the employees was not reasonable unless the company itself — management and unions — agreed to take full responsibil-ity for the change process. Our contribution would be to help with the design, by arranging different arenas for dialogue (*e.g.* the search conference, the steering group, and the project groups), by acting as sparring partners and advisors, and by following and documenting the process. As professional researchers, we had a special interest in learning about the process of decentralization, in analyzing the different dialogues that emerged in the process, and in improving the working conditions for women. This three year action research project was thus really a joint learning process. We learned about how different people, due to their positions, act when confronting a change process and we learned about the many different obstacles that delay a change process. While mirroring the process and discussing our roles in the research group, we learned a lot about our own actions and reactions as well.

Gender in action research

In the work at the laundry, our focus on gender was key to the changes. Through the process, we learned about men's and women's different way of communicating and interpreting changes and we learned to recognize both the manifest and the invisible gender power structure. This is not a mere add-on to action research; it was essential to the success of the project and we believe this is a general lesson from the case. Because such a case is infrequently made in the action research literature, I will develop it in considerable detail here.

In the foreword to *Human Inquiry: A Sourcebook of New Paradigm Research,* Reason and Rowan address gender in action research (Reason and Rowan, eds 1981). This book has many essays by different contributors who offer alternatives to orthodox methods. Despite their effort to achieve diversity in approaches, they wrote that it was not "until it was too late to do anything about it" that the issue about relationship between feminist scholarship and new paradigm research was raised:

> This is what concerns us: we just didn't think about it. We believe we have the awareness, and have acted on it in other contexts, but we didn't apply it here: we failed to respond to our own questions about being aware and questioning the patriarchial patterns which surround us. (p. xxii) …Again, we just didn't look hard enough. And this is rather curious, because throughout this book are references to new paradigm research being a move away from 'male' towards a 'female' approach to inquiry. So there seems to be a real danger that in new paradigm research men will take a 'female' way of looking at the world, and turn it into another 'male' way of seeing it: men may understand the words, but do they know the music? …" (p. xxiii)

In my opinion we, as action researchers and change agents, have a responsibility to be aware of the gendered worklife in order not to contribute to the development of still more male-dominated work organizations.

Why has gender been missed so frequently in action research?

The laundry project shows that there are differences and inequalities between men and women that have to be considered in change processes towards more decentralized and democratic work organizations, *i.e.* in the move from the old to the new paradigm. The different positions of men and women in society can, according to Holmberg (1993), be regarded either as a *problem of equality* or as a *condition of gender power.* The equality problem is politically defined and mostly concerns unequal conditions in work life and in the family. It is based on the assumption that men and women have a mutual interest in changing the unequal conditions in society and that this can be done by discourse, negotiation and law. This perspective claims gender neutrality and is based on the assumption that men and women are equal.

A gender power perspective, on the contrary, points out that there is a conflict between men and women and that they have different interests in changing the conditions between the genders. The gender power perspective centers on the patriarchal structure of society, where men (as category) dominate women (as a category) (Holmberg 1993). Holmberg's approach is supported by that of Jonasdottir who, from a Marxist perspective, states that the patriarchal structures are maintained through the fact that it is women's "right" to give love, care and health to men, while men have the "right" to take from women. Women's lack of freedom is here connected to both norms and gender and women's capacity to love is exploited.

Whether one agrees with these authors or not, it is reasonably clear that inequality between men and women is officially considered resolvable within our present type of society. In practice, equal opportunity policies have meant that women will be moved up to the level of men rather than expecting society to change to meet women's needs and conditions. When this sort of gender neutral thinking is used in a context that is not gender neutral, it creates confusion and contradictory organizational processes.

I believe that the laundry case shows that, to change gender power relations, men and women have to see the subtle patterns and processes that structure the relations between them. They have to become aware of the hidden structures behind the gender-segregated reality that are deeply rooted and integrated in the institutions of our society. Holmberg states that it is not in the official gender equality policy that the gender power structure is revealed. Rather it shows up in making women individually responsible to work for their own equality and by stating that there exists no formal hindrance for equal opportunity for men and women. This is where the social mechanisms that maintain the order and suborder between the genders become visible (Holmberg 1993) and these are the mechanisms we intervened in at the laundry.

Holmberg uses symbolic interactionism to understand how patriarchal structures are reproduced in society. The man/woman develops in interaction with society and others. The man/woman and society are intergrated and become each other's conditions of existence. Women and men are, by themselves and others, ascribed different characteristics and different roles, which they internalize in their identities as human beings. Thus men and women internalize gender hierarchy and power structure as a part of their gender identity. Women put themselves in a subordinated position in relation to men, and it is through this subordination that they are confirmed as sexual beings. For men, therefore, it is unproblematic to be superior to women. They have internalized this notion in interaction with society (including with women) (Holmberg 1993, p.73). Again, we addressed this in the way we structured the change process at the laundry and did so to good effect.

The Norwegian researcher Hildur Ve (1989) contributed to the understanding of this phenomenon by using the concepts of "technical limited rationality" and "rationality of responsibility," based on a Weberian theory of rationality. Ve means that Weber's concepts of means-end rationality and substantive rationality are too limited because they do not include the gendered division of labor that is the part of contemporary social reality now that women have entered the labor market in many different kinds of work. Ve and other Scandinavian researchers (Sörensen 1982, Waldén 1989, 1990, and Gunnarsson 1989) point out that, because of their different practical and social experiences based on the gender structured division of labor, men and women develop different types of rationality. These different rationalities are social constructions and should not be viewed as arising from biological differences between men and women.

Ve argues that the fundamental difference between these rationalities is that women follow a "rationality of responsibility" treating human beings as irreplaceable. Their aim is to optimize health and harmony for those who need it and eventually to make oneself superfluous. By contrast, the rationality Ve ascribes to men is called "technical limited rationality," which is linked to technical, economic and bureaucratic rationality in which human beings are objectified and replaceable. There is some support for this in industrial work life studies in Scandinavia which show different patterns of actions towards the tasks that men and women have to handle. For example, women in industrial work, compared to men, focus more on the users and the need for technology, than on the technology itself (Gunnarsson, 1989, Kvande-Rasmussen, 1991, Sörensen, 1982, Ljungberg van Beinum 1991, 1994, and Hansson, 1993 and 1994).

To explain these differences, Waldén (1989, 1990) uses the concept of "culture" and argues that, as a result of early socialization into the traditions and gender structure of their society, men and women figuratively can be said to end up living in different cultures. Women's culture is directed by need, its organization is organic and built out of a central order, where wholeness and continuity are key elements. Men, on the other hand, have been responsible for building and maintaining the society beyond the home — the state and large-scale social institutions — through production, technology and military protection. Built in this context, men's culture involves the principles of performance and replacement (Chodorow, 1978).

According to Ve, this male "technical limited rationality" is now diffusing to previously female-dominated sectors like education, health care, and the social services. Research in the social service and health insurance sector shows how badly this form of rationality functions in such arenas and how women's work in these arenas rapidly loses quality when it is hierarchically restructured. Through professionalization, specialization, and the use of scientifically structured languages, the valuable everyday knowledge that women once brought to the caring professions, often gets lost, a point also made by Josefsson (1991). The Norwegian researcher Berit Ås also focused on the ways men use their power through the language and how they make women invisible in the communication process (Ås 1981).

The Swedish linguistic researcher, Einarsson, shows how women and men, when they learn to talk, develop different languages and models for communication. For example, women's language is more concrete while men's is more abstract. He also shows that in a dialogue between men and women, women ask more questions, give more "positive minimal responses," and often use the pronouns *you* and *we*. Men often interrupt women, men question and discuss what women say, and they ignore what women say by not answering, by giving "delayed minimal response", or by answering without enthusiasm. Men also make more statements about facts and offer more opinions and suggestions (Einarsson 1984).

Thus women's language is more person-oriented, expressive, emotional and evaluative, while men's is more object-oriented, instrumental and focused on the definition of concepts. Women communicate more directly with others and, if there are different opinions in the group, they want to try to reach consensus. Women's communication is personal and concrete, and they verbalize emotions and experiences. By posing questions, they easily get others to talk and they are good at giving positive feedback.

Again, whether or not you agree with the substance of all of the above-cited perspectives, it should be clear that such gender perspectives were deployed in our action research intervention at the laundry. They created leverage for our thinking and enabled us to address gender issues in the work place in such a way that change in gender relations became an integral part of the overall change process.

Gender and action research

Where are gender research and action research necessarily connected? Two main issues link these fields: gender and democratic dialogue and gender and the kinds of behavior that promote successful action research processes.

Democratic dialogue

The core issue here is that the theory and methods of action research are based on the use of dialogue and communication. Through democratic dialogue, people come to mutual understanding, which is the fundamental basis for democratic development (Gustavsen 1992). But if the above-cited research is right, what then happens to these democratic dialogues if men and women use language differently and live in somewhat distinctive cultural worlds? The laundry case shows that much of the action research process necessarily centered on mediating these very different gender worlds for the good of the organization as a whole.

Gustavsen argues that it is only through dialogue that the linguistic resources will be developed that make it possible to create the common ground for the democratization of work. If we relate this to Einarsson's work and other linguistic research findings showing that men and women when they learn to talk develop different languages and models for communication, we can easily understand how the criteria for a democratic dialogue, if used in an orthodox way without considering the gender perspective, may work in an antidemocratic direction.

Action research and the "rationality of responsibility"

There is also a clear similarity between the democratic values that guide the action research framework and the kind of "rationality of responsibility" that is supposed to typify the world of women. When van Beinum states that "Content and processes are different perspectives of the same phenomenon. One cannot have one without the other. The content is the process" (van Beinum 1993), he is describing an approach that is very close to the picture feminist researchers have created of the behavioral styles of women. Similarly "women's culture" as defined by Waldén, Ve, Gunnarsson, Einarsson, Haavind, Hirdman, and Josefsson, is built on caring and maintaining human beings themselves, a central feature of action research processes.

The upshot of this is that, if we do not notice and try to understand the gendered division of labor, we can easily be led to think women do not choose to take on leadership positions of their own free will and look upon male management as the norm. When we have experienced the failures of the hierarchical structure, as in the case of the laundry, we may then look for a new paradigm guided by new values. But if we do not focus on women in particular and try to understand them in relation to men, there is no guarantee that the values that emerge in the action research process will not be simply a new male norm, used to create greater democracy among men but still excluding women.

As action researchers, we cannot exclude the gender dimension. Participatory processes in organizations, mutual enrichment, shared responsibility and joint understanding between researchers and practitioners require not just democracy but gender equality. By insisting on including gender in action research, I therefore am equating democracy with gender equality. However, descriptions of most action research projects seldom deal with the gender dimension. Rather, action research, with some exceptions, pretends to be gender neutral, *i.e.* it is based on the theory that men and women are equal. Of course, from a gender perspective, this leads to the maintenance of the male dominance by making the inequality between men and women invisible.

Conclusions

At the beginning of the laundry project, we had no specific focus on women or on the gendered organizational structure. As the process developed, however, the difference between men's and women's conditions, ways of thinking, acting and communicating became visible to all the participants — to the researchers as well as to the laundry workers, to women as well as to men. By adding the gender perspective to the redesign processes, it was possible to identify the different conditions for men and women in the organization and to take steps to use the capacities of women in a more effective ways.

By using the concept of democratic dialogue with a gendered perspective, Drejhammar and Rehnström (1990) worked with groups of women in different organizations on a project specifically designed for this purpose. By making it easier for the women to talk about their work experiences, needs and desires for the future in their own way, without hindrance and domination by male management and colleagues, they found that the women expressed many opinions about working conditions, management and organization that have led to new routines and an effective organizational development.

In our case, we did this kind of work in mixed gender groups. Perhaps a reason that we managed raise the gender issues effectively such groups was because women were both the majority in the work force and because the laundry was an organization that, both in the production process and in its relationship to consumers, was strongly affected by women's culture already.

Feminist scholarship points in many different political directions. My own view is that the way to reach equal opportunity for men and women in work life is not by polarizing them and stressing gender conflict. I think that improvements will be made only by helping men and women to understand each other's conditions and by bringing their diverse perspectives into work life reform. If we want the organizational paradigms to guide work life development and if we understand action research as a way to create democratic work organizations, then we all have a responsibility to include gender perspectives in action research with work organizations.

Notes

1.   For a discussion about the concept of paradigm, see Kuhn 1962.

2.   A more detailed description and analysis will be published by me with the title 'From collaborative inquiry to joint action-the Torup case'1999, in *Ideas and practices of action research and institutional journey*, Hans van Beinum (forthcoming).

Chapter 13

Learning to Learn

Participatory Action Research in Public Schools

Ann Martin

One of the biggest ideas in primary/secondary educational reform in the United States is restructuring. It is also the most recent idea to gain attention. The term refers both to the means — restructured school organizations — and to the end — restructured goals for education — namely, student outcomes that demonstrate the capacity for continuous learning, as opposed to performance on tasks such as examinations and papers. The reform is often described as "restructuring through shared decision making," which refers to the intent that the restructuring will be achieved through the collaboration of teachers, parents, support staff, and, where possible, students, who collaboratively will make decisions formerly made exclusively by administrators.

This chapter addresses the early stages of a restructuring effort in Binghamton, New York. In particular, it focuses on the use of participatory action research as a method to initiate and sustain the process of educational reform.

The Binghamton project had presented a challenge for action researchers even before I began as its consultant-researcher, for the New York State Commissioner of Education had dictated in August 1992 that by February 1994, all districts in the state would have to develop a participatory process for educational change. The challenge was in the requirement for participation. There is always a question whether an imposed structure can be a meaningful vehicle for cultural and organizational change. Action researchers today place high value on change processes that are developed *with* the local community (Elden and Levin 1991; Emery 1982). Change ordered from the top risks being superficial and mechanistic, never "owned" by those who are expected to change. One goal of my intervention in Binghamton was to develop ownership of the process among those on whom it was imposed.

Why PAR?

I undertook the project hoping that if shared decision making developed through participatory action, the participants could, at the very least, discover the scope and structures for shared decision making that made the most sense for their district. In this sense, it would be a research project as well. My role would be to enable collaboration to take place by offering the participants tools and skills for communication and participation and to provoke reflection that would lead the participants to learn.

Once the work began, however, I could see far greater potential in PAR as an approach to educational reform. The first argument for using PAR was that the nature of the change required was so enormous that the work had to be accomplished through discussions and consensus across many constituencies. PAR is founded on a faith in change through participation — not participation for its own sake, but participation aimed at building meaning through dialogue.

The second argument for using PAR was that the AR processes of inquiry, reflection, and knowledge development, are the very processes educators hope to teach students — and the very processes reformers claim have been slighted in public education. In the words of *A New Compact for Learning*, the document that spells out the expectations for reform in New York: "Our mission is not to keep school — it is to see that children learn. . . . While rudimentary skills and factual knowledge remain important, the larger goal is to nurture the quality of students' mental activity — the capacity to raise questions, generate hypotheses, solve complex problems, integrate learning, communicate effectively in a variety of forms (1991: 3-4).

Conceivably, the processes of inquiry and dialogue could sharpen the educators' focus on the significant reform they intended to accomplish by "nurturing the quality of students' mental activity" as they nurtured these qualities in themselves. At the same time, PAR might be able to help these educators see the distance between their theories and actual practice and thus make the first move toward lasting change.

Schools as Organizations

One feature of the current school reform movement is that an explicit connection is made between educational change and the participative process. The reformers in New York State proclaim, "We must reconceive the system itself" (*Compact* 1991: 2), yet reconceptualizing, much less transforming "the system," is a daunting undertaking. The current structure of American schools was not casually built and will not be easily dismantled.

As David Tyack and Elisabeth Hansot have noted (1983), standardization, professionalization, and bureaucracy became entrenched features of American schools during the Progressive Era (1890-1914). Schools and school systems were reorganized along corporate-managerial lines, with district superintendents at the top of the hierarchy, teachers (not to mention students) at the bottom, and a cadre of technical experts and middle-level supervisors in between. Since then, the fundamental structure has remained unaltered; in large part, U.S. schools still operate like outmoded industrial organizations (Chubb and Moe 1990).

In 1984, Theodore Sizer wrote that the system designed in the late nineteenth century for "social order" had created a bureaucracy that stifles initiative, relies on a high level of specialization that fails to treat students as whole people, and pays no attention to the enormous variability of students, assuming what is effective for one will be effective for another. Furthermore, "large, complex units need simple ways of describing themselves, so those aspects of school keeping which can be readily quantified . . . become the only forms of representation" (207). His example of this phenomenon is the state mandates that specify the number of minutes each student must spend on a given subject.

Even earlier, in a 1971 paper about schools as sociotechnical systems, Herbst blamed the production-model organization of schools for their inability to promote learning. His point, like Sizer's, was that schools segment learning into subject divisions and then treat the learning itself as a set of isolated tasks. This compartmentalization means that schools are set up for specialists to deliver a subject, which children are to receive and presumably commit to memory. On the one hand, the effect is to promote what Herbst called "determinate" tasks as the subject of teaching, which is accomplished through a predetermined process and has a predictable outcome. On the other hand, as Herbst points out, learning takes place when tasks are indeterminate, when the means for arriving at an outcome are matters for research and discovery.

In the bureaucracy Herbst and Sizer describe, teachers are at the bottom of a pyramid where there are no possibilities to alter the system. Moreover, as Michelle Fine argues (1992), such disempowered teachers, in particular those who work with disadvantaged young people, act out their disempowerment with students.

"Empowering People at All Levels"

Having heard the message of the revitalization movement in American industry, school reformers across the nation are adopting their version of participatory decision making, shared decision making (SDM), as the means to change.[1] The theory is that SDM gives those closest to the learner (*i.e.*, parents, teachers, and students themselves) a voice in the reform and ownership of the critical decisions that influence teaching and learning (Katz 1992; Fernandez 1993).

At the heart of this movement is the recognition that schools must prepare future generations for work that is no longer modeled on the rigid bureaucracies of educational systems devised in the nineteenth century. There is also a deep sense that schools have failed to instill an interest in learning, the very value that inspired the development of universal public education.

When groups of Binghamton teachers, administrators, parents, and support staff in project-related workshops were asked to draw visions of an ideal future for their schools, they drew schools with open doors, students and community people streaming in and out; they drew teachers in circles, reaching out to children; some drew children tall and straight — self-confident and able to face the future. Talking about their drawings, the workshop participants used phrases such as "children are continuous learners," "all children are successful," and there should be "a partnership of home, school, and community."

As I watched the drawings develop and heard people describe their efforts, I began to realize that what the educators had envisioned as appropriate learning for children was precisely what they, as adults, would have to do to create their ideal world. Like the brown, black, and red stick figures on their papers, the educators would have to join hands and work together, look outside their buildings for knowledge, end their isolation from each other, and reflect on their experience. For this to happen, I reasoned, not only was PAR appropriate, it was what they needed to succeed.

Reflective Learning: The Research in PAR

In my thinking, three constructs related to reflective learning define the research that takes place in PAR. The first construct is single- and double-loop learning, as described by Chris Argyris, Robert Putnam, and Diana McLain Smith, in *Action Science* (1987). In single-loop learning, actors change actions to achieve results they have not questioned, without examining the values that drive their actions. An example might be found in the decision to order new readers when test scores are low.

Double-loop learning, by contrast, occurs when actors are able to see the values that guide their actions and that it is possible to question those values. This is especially important when inconsistencies exist between what they say they want to do (espoused theory) and what is actually done. An oversimplified but useful example might be the claim that education is meant to foster curiosity (espoused theory) while in reality one-time performance, as exhibited in test results, is what counts (theory-in-use).

The second construct, consistent with single- and double-loop learning, is the ranking of first-, second-, and third-order change in organizational development, as described by Jean Bartunek and Michael Moch (1987). In first-order change, actions or even strategies may change, but the world views ("shared schemata") that drive them are unquestioned. If, for example, some children are not learning to read, the decision might be to keep them in first grade. In second-order change, there may be some modification of world view in order to improve outcomes. For example, the understanding that children are developmentally ready to read at different times might lead to stretching reading instruction over two or three grades. In third-order change, actors become aware of their underlying schemata, consciously question their validity and *negotiate with each other to arrive at new understandings*. Perhaps, it turns out, children learn to read when they encounter the *need* to read to accomplish a real task, an understanding that could lead to the complete redesign of elementary education. As with double-loop learning, third-order change implies ongoing development of new understandings, but this development occurs in an organizational context, in part as the result of dialogue by members of the organization.

The third construct is actually framed as a definition of the "research" in PAR: "an attempt to surface and organize the predominant interpretive tendencies within the group and subject them to a kind of self-conscious examination" (personal correspondence, Greenwood to Virginia Vanderslice, April 6, 1993). If we subscribe to these constructs, PAR becomes the sensible approach to the profound reform called for in *The New Compact for Learning*. To change a system designed to educate children, the ideas, theories, and values of the entire system must be examined, and, insofar as each actor in the system operates from a set of beliefs, it makes sense that these beliefs and ideas should be opened up for inquiry in a context of participatory or shared decision making. It is because such profound questioning of beliefs and values will be required for the restructuring of the system to take place and because collaboration will be required for the system to change that PAR methodology can be of great use.

The First Phase

The Binghamton project really began in 1991, when the school administration and the teachers union (BPTA) sought my help in learning a process of interest bargaining that could replace traditional adversarial negotiating. In April of that year, representatives of the two locals of the Civil Service Employees Association, the Binghamton Association of School Administrators, the Binghamton Teachers Association, the central administration, and the board of education participated in a workshop that became the forum for discussion at the leadership level of the district.

In the bargaining sessions that followed, the BPTA and the board of education agreed to institutionalize SDM in the labor agreement. The district formed a top-level steering committee, Excellence in Academics (EIA), composed of representatives of all the bargaining units, the board, and parents.

The work that followed took place at top administrative and school levels. The goal of the top-level group, which included the EIA committee, the superintendent and his assistants, and members of the board of education, was to develop a mutual understanding of what they were undertaking and how they would proceed. The goal of the administrative group, which was composed of principals and assistant principals, was to develop a particular understanding of what SDM would mean for their roles. Finally, the school group was composed of the members of the SDM committees at the district's ten schools, which reflected, on the school level, the composition of the EIA committee and included the administrators of each school. For this group, the goal was parallel, namely, to understand shared decision making and their roles as decision-making bodies.

In January and February 1992, each of these groups participated in its own workshops (one day for the administrators; two days for the EIA committee and for the school committees, which met in groups of two) to develop a shared sense of values and a vision for education. The EIA committee focused on the visions for the district, whereas the school committees focused on their visions for their particular schools.

Also included in the workshops was training in consensus and agenda setting. A great deal of effort was spent understanding the difference between educational goals and the process by which these might be accomplished (*i.e.*, shared decision making and school-based management, in which curriculum and expenditure decisions are made at the school rather than at the central level).

Because the implicit agenda for these groups was organizational change, it was imperative that they begin to question some of their assumptions. We started by using "force field analysis" to understand resistance to change — their own as well as others. A concept from the work of Kurt Lewin (1969), it builds on the assumption that agents will be more successful if they work to reduce resistance than if they exert force for change. For the first time, the participants began to identify conditions — such as lack of information, isolation, and the politics of board elections — that, if addressed, could overcome superficial signs of resistance.

It seemed essential, too, to build confidence and generate dialogue across roles and schools. The organizational structure Sizer and Herbst describe has fostered a culture in which teachers, isolated from decision making, consider it their right to teach as they see fit, resist administrative evaluations, and resent mandated curricula and standardized tests. The extent of this culture was clear when one teacher, resisting SDM, said it might be good to hang on to "the little power we have. If you [administrators] make the [decision], I can complain about it."

I reasoned that if the teachers and administrators could experience collegiality in confronting shared problems in the workshops, they might then see the possibilities for actually collaborating on educational change. I felt it would take months, however, of working together, getting organized, and developing strategies for joint decision making before I could realistically expect to see results.

Developments over the Next Eighteen Months

Two interventions with the school committees followed the initial workshops. The first took place six to eight months later. At that time, only half the schools had met the EIA committee's requirement to submit a plan that included their proposed method of operation and the educational issues they intended to address. The EIA committee struggled with issues of authority and accountability: Could it *require* plans? What should its role be if plans were not submitted? What if the plans were only on paper? What was really going on in the schools, and how was the committee to find out? The members of the committee were eager to avoid a watchdog role but felt responsible for change in the district.

A self-assessment was planned: the EIA committee would spend half a day with each school committee discussing the progress it had made (or failed to make). This would test my belief that by working together, the members of the committees could begin the unfreezing process of confronting their assumptions and habits, as well as take the first critical look at their committee's progress.

In the self-assessment workshops, held in October 1992, the school committees were asked (1) to hold up a mirror to their work and themselves as groups at that time and a year earlier, (2) to define their missions as they had come to see them, and (3) to identify preliminarily some observable results they could expect. The "outcomes" approach was a deliberate effort to tie their organizational change work to the large-scale, ongoing district-level work on identifying outcomes for the educational process in Binghamton.

The self-assessment workshops were followed in March 1993 by a half-day workshop for the EIA committee entitled "Moving from Outcomes to Action," intended to serve as a model for the EIA group to use with school committees. As another means for addressing the EIA committee's concern with the schools' progress, a liaison member or members were chosen to interact with each school committee.

Curious to know what, if anything, had changed after the self-assessment meetings, three Cornell University graduate students and I interviewed committee members from four schools in April and May 1993.[2] The interviews were designed to take a closer look at whether the SDM committees were addressing educational issues, to see whether committee members thought of themselves as "researchers," to look for evidence of cultural change, and to find out where, if anywhere, the process was getting stuck. The follow-up to the interviews — feedback to the school committees from which members were interviewed; group discussion and reaction; and a joint dialogue with the EIA committee on what the school committees have learned and what issues still need to be addressed — will be the next step in the project.

What Was Learned

As I went into the self-assessment meetings, two questions were on my mind. The first question was whether the committees had, in fact, just gone through the motions of establishing committees and procedures in order to meet the require-ments of yet another mandate. The second question was whether they had engaged in a "determinate" task or whether there was some element of discovery in their work on which we might build. These were, of course, questions at the core of participatory action research.

Based on what occurred in Binghamton in the first year, it appears that given enough latitude, a mandated process develops its own character and conviction. In fact, dictated change seems to have created the opportunity for learning, whether the learning was intended or not. In the following sections, I discuss more specifically what was learned.

Participative Process Itself

Because none of the committees had done very much in the way of educational decision making at the time we began the self-assessment sessions, I expected to hear a lot of comments reflecting discouragement and disillusionment. Instead, participants expressed support and enthusiasm for the *process*. The groups had used consensus- and agenda-development processes to develop a vision — the operational and ground rules for their work — and to agree on which educational issues to tackle. Even where the processes had failed to yield perfect decisions, group members had discovered the advantages of collaboration; they had devel-oped their skills in working together *and* a positive outlook on their future ability to make joint decisions.

In the dialogues prompted by asking them to look in an imaginary mirror, most of the groups also expressed doubts about their ability to succeed in their tasks. Few of the committees have actually initiated major changes in education. The one committee that may have actually initiated such change, the high school committee, is reluctant to see its accomplishments as significant. These fears are well founded and show an enhanced understanding of its task, as illustrated in such comments as "It's big and complex now" and "We're on a train going uphill; we've slowed down because we have a bigger task." Such remarks are encouraging from the action research perspective because they show evidence of a new understanding that the work will require puzzling through the complexities of collaboration, perhaps even having to "surface and organize the predominant interpretive tendencies within the group" (personal correspondence, Greenwood to Vanderslice, April 6, 1993).

The committees were closer to undertaking the fundamental reform of education now that they understood the enormity of the undertaking. Some may still fail to attempt real change in their schools, but they are all grappling with *how* to attempt it, a state that is considerably more promising than our worst fears for groups that were established with no opportunity to decide whether this was the best structure and no say in their agenda.

Looking back, it is possible to see how this realization developed. Once the committees were formed for each school, they began asking how they would accomplish change. It became evident that as groups of ten or twelve people in each school, they could not come up with all the ideas or make all the decisions. They faced skepticism in their schools over whether anything could ever change and whether the various powers that be would ever "let" teachers have a say in what goes on in their schools. They soon understood that their job required the cooperation and collaboration of all their constituents. They realized that, not unlike the action researcher working with them, they must be sensitive agents in the participative process. They realized that the committee itself would not accomplish reform but rather would set the stage for a broader participative process. Their mission was not to replace the single authoritarian figure in the school (the principal) with a group decision-making body but, in a role similar to that of action researchers, to promote inquiry, reflection, and action based on what was learned. Understanding this, the teachers have taken the first steps on the road to fostering change.

The follow-up interviews supported the optimistic discussions that took place during the self-assessment sessions: working together had enabled the teachers to develop new ideas and accomplish results they had felt unable to achieve in the past. One special education teacher reported "a new perspective, an air, a new atmosphere." When the interviewer asked what had made this new air possible, the answer was "access and freedom to pursue knowledge with others." A teacher from another school spoke about "breaking down walls" and "sharing good practice." Although others uttered disclaimers such as "I don't know that [the reforms] will impact on instruction" and "We haven't made any decisions yet that actually affect the classroom teacher," these remarks do not stand in the way of evidence that the participative process *has* touched on how education is construed in the schools.

Developing Self-Awareness

In the course of the self-assessment, the Binghamton High School committee confirmed what Herbst had seen years before in Norway. School staff members spoke of personnel in different areas knowing very little about each others' jobs, of a guidance office divided according to grades, which discouraged communication about students, and of departments that met separately, missing the chance to know what students learn in other disciplines. In describing what they hoped to accomplish, one teacher said, "to eliminate cynicism of teachers and replace it with a sense of control." Autonomy behind the classroom door has left teachers with no sense of control over the educational process. Shared decision making offers more knowledge and, therefore, more control.

We found evidence that the committees do engage in data collection, although there is no talk of "research." At least two have surveyed their staffs to discover staff priorities and interests. What has not developed, apparently, is any sense that student needs or accomplishments or attitudes might be used as data for their work. In other words, there is no evidence of the learner-centered environment.

Interviewees did report significant personal change as a result of their work on the SDM committees. An administrator who does a lot of trouble-shooting reported that his decisions were now "more kid-oriented; I'm more flexible . . . don't automatically come down on the side of the teacher." A skeptical teacher said: "I like to hide. Maybe that's the best thing. . . . It's gotten me to the point where I can't do that." A parent reported that she had "grown to feel that I'm a valued person." A principal reported that he felt he had become "a better listener . . . hearing greater diversity." A support staff member said that teachers "know our needs now" and "you see things getting done." If we can accept that personal change opens the way to new perspectives, the process is creating the conditions for further change.

Educational Change

The fact remains that most of the school committees have not tackled major decisions that directly affect education — although issues in education are being discussed. In a school where no one could point to educational change as a result of the committee's work, one teacher did refer to discussions she found exciting; her example was an idea considered by a subcommittee that teachers might move from classroom to classroom so they could be teaching "from your expertise . . . share what you're best at."

Educational change is evident at the high school, which is experimenting with a radically new way of scheduling students. Called the Copernican Plan, it was piloted in the ninth grade and has now been extended to the tenth grade: students concentrate on two subjects at a time rather than the traditional four or five; the number of weeks spent on each subject is shorter, but the work is more concentrated and, according to theory, more integrated.

Equally important, the committees seem poised, ready to act, on their understanding of the gap between the visions they drew and current conditions. They are aware of their own hesitancy and that they are not taking action where it is needed. When asked what is holding them back, they talk about two closely connected fears — their powerlessness and their fear of consequences. A year earlier they often pointed to resistance and apathy from their colleagues — teachers who had been "around too long" or "just don't want to change" — and parents who "don't care" as reasons meaningful change might not occur. Now they recognize their own responsibility in the situation, and it is this recognition that may allow for the risk and confrontation that will make room for double-loop learning. PAR methodology has brought them to this point of discovery.

Action research also presents a possible approach to dealing with the powerlessness and fear of consequences the committee members describe. Committee members often cite their own lack of authority and/or expertise when they confront what they have not done yet. They express frustration with responses that will empower them: "Test and find out" or "Ask the EIA committee so they are forced to address the issue." These participants would much rather have someone tell them the answers or be able to follow some well-established pattern. But answers do not exist, and because shared decision making in schools is new, there are few patterns. The participants *must* construct their own system.

Accountability

The fear of consequences is an even greater challenge to action research. The specter of accountability for poor results haunts all levels of a school system, dampening innovation and discouraging risk taking. For the individual teacher, to experiment is to risk failure and blame. It is safer to do what has been done over and over, even though it is patently clear that it does not promote learning for some children. For a principal, fostering experimentation involves the same risk on a larger scale. She or he must be "accountable" to the public as well as to the administration.

For a school, to face and really try to change what is not working for children — as might be the case in shared decision making — the risks are simply multiplied by the number of staff members and administrators involved. They may all be censured or, worse still, lose their jobs because of public outcry. The tenure system protects employment for those who have tenure, but it does not protect a school from being closed by a vindictive board of education. For a superintendent of schools, subject to the whim of an elected board, innovation always means putting her or his job on the line. Of course the same goes for the elected board, whose members will be replaced if there is controversy (not to mention radical change) in the district.

To be fair, when worried teachers and school administrators ask about "accountability" in shared decision making, they are asking on two levels. One is, simply: who will (or can) bear the consequences for children if they fail? The stakes are high when you are teaching young people. Teachers will say that they always live with this fear because they know they fail some children. What they want to do is succeed with more children.

The more pressing worry is the second one: who will (or is willing to) bear the political repercussions if they fail? It is the fear of being shut down by the system — whether it's a "no" from the principal when the committee thought it had the power to decide or a "no" from the superintendent because the board of education does not understand or a "no" from the state education department that finds some innovation incompatible with mandates designed to assure equal opportunity across the state.

What, then, can action research offer people struggling with the tension between change and accountability? It is possible that the participatory process itself will create an expectation of shared rather than individual accountability. This spreads the burden of blame, but if blame is still the outcome of shared accountability, then the old closed system of thinking has not changed: a single authoritarian figure is replaced with a group; poor performance gets punished; the performer learns not to try again. Is it any more useful for a whole school to be blamed for lower test scores than a principal? I suggest that it is not enough to switch the focus for accountability from individuals to a group; instead, the definition of accountability itself needs to be changed to be consistent with learning.

Learning

The notion of organizational learning as defined in the work of Argyris, Putnam, and Smith (1987) holds out the possibility of developing a system of accountability consistent with viewing children as learners rather than performers, consistent, moreover, with the idea that students should learn to learn. The work on "alternative assessment" in the educational community already addresses this issue with systems for measuring student progress that place importance on development rather than the scores or ratings of one given moment. But this discussion has yet to extend to accountability for professionals. Are they "performers," or is it legitimate to think of professionals as learners, too?

One idea I brought to Binghamton is the "Plan-Do-Check-Act" cycle, a diagrammatic developed by the statistician Walter Shewhart and introduced by total quality management *guru* W. Edwards Deming (Walton 1986). The point of the cycle is that it *is* a *cycle*, one that represents continuous improvement. It depicts an ongoing process of inquiry and reflection, although such a process could also apply to single- as well as double-loop learning.[3] Once you are acting, you are already planning new actions that you will observe and correct in action, and so on.

The usefulness of the cycle as a metaphor for educators is its message about progress and change as ongoing, in contrast to what they have previously been told concerning educational reform, which is "try and toss it out." One teacher described the skepticism arising out of the blame routine: "The faculty is saying to the administration, 'Prove to us that we're going to be listened to — prove to us that this isn't a waste of money for something that's going to be put on the shelf.'"

I suggested that the Binghamton groups redefine accountability in terms of *joint* responsibility for *continuous improvement*. The idea is clearly attractive to them, but so far they have connected it with their local experience in only a limited way, in their references to continuous improvement in their collaborative work and in their comments about confronting beliefs and habits: "We thought we understood consensus, but . . ." and "We had to face the fact that the administrator was running the show." It will be another bigger step to think of the work of educational change in the framework of continuous improvement.

Conclusions

School committees engaged in restructuring need courage to proceed in spite of the enormous risks, political and otherwise, of changing the system. There is an assumption of collective learning in PAR that supports the idea of accountability as learning-based rather than blame-based. In the Binghamton project, I have made it clear that my agenda is for the committees to see themselves primarily as learning about and not "doing" shared decision making. They are not producing a predictable result with tested methods; they are "making the road by walking" (Horton and Freire 1990: 6).

The concept of continuous improvement echoes educational philosopher John Dewey's idea that learning results from the interaction of observation and experience. The interaction of observation and action, processed in dialogue, is exactly what one expects with PAR. The hope is for a combination of research and action that leads to new observations, new opportunities for research, new action, and so on, continuing long after the outsider who introduced the cycle has left.

PAR makes particular sense when the problem is that educational practices are not meeting the needs of children. Wave after wave of educational reform has failed to change the organizational structure of schools or to alter the factory model in which education is an item to be delivered. Each wave has been introduced to teachers who continued to work in isolation on narrowly defined tasks with neither the time nor the opportunity to address learning as a whole. By insisting on participation and collaboration, PAR breaks up a rigid structure. By insisting on the importance of participant knowledge, PAR requires that teachers access what they know of learning. By insisting on research, PAR opens the possibility for educators to observe and reflect on their own work. In Herbst's terms, it frees them to approach their own undertaking as an *indeterminate* task (1971).

There is evidence in our interview data that several members of Binghamton's SDM committees are approaching their task of collaboration in this way. What remains to be seen is whether they dare undertake educational reform in the same manner. Whether the PAR process can carry them through the next step is an open question.

For educational change to take place, there must certainly be interaction between research and action, but we must be cautious that the "learning" goes beyond the "first-order" selection of alternative actions to replace ineffective ones. Michael Fullan warns that innovation in education is multidimensional: it involves new material, new approaches, and new or altered beliefs. "Change in teaching approach or style in using new materials presents greater difficulty if new skills must be acquired and new ways of conducting instructional activities established," he writes. "Changes in beliefs are even more difficult; they challenge the core values held by individuals regarding the purposes of education" (1991: 42).

Based on the early work at Binghamton, I believe PAR is the most promising way to lead educators to confront and alter their unstated assumptions about learning. Inquiry and reflection, with the help of an outsider, have led them to question their culture and express genuine dissatisfaction with their reluctance to grapple with educational issues.

The ability of educators to reconceptualize education may be linked to their ability to see their own learning as continuous, indeterminate, and based on inquiry. As I listen to the Binghamton shared decision-making committees, I wonder whether their members believe they or their peers, who must also be active participants, can learn. They want to reform education to support children's experimentation in learning, but they are afraid to risk experimentation on their own. They identify self-esteem as a critical value in education, but they recognize little of it in their colleagues. In fact, lack of self-esteem was so clear to two committees that they listed self-esteem for school staff as one hoped-for outcome of their work.

PAR offers these committees a chance to consider their work in the context of what they know about learning: that self-esteem is critical, that one learns best through experience, that experience combined with reflection can lead to new knowledge, and that one learns best of all by teaching others. If they engage in reflection, they may be able to examine the tacit values and assumptions that have guided their actions and then realign so that the educational programs they offer are consistent with their espoused beliefs. This will be a sort of third-order change, arrived at in shared decision making, worked out in dialogue and negotiation.

It is too early in the project to conclude whether it is successful. The groups still hesitate to make decisions. There is some hope from the early experience — but the challenge continues to be how to "teach" these educational leaders to be learners.

Notes

1. Although we do not find documents such as *The New Compact for Learning* beginning with calls to emulate Japanese management practice in the schools, observers of the latest school reform note the connection between economic competition and education. "The education linkage with economic growth maintains its hold on public opinion in 1988, and 'competitiveness' is a *cliché* in Washington and state capitals" (Kirst 1988: 21).

2. Three of the schools were "self-selected." I made an extra effort to include the high school because it is the only high school and certainly the most complex school in the system. Five of the ten schools responded to my letter describing the interview and dialogue process we hoped to follow, but as of this writing, we have had to limit our data gathering to four schools.

3. I am grateful to René van der Vlist of Leiden University for pointing out the single dimension of the Shewhart cycle and the potential limitation of using it as a metaphor for organizational learning. Its usefulness in the context of educators is as an image of hope rather than defeat. If mistakes are made, they have not failed but can continue on. The nature of the corrective action needed for educational reform is, indeed, more complex than a simple process adjustment such as one might find in industry. Even with double-loop learning, however, it is useful to think of the process as continuous.

Chapter 14

How About a Dialogue?

The Communicative Perspective Meets the Socioecological Perspective

Henrik Dons Finsrud

Within the action research community, several traditions have arisen over the past two decades. On the Scandinavian scene, the two dominant traditions are the communicative perspective, developed mainly by Björn Gustavsen (1992), and the socioecological perspective, developed mainly by Eric L. Trist and Fred Emery (Emery and Trist 1972; Trist 1983, 1986).[1] Both perspectives have been evident in national work reform programs, including the LOM program in Sweden (Naschold 1993) and the Norwegian Worklife Centre (SBA) program in Norway (Davies *et al.* 1993), and are at the forefront of work life reform efforts throughout Scandinavia.

Yet, however central and well articulated the two action research perspectives may be, they have been developed, presented, and propounded without any substantial discussions of their similarities and differences. This chapter is an attempt to start such a discussion and thereby to improve action research. Having conducted research from both perspectives, and therefore having witnessed those similarities and differences from a practical standpoint, I have seen areas in which a closer comparison could lead to improved research practice.

Generally speaking, these AR positions address the broad issue of industrial development by pursuing participative democracy and organizational productivity and change simultaneously. In so doing, both perspectives increasingly focus on regional change efforts and on the importance of the network concept as an organizing principle. This is in line with emerging trends in action research in which we observe a general shift in the research and development focus from single organizations toward network development in regional contexts (Chisholm and Elden 1993). The development of collaborative structures as such (*i.e.*, networks, clusters) is, to an even greater extent than ever, seen as an important

strategy for industrial development, not only within the action research community but also within management circles and the economic disciplines (Axelsson
and Easton 1992; Piore and Sabel 1984; Porter 1990; Storper and Scott 1992).

Because the aim of this chapter is to start a discourse between proponents of
these two central AR perspectives, it does not address directly the differences in
their theoretical underpinnings (a theory of communication and an open systems
theory, respectively). Instead, it focuses on how their AR strategies, research
practices, and conceptual apparatuses influence the construction of the field and
hence the new practices that may evolve. It is important to bear in mind that the
purpose of doing action research is not only to contribute new knowledge to the
scientific community but simultaneously to improve practice. Even more, it is
through developing practice in the field that new knowledge is generated (Elden
and Levin 1991).

Action Research and the Interorganizational Level

It is possible to identify different traditions in action research, such as action
science (Argyris, Putnam, and Smith 1987), participatory action research (Whyte
1991), participatory research (Brown and Tandon 1983; Fals Borda 1987), sociotechnical systems theory and social ecology (Thorsrud and Emery 1970; Herbst,
ed., 1971; Trist 1981, 1986), democratic dialogue or the communicative perspective (Gustavsen 1992), and maybe others. Clear and absolute distinctions do not
exist, however, because each tradition has multiple dimensions and they partly
overlap. To a degree, they share values and history and have influenced each
other. For instance, PAR has been influenced particularly by the development of
sociotechnical analysis and by research in work democracy in Norway, represented by, respectively, Trist and Thorsrud (Whyte, Greenwood, and Lazes 1991:
21).

The distinctions between the traditions are also blurred by the fact that
practitioners who describe themselves as being part of a certain tradition often
differ significantly among themselves in their actual approaches. Still, given this
interwoven background and kinship, it is possible to identify important differences in thinking that influence the way action research is done and hence the
knowledge produced and the quality of the practical solutions. These differences
become clearer and of greater relevance when the different approaches address
the same kind of fields or the same kind of issues with a similar overall ambition.

Historically, most action research efforts in work life have been directed
toward changing single organizations, or even parts of single organizations; the
interorganizational level has received less emphasis. Inquiry into this level implies focusing on the interactions and interdependencies between organizations

and the processes by which they can be developed. The rationale for shifting the focus from single organizations to the level between organizations differs from approach to approach, but generally it reflects a realization that change within an organization cannot be fully understood, facilitated, and sustained without considering the external relations of the organization, that is, without putting the change efforts into a larger context. Thus, the unit of analysis and change becomes the organization in and with its environment (van Beinum 1993).

The increasing interest in interorganizational relationships also reflects the nature of the problems with which societies are struggling. Increasingly, problems or problem areas are typically of such a complex nature that they cannot be solved by any single organization alone; they demand collaborative efforts involving several organizations. Regional industrial development is one such broad and complex area, and it is gaining increased attention from action researchers. As pointed out by Max Elden and Rupert F. Chisholm (1993), the complexity surrounding regional change efforts makes it very difficult to analyze, understand, and intervene in the systems involved. Thus, one of the central challenges for action researchers is developing methods, concepts, and strategies for carrying out action research in such large, complex, and loosely coupled social systems.

Without attempting to describe fully the communicative and the socioecological perspectives, I will briefly sketch their main characteristics to highlight their differences. By "perspective" I mean an overall framework that includes theoretical underpinnings and an underlying philosophy, values, concepts, methods, and strategies for change.

Communicative Perspective

The communicative perspective has been developed mainly by Björn Gustavsen, Per H. Engelstad, and Øyvind Pålshaugen at the Work Research Institute in Oslo and has been operationalized on a large scale in the Swedish LOM program.[2] The perspective has been described in several recent publications (Gustavsen 1992, 1993; Engelstad and Gustavsen 1993; Pålshaugen 1991, 1995) and will therefore not be described extensively here. As indicated by its title, this tradition is based on a theory of communication and on what is referred to as the "linguistic turn" in philosophy represented by such authors as Jürgen Habermas, Ludwig Wittgenstein, and Michel Foucault.

One of the central starting points of this approach is the need to achieve a broad scope in the change process by building up a critical mass of organizations involved in these processes (Engelstad and Gustavsen 1993: 219-20). Arguing that it is not possible to rely on "the force of the good example," in reference to experiences with experimental approaches in the Norwegian Industrial Democracy Program in the late 1960s, Gustavsen (1992) and others promoted the communicative tradition partly in reaction to the weaknesses and mistakes uncovered in the earlier phase in the history of sociotechnical design.[3] A central idea is that organizations can learn directly from each other through the exchange of experiences. This leads to the use of networks as the main means of organizing and managing the work reform process.

According to proponents of the communicative perspective, networks are the support structure for organizational development, primarily linking organizations to a network of competence centers (*i.e.*, researchers), but also linking organizations directly to each other so that they may exchange ideas and experiences gained through their own development work. The strategy aims at establishing groups or clusters of enterprises, preferably starting with four enterprises in each cluster, linking them to researchers, and subsequently linking the clusters into networks. The content of the development process — the design element — is of minor importance: "Ideally a network should work on as broad a range of topics as possible, to maximize the scope and variety of the experience available within the network" (Engelstad and Gustavsen 1993: 230).

Emphasizing the importance of good communication or good processes, the theoretical core is a theory of communication. An idea of good communication called "democratic dialogue" is the point of departure (Gustavsen 1985, 1992), and the notion of the reorganization of discourses (Pålshaugen 1991) brings process to the foreground.

A specific and rather detailed methodology for organizational change projects has been developed, including principles for involving the whole organization in the change effort; use of a particular type of conference called a "dialogue conference" (Gustavsen and Engelstad 1986, Engelstad 1996); establishment of a development organization within each organization; establishment of a strategy forum as part of the internal development organization to act as the link between the enterprise and the research network; and collaboration among enterprises through dialogue conferences.

On the regional network level, the research team sets up a strategy forum that guides and develops regional development activities. A composite body based on broad representation of the relevant parties, typically including labor market parties, researchers, and the project enterprises, the regional strategy forum serves as a place to discuss and evaluate project developments and program strategy. The experience gained in the LOM program further emphasized the development of networks on a regional basis, including networks among enterprises and among researchers.

Socioecological Perspective

The socioecological perspective has been developed mainly by Emery and Trist (Emery and Trist 1965, 1972; Trist 1976, 1983, 1986), but this approach and the systems thinking behind it have been clearly evident in action research programs undertaken at the Work Research Institute since the 1970s, although they are often given little attention in overviews of the historical development of Norwegian action research. A well-documented and much-referred-to example of a socioecological program is the action research program carried out at the Work Research Institute over a ten-year period from about 1970 of the Norwegian shipping industry (Johansen 1978; Thorsrud 1981; Walton and Gaffney 1991). The socioecological approach has also been an important part of the strategy followed by the Norwegian Worklife Centre (STBA) (Brundtland 1989; Hanssen-Bauer 1991; Qvale 1989, 1991).[4] The strong links between sociotechnical and socioecological thinking, moving from the intra- to the interorganizational level, is demonstrated above all by the fact that Emery and Trist were the pioneers in developing both sets of ideas. Oguz N. Babüroglu (1992) clearly shows this in tracking what he calls the Emery-Trist Systems Paradigm.

Social ecology refers to the organizational field created by a number of organizations, whose interrelations compose a system at the level of the field as a whole. In other words, social ecology is concerned with the intermediate level between the socially "micro" and the socially "macro." The overall field becomes the object of inquiry (Trist 1983).

Basic to this perspective is a recognition of the interdependencies between the organization and its environment. Organizations and their environments are complementary; they determine each other. Consequently, the unit of change is not the organization as such but the organization in and with its environment. Changes in single organizations are interrelated with changes in their environments — single organizations find themselves in tightly woven relationships with other firms, government regulatory bodies, central training institutions, labor organizations, and so forth. This means that problems associated with organizational development and work redesign cannot be tackled effectively at the level of a single enterprise but must be dealt with at the interorganizational level.

At the same time, the overall environment moves toward increased complexity and speed of change and, at certain points, creates a level of contextual commotion, unpredictability, and turbulence that Emery and Trist have called a "turbulent environment" (1965). This is reflected in a set of meta-problems or problem areas that are too extensive and too many-sided to be dealt with by any single organization, such as unemployment, industrial development, environmental issues, and poverty. Regulation and reduction of this turbulence and the handling of complex problem areas require collaboration by groups of organizations through the development of nonbureaucratic, self-regulating, interorganizational domains. According to Trist, this self-regulation must be of a democratic nature, and, as in the communicative perspective, the core values are those associated with participative democracy.

Interorganizational domains are functional systems of which the single organization is a part, and the domains occupy a position in the social space between the society as a whole and the single organization. Domains are cognitive as well as organizational structures and have boundaries, direction, and identities. Put more simply, domains can be thought of as the set of actors that become joined through a common problem or interest (Gray 1985). Formation or development of these domains is central in the socioecological perspective, and designing processes to facilitate the development of domains becomes a focal point.

According to Trist (1983, 1985), four intervention strategies in the development of interorganizational domains are of special importance. The first such strategy is the network initiative, in that "networks constitute the basic social form that permits an interorganizational domain to develop as a system of social ecology" (1983: 279). Networks are nonhierarchical, voluntary, unbounded social systems at the level between organizations. Networks will be constituted across levels and sectors (both public and private), as well as within, in order to facilitate the development of common ground and the coordination of resources.

The second intervention strategy Trist accords special importance is the search conference. Bringing stakeholders together in a participative and voluntary manner, search conferences enable shared appreciation to evolve and emergent domains to develop more coherently. They are also an important way to support action learning among a large group of people.

The third intervention strategy Trist mentions is the development of suitable referent organizations. Referent organizations are organizations at the domain level, designed to provide leadership to the multiorganizational domain without taking over any of the functions of the constituent organizations. There are several varieties of referent organizations, and many domains have more than one. They have three broad functions: regulation of present relationships and activities and establishing ground rules and maintaining base values; appreciation of emergent trends and issues and developing a shared image of a desirable future; and infrastructure support through sharing information and resources and creating special projects and other activities.

The fourth intervention strategy Trist says is of special importance is to convene the extended social field. It is very important that the referent organizations remain in sensitive contact with the extended social field of the domain. Members of the domain community must become part of the learning-appreciation process and must be convened at critical junctures. The importance of regulation by stakeholders can scarcely be overemphasized. The regional dimension is also emphasized in this perspective: "Locales such as regions and communities may constitute our most accessible learning theatres for building domains" (Trist 1983: 275).

Regional Industrial Development: The Case of Aust-Agder County

To illustrate the complexity and the changes, structures, and actors in a regional field, this section provides a short description of an industrial development case from Aust-Agder County in Norway. On the coast in southern Norway, Aust-Agder is a small county with only ninety thousand inhabitants. Its industrial profile includes electronics, maritime industries, and a woodworking industry, all mainly involving small and medium-sized enterprises.

From 1990 to 1995, a research team from the Work Research Institute followed and participated in industrial development efforts in the county, focusing on network formation between enterprises, competence centers, and the public sector. In this period, the county went through a rather remarkable change in industrial development, only partly due to researcher involvement.

In what was a noncollaborative, fragmented, nonstrategic industrial area consisting of uncoordinated single actors both in the private and public sectors, there are now a number of enterprise networks that have become arenas for joint policy making; a resourceful, coordinated, and active public sector that relates to the needs of industry; and competence institutions — all integrating their efforts and gradually becoming more able to address issues of work life concern in the region (Finsrud et al. 1993).

The county level in Aust-Agder gained an important role in industrial development through what is referred to as the Free-County Experiment. The main goals of this experiment have been to achieve closer coordination of the county's political and administrative systems and a strengthening of the county economically, and thus politically, in the area of industrial development by decentralizing the administration of the different national funds to the county level. These funds amounted to US$20 million in 1992.

Revitalized through the Free-County Experiment, the Agency for Industrial Development has taken a leading role in reshaping the public support system so that it relates better to the needs of industry. A strategy process at the county level involving a number of enterprises, competence institutions, politicians, and public agencies has resulted in three larger programs for the future. Within these programs, a number of projects are being developed by the key stakeholders, focusing on competence development and organizational development in general. Enterprises and the public administration have also started to collaborate in strategy development on a subregional level through a structure of four subregional boards, each relating more closely to local conditions. A regional structure linking the municipality to the county level is thus evolving — integrating and coordinating public efforts in interaction with industry.

In addition to this reorganization of the public administrative field, several networks between enterprises have emerged, creating new opportunities for organizing and intervening in the interorganizational field. The growing number of network initiatives reflects an increasing realization that collaborative strategies are important in improving competitiveness. The networks range from learning, competence, and policy-making networks to industrial networks along the value chain, and they operate both within and across branches. They are typically nonhierarchical. The five largest range in size from fifteen to forty members, with some enterprises being members of two or more networks. Adding up all these changes gives us a picture of a regional field pursuing a set of collaborative strategies in order to improve industrial development.

Communicative Perspective Meets the Socioecological Perspective

The communicative and the socioecological perspectives are different, even if closely related, yet this is not always recognized. For example, Hans van Beinum describes the Swedish LOM program as "representing the emergence of the socioecological approach" (1993: 173). Treating the LOM program as a socioecological approach is too imprecise if one wants to discuss the actual concepts and strategies it applied. Addressing the interorganizational level alone does not make the LOM program an example of the socioecological approach. Yet LOM did have certain socioecological characteristics, such as an interorganizational orientation, a focus on broadly based societal development, network building, and the links between micro and macro development.

The two perspectives also have other important similarities, such as shared values, a focus on participation, and the use of conferences. Their research strategies and central concepts reveal some important and interesting differences, however (see table 1). Socioecological thinking, to my knowledge, was never put forward as a central and guiding perspective for the LOM program in other publications (Naschold 1993; Gustavsen 1992; Engelstad and Gustavsen 1993). On the contrary, the LOM program has been presented as the key example of a communicatively-oriented work reform project. Since the proponents of these perspectives generally view them as separate and distinct, I will continue to regard them as such, but without denying their important similarities.

Still, it is worthwhile to examine them comparatively because, for example, the communicative tradition pays little attention to later attempts to refine the sociotechnical approach in a socioecological direction. Instead, its argument for the importance and relevance of the communicative turn refers to shortcomings of the experimental approach in the Industrial Democracy Program (IDP) before 1970 (Thorsrud and Emery 1970), largely ignoring alternatives developed later on (Gustavsen 1992: 12-30). This point is also made by Jon Hanssen-Bauer (1991).

It seems quite evident, for example, that the Shipping Research Program carried out at the Work Research Institute in the 1970s, which brought a "whole" industry into the change effort through a multilevel, network-based strategy along socioecological lines, provides an alternative both to the experiments of the 1960s and to a strictly communicatively oriented strategy (Thorsrud 1981; Walton and Gaffney 1991).

Table 1. Differences between the Perspectives

Characteristics of approaches to interorganizational development	Communicative Perspective	Socioecological Perspective
Content focus	Organization development	Handling of shared problems
Diffusion strategy	Achieve critical mass and broad scale development through learning networks	Change efforts linked to multilevel domain formation through a variety of network constructs
Managing and structuring the inter-organizational field	Establishing of regional strategy forum Prescribed cluster and network initiatives	Domain development Design of referent organizations Emergent network initiatives
Networks	*Purpose:* Exchange of experience *Function:* Support structure for intra-organizational development projects	*Purpose:* Handling of shared problems *Function:* Organizing at the inter-organizational level, development of common ground and coordination of resources.
Regional dimension	Transactional environment: organizations and their directly relevant support structure	Contextual environment: Complex sets of interrelations in domains that are multilevel and cross sectoral.
Role of the researcher	Primarily facilitator of processes	Facilitator of designs and processes

Table 1 sums up the main differences between the two approaches. Below, these differences are discussed more in depth by focusing on an issue both examine: regional industrial development. I will use the case from Aust-Agder County to illustrate the socioecological perspective and my own experience in working on a regional project to portray the communicative perspective.

I will show that the way concepts are developed and understood have important consequences for the construction of the field and that different concepts lead to the development of different field constructs. Closely linked to this are the different roles of the researcher in each framework. Using the framework from Table 1, we can see how these viewpoints influence the action research strategies in regional settings.

Content Focus

While the communicative perspective focuses on promoting organizational development, the socioecological perspective has a more general focus, namely, the handling of shared problems at the interorganizational level — problems that have to be defined by the actors themselves. The shared problem in any specific situation may well be one of organizational development, but that is not predefined. Thus, the foci are overlapping but the communicative perspective can be said to have a more limited content focus. Still, the two perspectives coincide on the issue of interorganizational development in regional contexts.

Diffusion Strategy

The issue of the diffusion of change beyond the single enterprise is central in Scandinavian action research and is linked to the notion of work life reform. How to use limited resources to have maximal national impact on participative democracy and productivity is seen as one of the main questions (Qvale 1994). Thus, strategies for diffusion have been fundamental to the design of national programs (IDP, LOM, SBA).

Not being able to rely either on the impact on work life of academic publications or on the "lighthouse" effect of the single, successful enterprise, strategies for diffusion of change have taken other forms. According to proponents of the communicative perspective, the assumption is that concrete solutions cannot successfully be copied but that ideas, experiences, and concepts can and should be exchanged in order to speed up learning processes and thereby support organizational development. Achieving a critical mass of enterprises involved in change efforts and linking these enterprises into learning networks then becomes the basic diffusion strategy. Rather than viewing this as "diffusion," Gustavsen (1992: 28) sees this as "restructuring in parallel."

Given the interwoven nature of the single organization in its environment, the basic concept of diffusion in the socioecological perspective is that changes in enterprises have to lead to and be part of changes in their domain (*i.e.*, change has to be diffused or spread by leading to relevant changes in their institutional environment) (Qvale 1994). As in the Norwegian SBA program, developing the domain as a diffusion strategy often means applying a multiple strategy involving organizations at different levels (Hanssen-Bauer 1991), such as the enterprise, networks of enterprises, the education system, labor market parties, regulatory bodies, and various local, regional and national authorities. The strategy followed in the SBA also included developing regional networks as mechanisms for diffusion (Hanssen-Bauer and Snow 1994).

The diffusion strategy from the socioecological perspective may imply seeking to work with a region, a sector, or an industry and its institutions. In the Shipping Research Program, it meant building a network of ship owners; ships, shipyards, R&D centers, and the education system; and representatives of the employers' confederation, the unions for seamen, the government control agency, the relevant ministries, and the classification institution (*e.g.*, Thorsrud 1981; Walton and Gaffney 1991).

These two different diffusion strategies clearly influence how development at the interorganizational level is approached and thus how the field is constructed. From the communicative perspective, learning networks are the clearest embodiment of the diffusion strategy; from the socioecological perspective, domain formation takes on a central role.

Managing and Structuring the Interorganizational Field

From both perspectives, participatory development of an interorganizational field implies building structures and institutionalizing certain functions at the interorganizational level — structures and functions that enhance the capacity for self-management. In the socioecological perspective, the central concepts are domains and referent organizations; in the communicative perspective, their "counterpart" is the "strategy forum."

The concepts of domain and referent organizations provide a framework and a direction for structuring and intervening in the interorganizational field. This framework goes beyond the idea of networks, which are just one of the strategies for developing domains. Multiorganizational domains are developed through collaborative efforts to define and deal with shared problem areas. Problem areas, and hence the domains, can be overlapping and typically bring together different levels and sectors.

In the case of Aust-Agder, for instance, closely linked or overlapping problem areas as defined by the actors themselves are unemployment, industrial development, and competence development in industry. These issues are understood as subsets of each other; improving industrial development will be an important way to reduce unemployment, and competence development in a broad sense will contribute to industrial development. Formulations and operationalizations of these shared concerns through collaborative processes bring together different sets of stakeholders, who form overlapping domains. Thus, a variety of collaborative structures and concrete development programs and projects may emerge.

For instance, a shared concern about competence development in industry brought together the region's leading competence institutions (an R&D institute, a district university, and consulting firms), a number of enterprises already forming enterprise networks for learning and development purposes, and central politicians and representatives of public agencies from the county and municipal level. Through a number of conferences, workshops, meetings, and project groups and by linking up to national financial sources, a wider range of concrete, collaborative development efforts have begun to emerge. Groups of enterprises and competence institutions collaborate on a number of training and development issues, such as quality assurance, just-in-time marketing and export, and training of management, foremen, and workers. Representatives from different public offices and agencies have formed teams at the municipal level, working with groups of smaller enterprises to design tailor-made training programs and to provide links to competence institutions and various funding sources at the county level.

These new, problem-driven ways of using public financial and personal resources are replacing a prespecified grant and budget system and the traditional separation among public agencies. Instead of focusing on areas of responsibility and the boundaries between agencies, the participants are increasingly paying attention to their shared concerns. This has been achieved not through education, infrastructure, national support programs, unemployment benefits, or public budgets per se but primarily by bringing the enterprises and their expressed needs into focus. This has been done by involving a number of enterprises in continuous strategy development processes together with politicians and public agencies, both at county and municipal levels.

Repeatedly, discussions of the needs and interests of the enterprises and of the region have led to the development of programs and projects that integrate previously uncoordinated resources. This increased coordination and integration of public activities in the field of industrial development is strengthened by the county budget structure itself. Because the money is held together in one fund, the participants will not receive funding unless they can agree on joint strategies.

This example reflects how the design of the process and the structures are emergent, not specified beforehand. The process is based on participation by the stakeholders and driven by the nature of the actual problem or task at hand. The field construct emerging through a domain orientation is multidimensional and multilevel, bringing in a wide set of stakeholders from different sectors and levels and recognizing and developing their roles in the regional field.

This is further augmented through the concept of referent organizations, which may be thought of as organizations at the domain level that undertake certain functions on behalf of their domain. There are different types of referent organizations, and there can be more than one in the same domain.

This is the case in Aust-Agder, where several organizations take on referent functions in the domain of industrial development. Examples are the forums for joint strategy development, the boards of the five largest enterprise networks, and the Agency for Industrial Development. Successful or not, all of these groups take on functions on behalf of their organizations. These include activities such as policy making and policy influencing in the larger system, attracting financial and professional resources to the domain, initiating projects, supporting cluster and network formation, and providing information distribution and the exchange of experiences among the stakeholders. Through these activities, the referent organizations assist in reducing fragmentation in the domain and generate collaborative efforts among the stakeholders. The functioning and mutual coordination of the referent organizations in Aust-Agder may not be optimal, but it illustrates that through a socioecological perspective, interorganizational dimensions or characteristics are catalyzed to provide a framework for doing action research in such fields.

If we look at the strategy followed in the communicative perspective, the element that corresponds to the referent organization is the regional strategy forum, which links the development projects, the clusters, and the networks to a wider set of regional stakeholders and develops strategies on a higher level. In socioecological terms, the strategy forum performs some of the functions of a referent organization, but whereas the regional strategy forum is prescribed in the communicative approach, referent organizations emerge in the socioecological perspective. Their actual design, how many there are, and who participates in them emerge out of the actual field situation.

Networks

The socioecological perspective arrives at the concept of the network by identifying the interorganizational level as the critical one for handling complex problem areas. The functions of networks are therefore broadly understood as being the development of a common ground and the coordination of resources. A broader concept of network is therefore relevant. The development of a community or a region, for example, often requires participation by a wide set of actors: business, labor, education, research, consulting, public agencies, politicians, and other groups and organizations.

Networks are often cross-sectoral, and the handling of shared problems or actions will typically be a core task in network collaboration. Implicit is the idea that a variety of purposes and hence participants and designs are relevant. Networks may therefore be established to handle such matters as the exchange of experiences, information sharing, policy making, collaborative problem solving, or more business-related issues — as well as combinations of these concerns. The Jamestown project in New York (Trist 1986) and more recently the Baldwin project in Harrisburg, Pennsylvania (Chisholm 1993), are examples of programs in which the concept of networks was grounded in the socioecological perspective.

From the communicative perspective, the exclusive purpose of networks is to enable program participants to exchange experiences; that is, they perform as learning networks. Networks are viewed primarily as support structures for intraorganizational development projects, and the need to achieve greater scope in organizational change is the primary motivator for establishing them. The network in the Karlstad case in the LOM program is an example of a network that was formed based on the communicative perspective. It has been evaluated according to the quality of the relationship between the enterprise development projects and the (researcher) network (Engelstad and Gustavsen 1993). "Good quality" requires that there be at least two persons on each side: two from the enterprise, two from the researcher network.

In the data for this case, there is a strong correlation between the quality of the project-to-network relationships and the combined outcome measures in each development project. The conclusion put forward is that these data directly support the notion of network building as a viable means for promoting locally managed development processes (Engelstad and Gustavsen 1993: 242). Although I share this view of the potential of networks, another reasonable interpretation of the same data would be that stronger relationships between the researchers and the people in the projects led to better results in the change projects. This would hardly be surprising.

Experience from working for two years on a regionally-oriented project using the communicative perspective to try to establish networks between enterprises engaged in change efforts showed the difficulties and often insufficiencies of building networks based solely on the exchange of experience (see Gustavsen 1993). The clusters established around common development tasks, such as the development of middle management and quality assurance, ended up having only rudimentary contact after the researchers withdrew. Where a cluster has continued to develop on its own, it is because the enterprises very soon were not just exchanging experience but tackling such business matters as marketing, sales, purchasing, and production. Similar findings are reported in the evaluation of the LOM program. Only 27 percent of the clusters had postproject contacts. "The conclusion is that it is hard to establish networks based on organizational development experience between organizations" (Naschold 1993: 69).

These comments do not imply a rejection of the importance of exchanging experiences and developing communicative structures. Rather, it means that the network construct, as used in my example, had some clear shortcomings and must be further developed — probably along the lines indicated above, in which the exchange of experience becomes just one of the purposes of a network relationship. The same conclusion is drawn by Jon Hanssen-Bauer and Svein Ole Borgen (1991), building on their background in the SBA program. They argue that the most well-functioning networks contain both a learning and a business element, whether they start as learning or business networks.

As illustrated above, in an action research project, the different purposes and rationales behind the network constructs lead to the development of different networks with different participants. The socioecological perspective maintains a wider concept of network, in which the participants, the concrete purpose(s), and the design of the specific network have to emerge out of the field situation. This allows for a variety of network constructs to develop, including — but not limited to — networks for the exchange of experiences. Having the exchange of experiences as the primary purpose for establishing network relations, as in the communicative perspective, is a much narrower approach, limiting the participants in the network to representatives of enterprises and researchers directly involved in the AR project.

Regional Dimension

The concept of region, or rather the use of the term "region," since it is not explicitly developed as a concept in either perspective, reflects how the field as a whole is perceived. Furthermore, the regional dimension represents the relevant overall field of inquiry and thus partly mirrors the diffusion strategies in the two perspectives.

Being an open systems approach, social ecology tries to take into consideration the complex set of interrelations that exist between organizations (public and private) and between sectors and levels. Some examples of activities aimed at building domains and designing relevant referent organizations within a regional setting are collaboration between work life and educational institutions; the structuring of the competence system; the development of business and learning networks; and the initiation of strategic processes involving a wide set of participants. The scope of the interorganizational domains will typically extend beyond the scope of the regional dimension referred to here. This broader approach reflects the importance of the contextual environment in socioecological thinking (Trist 1976).

In Norway, "region" often refers to one or a few counties or, in some cases, to parts of several counties. The county plays an important role in regional industrial development in the Norwegian context, where the public support system is organized according to the county and municipal structure, with the county representing the economic, political, and administrative level between the state and the municipality. As a result of the Free-County Experiment, in which the handling of national funds is delegated to the county level, the county level in Aust-Agder has increased its importance in industrial development. Nevertheless, the concept of regions in matters of industrial development is not limited to the county as such. Even if the county is a central entity in regional thinking and an important level for industrial development, other forces — such as markets, competence structures, and industrial structures — will emphasize the need for regional thinking and solutions that exceed county borders.

From the communicative perspective, the relevant regional field is made up of the enterprises and the directly relevant support structure of researchers and institutions. As such, it represents an organizational set or transactional environ-ment for the enterprises in matters of organizational change. Links to the national level, as in the LOM program, are strong, but mainly they form part of the researcher network and program structure. In other words, from the socioecologi-cal perspective, the development of a wider regional field is important. The communicative perspective does not emphasize the contextual environment to the same extent.

Role of the Researcher

A paradox in the communicative perspective, related to the problem of experi-ence-based networks, is the role of the researcher in the networks. Ideally, the researchers design arenas in which democratic dialogue can take place. They do not interfere with content and strongly emphasize that the enterprises have responsibility for progress.

Experience from working with this approach shows that, on the contrary, the networks come to rely heavily on the researchers. The researchers, to a large extent, become the link in the networks. They represent the connections to the other enterprises. In some cases the network contains single enterprises linked to a network of researchers and not to each other, as in the Karlstad example, in which six out of fourteen were single-organization projects and eight were cluster projects (Engelstad and Gustavsen 1993: 239). As pointed to in the LOM evalua-tion cited above, when the researchers left, most of the clusters ceased to function as clusters (Naschold 1993). It appears, therefore, that the ideal of self-sustaining enterprise networks is hard to create, and strategies for making the researchers become superfluous need to be given more attention.

Experience from working in a loosely coupled, complex field, such as Aust-Agder, indicates that if an action researcher does not know the field in which he or she is operating — the actors, the politics of the system, and the problems and issues at stake — the researcher will be unable to intervene in a fruitful manner. Field knowledge and sensitivity are demanded concerning such issues as when and where to arrange conferences, workshops, and meetings; which topics to bring to the table; whom to try to involve as participants; and generally what initiatives to take.

Creating good processes for change presupposes knowledge of the field and of the change (*i.e.*, the content or design element). Thus, the design of the change processes cannot be detached from the processes; the design and the process elements are intertwined. These requirements necessitate that the researcher be clearly involved with the field, as argued for in the socioecological perspective.

In the communicative perspective, the role of the researcher is more distant (Pålshaugen 1991); he or she focuses almost exclusively on the reorganization of discourses and processes and therefore does not "need" a closer involvement with the field. The content of change efforts is left to the participants in the field, while the researcher focuses on developing good communication or good processes. In this case, the researcher's role evolves based mainly on his or her work with single organizations. Working with these single organizations, it may be easier to rely on previous experience as the background for initiating processes aimed at change.

Some experienced action researchers will say that they tend to know the nature of the work in the enterprises, the organizational and power structures, the roles, the typical problems, the prevailing productivity concepts (just-in-time, TQM), and so on. Still, it seems that as we move to the interorganizational level, the more distant role for the researcher is inadequate for doing action research.

Conclusions

Having compared the concepts and strategies around the issue of the field construction for interorganizational development does not mean that I have made a global comparison of the two perspectives. Such a comparison would encounter major problems because the two perspectives have different theoretical points of departure and different epistemological foundations. The intent here was to compare the extent to which these two perspectives represent a framework for doing action research on regional industrial development, with particular emphasis on their ability to grasp the complexity of such a field.

The comparisons of the different concepts show that the socioecological perspective appears to be conceptually stronger for work at the interorganizational level and provides a more comprehensive field construct than does the communicative perspective. The complex set of network relations in the Aust-Agder field, in which a number of public agencies, competence environments, and enterprises engaged in the development of joint strategies, programs, and projects, clearly indicates the need for an approach to networks and regional industrial development that is able to reflect and relate to a wide set of interrelated actors involved in collaborative change processes on different levels.

At its current stage of development, the communicative perspective falls short of accounting for this complexity. The communicative perspective has its strengths at the intraorganizational level and is not as well developed on the interorganizational level. This conclusion is supported by Frieder Naschold's evaluation of the LOM program: "The overall conclusion must be that the interorganizational development level is — in both quantitative and qualitative terms--considerably below that of intra-organizational development" (1993: 69). One must add that the communicative perspective originally focused on methods and strategies for intraorganizational development. As action research addresses issues at the interorganizational level and as the communicative approach is used to address industrial development more generally, a more complex approach will have to be developed to better reflect the stakeholders, structures, and dynamics of a regional field.

Thus, however incomplete it may be, the socioecological field construct created by the concepts of domain, referent organizations, and networks seems more able to capture the complexity of the field and function as an action research perspective for industrial development. In that the communicative perspective is central in Scandinavian action research — being the basis for "Enterprise Development 2000," a national research program on enterprise development in Norway (see Gustavsen and Mikkelsen 1993), it seems highly relevant to point to the good qualities of the socioecological perspective, qualities that suggest a direction for further development of the communicative perspective and that offer a powerful approach in their own right.

Acknowledgments

This essay was written during my participation in the ACRES program, during which Davydd Greenwood, in particular, gave me valuable comments on an early version. Øyvind Pålshaugen and Per Engelstad have commented constructively on my presentation of the communicative perspective. Thoralf Ulrik Qvale and Hans van Beinum have also given me very helpful comments, and I am indebted to Oguz Babüroglu for his thorough and constructive comments toward the end.

Notes

1. I am classifying the action research variants quite differently from van Eijnatten (1993), who overlooks this line of development completely, however present it is in the literature to which he is referring. In addition, he places examples of socioecological research programs both in the participative design category (Norwegian shipping industry program, page 55), under the democratic dialogue heading (SBA, page 69), and as part of "modern STSD in North America" (Trist's Jamestown project, page 78).

2. The LOM program, which lasted from 1985 to 1990, encompassed about 150 organizations, public and private, and close to 60 researchers. Gustavsen was the main architect behind the program (Naschold 1993).

3. The communicative perspective has its historical, though not its conceptual, roots in socio-technical thinking and in Scandinavian work life traditions. In spite of the rather weak conceptual links to sociotechnical systems design, van Eijnatten (1993) chooses to classify this perspective, or democratic dialogue as he calls it, as a variant of the sociotechnical systems design paradigm.

4. STBA was a five-year program (1988-93) initiated and financed jointly by the Norwegian government and all the main labor market organizations. The purpose of the program was to promote productivity in private and public enterprises through the application of participative methods for change.

References

Abercrombie, N., et al. 1988. *Dictionary of sociology.* London: Penguin Books.

Acker, J. 1988. Class, gender and the relations of distribution. *Signs* 13: 473-97.

Addams, J. 1910. *Twenty years at Hull-House.* New York: Macmillan.

Addams, J. 1930. T*he second twenty years at Hull-House: September 1909 to September 1929, with a record of a growing world consciousness.* New York: Macmillan.

Alpert, D. 1985. Performance and paralysis: The organizational context of the American research university. *Journal of Higher Education* 56(3): 243–81.

AMFO (Swedish Work Environment Fund). 1991. Activity plan for 1991 (in Swedish). Stockholm.

Appalachian Alliance Task Force. 1983. *Who owns Appalachia?* Lexington: University Press of Kentucky.

Arbetsorganisation och produktivitet, Expertrapport nr 5 till Produktivitetsdelegationen, 1991. Stockholm: Allmänna förlaget

Argyris, C., R. Putnam, and D. M. Smith. 1987. *Action science: Contents, methods and skills for research and intervention.* San Francisco: Jossey-Bass.

Ås, Berit; *Kvinner i alle land. Håndbok i frigøring,* Oslo: Aschehoug, 1981

Aubert, V. 1985. *The hidden society* (in Norwegian). Oslo: University Press.

Axelsson, B., and G. Easton. 1992. *Industrial networks: A new view of reality.* London: Routledge.

Babüroglu, O. N. 1992. Tracking the development of the Emery-Trist systems paradigm. *Systems Practice* 5(3): 263-90.

Barth, F. 1981. *Process and form in social life.* London: Routledge.

Bartunek, J. and M. Moch. 1987. First-order, second-order, and third-order change and organizational development interventions: A cognitive approach. *Journal of Applied Behavioral Science* 23(4): 483-500.

Bauman, Z. 1991. *Modernity and ambivalence.* Cambridge: Polity Press.

Bauman, Z. 1993. *Postmodern ethics.* Oxford: Blackwell.

Beinum, H. van. 1990a. *Observations on the development of a new organizational paradigm.* Paper presented at the Seminar on "Industrial Democracy in Western Europe," Cologne.

Beinum, H. van. 1990b. *Observations on the development of a new industrial paradigm.* Stockholm: Arbetslivscentrum.

Beinum, H. van. 1993. The kaleidoscope of workplace reform. In *Constructing the new industrial society,* edited by F. Naschold, B. Gustavsen, and H. van Beinum. Assen/ Maastricht: van Gorcum.

Beinum, H. van. 1996. Om aktionsforskningens udvikling I Europa, et perspektiv (On the development of action research in Europe – a perspective) in Aktionsforskning, Kurt Aagard Nielsen and Peter Vogelius eds. Copenhagen: Arbejdsmiljöfondet.

Beinum, H. van. 1997. Zur Praxis der Arbeitsforschung in "Aktionsforschung und industrielle Demokratie", ed. Werner Fricke. Bonn: Fried-Ebert Stiftung.

Beinum, H. van. forthcoming. *Ideas and practices of action research and institutional journey,* Amsterdam/Philadelphia: John Benjamins Publishing Company.

Beinum, H. van, C. Faucheux, and R. van der Vlist. 1996. Reflections on the epigenetic significance of action research. In *Beyond theory,* edited by S. Toulmin and B. Gustavsen. Amsterdam: John Benjamins.

Beinum, H. van, and Pålshaugen, Ø. 1996. Introducing 'concepts and transformation': Editorial. In *Concepts and transformation* 1. Amsterdam: John Benjamins.

Bender, T. 1987. *New York intellectual: A history of intellectual life in New York City from 1750 to the beginnings of our time.* Baltimore: Johns Hopkins University Press.

Bender, T. 1993. *Intellect and public life: Essays on the social history of academic intellectuals in the United States.* Baltimore: Johns Hopkins University Press.

Benson, L., and I. Harkavy. 1991. Progressing beyond the welfare state. *Universities and Community Schools* 2(1/2): 228.

Berger, B., and H. Kellner. 1981. *Sociology reinterpreted* (in Danish). Aalborg, Denmark: Linhardt and Ringhof.

Berger, P. and T. Luckmann. 1983. *The social construction of reality: A treatise in the sociology of knowledge* (in Danish). Aalborg, Denmark: Linhardt and Ringhof.

Bergman, S. J. 1993. Mutuality in relationships: A challenge for today's men (in Swedish). *Women's Science Journal* 1.

Berk, R. A. 1988. How applied sociology can save basic sociology. In *The future of sociology*, edited by E. F. Borgatta and K. S. Cook. Newbury Park, Calif.: Sage.

Bernstein, H. J. 1987. Idols of modern science and the reconstruction of knowledge. In *New ways of knowing: The sciences, society, and reconstructive knowledge*, edited by M. G. Raskin and H. J. Bernstein. Totowa, N.J.: Rowman and Littlefield.

Boglind, A., *et al.* 1981. Unions in company crisis (in Swedish). Department of Sociology, Gothenburg University. Unpublished research report.

Bok, D. 1982. *Beyond the ivory tower: Social responsibilities of the modern university.* Cambridge: Harvard University Press.

Bok, D. 1990. *Universities and the future of America.* Durham, N.C.: Duke University Press.

Booth, C. 1891. *Life and labour of the people in London*, vol. 2. London: Williams and Northgate.

Bortoft, H. 1986. *Goethe's scientific consciousness.* Institute for Cultural Research 2. London: Octagon Press.

Box, I. 1989. *The social thought of Francis Bacon.* Lewiston, Me.: Mellon.

Boyer, E. L., and F. M. Hechinger. 1981. *Higher learning in the nation's service.* Washington, D.C.: Carnegie Foundation for the Advancement of Teaching.

Bråthen, S. 1973. Model monopoly and communication systems: Theoretical notes on democratization. *Acta Sociologica* 16(2): 98-107.

Bridger, H. 1990. The discovery of the therapeutic community. In *The social engagement of social science,* vol. 1, *A Tavistock anthology,* edited by E. Trist and H. Murray. Philadelphia: University of Pennsylvania Press.

Brokhaug, I. K. 1985. Development work in local communities (in Norwegian). *Sociology Today* 2.

Brown, D., and Tandon, R. 1983. Ideology and political economy in inquiry: Action research and participatory research. *Journal of Applied and Behavioral Sciences* 19(3): 277-94.

Brox, O. 1966. *What happens to north Norway?* (in Norwegian). Oslo: Pax.

Brox, O. 1990. *Practical social science* (in Norwegian). Oslo: University Press.

Brox, O. 1992. Acquisition of real property and buy-outs of firms: The concession laws (in Norwegian). In *The EEA agreement and the consequences for Norway.* Oslo: Nei til EU.

Brundtland, G. H. 1989. The Scandinavian challenge: Strategies for work and learning. In *International handbook of participation in organizations,* vol. 1, *Organizational democracy: Taking stock,* edited by C. J. Lammers, and G. Széll. New York: Oxford University Press.

Bulmer, M. 1984. *The Chicago school of sociology: Institutionalization, diversity, and the rise of sociological research.* Chicago: University of Chicago Press.

Bulmer, M., and J. Bulmer. 1981. Philanthropy and social science in the 1920s: Beardsley Ruml and the Laura Spelman Rockefeller memorial, 1922–29. *Minerva* 19: 347–407.

Burrell, G., and G. Morgan. 1979. *Sociological paradigm and organizational analysis.* London: Heineman.

Center for Educational Research and Innovation. 1982. *The university and the community: The problems of changing relationships.* Paris: OECD.

CAU Annual Reports and Activity Plans. 1986-1993. Halmstad: Halmstad University.

Chien, I., S. W. Cook, and J. Harding. 1948. The field of action research. *American Psychologist* 3(2): 43–50.

Chisholm, R. F. 1993. The new Baldwin corridor coalition: A vision based effort to develop a twenty-first century industrial community. Paper presented at conference of the Academy of Management, Atlanta, Georgia.

Chisholm, R. F., and M. Elden. 1993. Features of emerging action research. *Human Relations* 46(2): 275-98.

Chisholm, R. F., and M. Elden, eds. 1993. International Dimensions of Action Research: A Source of New Thinking about Inquiry that Makes a Difference, *Human Relations*, special issue, 46(2): 275-98.

Chodorow, N. 1978. *The Reproduction of Mothering.* Berkeley: University of California Press.

Chubb, J. E., and T. Moe. 1990. *Politics, markets, and America's schools.* Washington, D.C.: Brookings Institution.

Churchman, C. W. 1979. *The systems approach and its enemies.* New York: Basic Books.

Clapp, E. 1939. *Community schools in action.* New York: Viking.

Clegg, S. 1990. *Modern Organizations - Organization Studies in the Postmodern World.* London: Sage Publications.

Cohen, A., D. Greenwood, and I. Harkavy. 1992. Report of the proceedings of the conference on social research for social change: Varieties of participatory action research. *Collaborative Inquiry* 7.

Cohen, S. P. 1991. The Pittsburgh survey and the social survey movement: A sociological road not taken. In *Social survey in historical perspective*, edited M. Bulmer, K. Bales, and K. K. Sklar. New York: Cambridge University Press.

Cole, R, H. and H. van Beinum. 1993. *Constructing the new industrial society.* Assen: van Gorcum.

Cole, R., P. Bacdayan, and J. White. 1993. Quality, participation, and competitiveness. *California Management Review* 35: 68-81.

Coleman, J. S., *et al.* 1966. *Equality of educational opportunity.* Washington, D.C.: U.S. Government Printing Office.

Coles, R. 1989. *The call of stories.* Boston: Houghton Mifflin.

Cox, M. W. 1990. Rethinking the American school. *Chalkboard* 38(2): 10-12.

Critchley, S. 1992. The Ethics of Deconstruction: Derrida & Levinas. Oxford: Blackwell Publishers.

Czarniawska-Joerges, B. 1993. *The three-dimensional organization.* Lund: Chartwell Bratt.

Dahlgren, L. 1993. The researcher as participant (in Swedish). In *Participant-oriented research*, edited by J. Holmer and B. Starrin. Lund: Studentlitteratur.

Davies, A., et al. 1993. *Evaluation report — commissioned by the board of the SBA program*, Vol. 1, *Executive summary and main report.* Oslo: Norwegian Worklife Center.

Davis, C. 1996. Lévinas – An Introduction. Cambridge: Polity Press.

Davis, L. E. and J. Taylor. 1972. Design of Jobs. Harmondsworth: Penguin.

Deegan, M. J. 1988. *Jane Addams and the men of the Chicago school, 1892–1918.* New Brunswick, N.J.: Transaction Press.

Deetz, S., and A. Kersten. 1983. Critical models of interpretive research. In *Communication and organizations,* edited by L. Putnam and M. Pacanowsky. Newbury Park, Calif.: Sage.

Dewey, J. 1902. The school as social center. *National Education Association Journal of Proceedings and Addresses* 41: 373-83.

Dewey, J. 1910. *How we think*. New York: Heath.

Drejhammar, I. and Rehnström, Kerstin. 1990. *Arbetsledning i dialog om jämställdhet,* in Eriksson, K., ed. *Självständighet och delaktighet - nyckelord för ledare,* Stockholm: Arbetsmiljöfonden.

Ebeltoft, A. 1991. *Dialogkonferanser.* Report 1/91. Oslo: Work Research Institute.

Eduards, M. 1992. *Den feministiska utmaningen - Kvinnors kollektiva handlande,* in G. Åström & Hirdman, eds. *Kontrakt i kris. Om kvinnors plats i välfärdsstaten.* Stockholm.

Ehrenreich, J. 1985. *The altruistic imagination: A history of social work and social polity in the United States.* Ithaca, N.Y.: Cornell University Press.

Eijnatten, F. M. van. 1993. *The paradigm that changed the workplace.* Assen/Maastricht: van Gorcum.

Eikeland, O. 1990. *Experience, dialogics, and politics* (in Norwegian). Oslo: Work Research Institute.

Einarsson, J. 1984. *Särart i samspråk - Om kvinnlig och manlig samtalsstil,* Språk och kön i skolan 9, Lund: Lunds universitet.

Einarsson, J. 1993. Lecture at Halmstad University, May.

Einarsson, J., and T. G. Hultman. 1984. *Good morning, boys and girls* (in Swedish). Malmo: Gleerups.

Elden, M. 1979. Three generations of work-democracy experiments in Norway. In *The quality of working life in Western Europe,* edited by G. Cooper and E. Mumford. London: Associated Business Press.

Elden, M. 1983. Democratization at work. *Journal of Occupational Behavior* 4: 21-34.

Elden, M., and R. F. Chisholm. 1993. Emerging varieties of action research: Introduction to the special issue. *Human Relations* 46(2): 121-42.

Elden, M., and M. Levin. 1991. Cogenerative learning: Bringing participation into action research. In *Participatory action research,* edited by W. F. Whyte. Newbury Park, Calif.: Sage.

Elster, J. 1989. *Nuts and bolts for the social sciences.* Cambridge: Cambridge University Press.

Emery, F. E. 1959. *Characteristics of socio-technical systems.* London: Tavistock Publications.

Emery, F. E. 1977. *Futures we are in.* Leiden: Martinus Nijhoff.

Emery, F. E. 1986. The next generation of issues that confront out human futures. *Quality of Work Life* 3(1-2): 95-104.

Emery, F. and M. 1974. *Participative Design: Work and Community Life,* Canberra: Australian National University.

Emery, F. E., and E. Thorsrud. 1976. *Democracy at work: The report of the Norwegian Industrial Democracy Program.* Leiden: Martinus Nijhoff.

Emery, F. E., and E. Trist. 1965. The causal texture of organizational environments. *Human Relations* 18: 21-32.

Emery, F. E., and E. Trist. 1972. *Towards a social ecology.* London: Plenum Press.

Emery, M. 1982. *Searching.* Canberra: Australian National University, Centre for Continuing Education.

Emery, M. 1989a. *Participative design for participative democracy.* Canberra: Australian Naional University, Centre for Continuing Education.

Emery, M. 1989b. *A Training Workshop on the Theory and Practice of Search Conferences,* in Emery, F. and M. 1989. Participative Design for Participative Democracy. Canberra: Australian National University.

Engelstad, P. H. 1993. The dialogue conference: A method for research-supported enterprise development (in Swedish). In *Participant-oriented research,* edited by J. Holmer and B. Starrin. Lund: Studentlitteratur.

Engelstad, P. H. 1996. The development organization as communicative instrumentation: Experiences from the Karlstad program. In *Beyond theory,* edited by S. Toulmin and B. Gustavsen. Amsterdam: John Benjamins.

Engelstad, P. H., and B. Gustavsen. 1993. Swedish network development for implementing national work reform strategy. *Human Relations* 46(2): 219-48.

Engelstad, P. H., and L. A. Ödegaard. 1979. Participative redesign in Norway. In *Working with the quality of working life.* Leiden: Martinus Nijhoff.

Eriksson, K., and S. J. Holmer. 1982. Universities and unions: A survey of academic training courses for blue-collar union representatives. Department of Sociology, Gothenburg University. Research report.

Eriksson, K and J. Holmer, 1991. *Studiecirklar som stöd för förändring av arbetslivet,* Göteborgs Universitet and Centre for Worklife Development, Halmstad University.

Eriksson, K., and S. J. Holmer. 1992. Study circles as a support for changes in working life. Halmstad University/Karlstad University. Research report.

Eriksson, K., et al. 1993. Product development and conducive work in creatively coordinated production. Center for Working Life Development, Halmstad University. Research report.

Erlandson, D. A., et al. 1993. *Doing naturalistic inquiry: A guide to methods.* Newbury Park, Calif.: Sage.

Everett, S., ed. 1938. *The community school.* New York: Appleton- Century.

Fals Borda, O. 1987. The application of participatory action research in Latin America. *International Sociology* 2(4): 329-47.

Fals Borda, O., and Rahman, M. A. 1992. *Action and knowledge.* New York: Apex Press.

Faucheux, C. 1994. Wozu Brauchen Wir Aktionsforschung? (in German). In *Arbeit und Technik,* edited by W. Fricke. Bonn: Friedrich Ebert Stiftung.

Ferguson, K. 1984. *The feminist case against bureaucracy.* Philadelphia: Temple University Press.

Fernandez, J. 1993. *Tales out of school: Joseph Fernandez's crusade to rescue American education.* Boston: Little, Brown.

Fine, M. 1992. *Framing dropouts: Notes on the politics of an urban public school.* Albany: State University of New York Press.

Finsrud, H., *et al.* 1993. *Competence milieus for industrial development in Aust-Agder* (in Norwegian). Report 5/93. Oslo: Work Research Institute.

Fitzpatrick, E. 1990. *Endless crusade: Women social scientists and progressive reform.* New York: Oxford University Press.

Fivelsdal, E. 1971. On Max Weber's sociology: An introduction (in Norwegian). In *Power and bureaucracy,* edited by M. Weber. Oslo: Gyldendal.

Freire, P. 1970. *The pedagogy of the oppressed.* New York: Herder and Herder.

Fricke, W. 1983. Participatory research and the enhancement of workers' innovative qualifications. *Journal of Occupational Behaviour* 4: 73-87.

Friis, S. 1991. Dependencies in researcher on user controlled information systems development. In *Human jobs and computer interfaces,* edited by M. I. Nurminen and G.R.S. Weir. Amsterdam: North-Holland.

Friis, S. 1994. The PROTEUS approach: A short presentation of background, principles, and methods. In *AI and society.* Berlin: Springer Verlag.

Fullan, M. G., with S. Stiegelbauer. 1991. *The new meaning of educational change.* New York: Teachers College Press.

Gardell, B. 1980. Psychosocial aspects of industrial production methods. In *Society, stress, and disease* 4, edited by L. Levi. London: Oxford University Press.

Garfinkel, H. 1967. *Ethnomethodology.* Englewood, N.J.: Prentice Hall.

Gaventa, J. 1980. *Power and powerlessness: Quiescence and rebellion in an Appalachian valley.* Urbana: University of Illinois Press.

Giddens, A. 1990. *The consequences of modernity.* Cambridge: Polity Press.

Gilligan, C. 1982. *In a different voice.* Cambridge: Harvard University Press.

Gilligan, C., *et al.* 1988. *Mapping the moral domain.* Cambridge: Harvard University Press.

Gilman, D. C. 1898/1969. *University problems in the United States.* New York: Garret.

Glaser, B. G., and A. L. Strauss. 1967. *The discovery of grounded theory: Strategies for qualitative research.* Chicago: Aldine.

Gordon, L. 1992. Social insurance and public assistance: The influence of gender in welfare thought in the United States, 1890–1935. *American Historical Review* 97: 19-54.

Gray, B. 1985. Conditions facilitating inter-organizational collaboration. *Human Relations* 38(10): 911-36.

Greenberg, J., and S. Mitchell. 1983. *Object relations in psychoanalytic theory.* Cambridge: Harvard University Press.

Greenwood, D. J. 1989. Paradigm-centered and client-centered research: A proposal for linkage. *Proceedings of the Forty-Second Annual Meeting of the Industrial Relations Research Association.*

Greenwood, D. J., and J. L. González, *et al.* 1992. *Industrial democracy as process: Participatory action research in the Fagor cooperative group of Mondragón.* Assen/Maastricht: van Gorcum.

Greenwood, D. J., W. F. Whyte, and I. Harkavy. 1993. Participatory action research as a process and as a goal. *Human Relations* 46(2): 175-92.

Gruber, H. E. 1989. Creativity and human survival. In *Creative people at work,* edited by D. B. Wallace and H. E. Gruber. New York: Oxford University Press.

Guba, E. G. 1978. *Towards a methodology of naturalistic inquiry in educational evaluation.* Monograph 8. Los Angeles: UCLA Center for the Study of Evaluation.

Guba, E. G., and Y. S. Lincoln. 1989. *Fourth generation evaluation.* Newbury Park, Calif.: Sage.

Gunnarsson, E. 1989. *Kvinnors Arbetsrationalitet och Kvalifikationer,* arbetsrapport nr 6 in Qvist-projektet, Stockholm: Arbetslivscentrum.

Gustavsen, B. 1983. The Norwegian work environment reform: The transition from general principles to work-place action. In *Organizational democracy and political processes,* edited by H. Crouch and F. Heller. Chichester: Wiley.

Gustavsen, B. 1985. Workplace reform and democratic dialogue. *Economic and Industrial Democracy* 6(4): 461-79.

Gustavsen, B. 1990. *Toward better working life: Strategies and methods in local development work* (in Swedish). Stockholm: Swedish Center for Working Life.

Gustavsen, B. 1992. *Dialogue and development: Theory of communication.* Assen/Maastricht: van Gorcum.

Gustavsen, B. 1993. Creating productive structures: The role of research and development. In *Constructing the new industrial society,* edited by F. Naschold et al. Assen/Maastricht: van Gorcum.

Gustavsen, B. 1996. Development and the social sciences: An uneasy relationship. In *Beyond theory,* edited by S. Toulmin and B. Gustavsen. Amsterdam: John Benjamins.

Gustavsen, B. and P. Engelstad. 1986. The Design of Conferences and the Evolving Role of Democratic Dialogue in Changing Working Life. *Human Relations,* Vol. 39, No. 2: 101-116.

Gustavsen, B., and G. Hunnius. 1981. *New patterns of work reform: The case of Norway.* Oslo: University Press.

Gustavsen, B., and L. N. Mikkelsen. 1993. Enterprise Development 2000: Conceptually managed productivity development and organizational renewal in working life (in Norwegian). Program proposal. Work Research Institute/Research Council of Norway.

Gustavsen, B., and A. Sandberg, eds. 1984. *Work life change programs: National experiences of research support* (in Swedish). Stockholm: Swedish Center for Working Life.

Haavind, H. 1992. We must search for the changed meaning of gender (in Swedish). *Women's Science Journal* 3.

Hackney, S. 1986. The university and its community: Past and present. *Annals of the American Academy of Political and Social Science* 488: 135–47.

Hackney, S. 1992. Universities and the schools: Hanging together or hanging separately? Address at Bank Street College, New York, May 2.

Hall, B. 1978. *Creating knowledge: Breaking the monopoly — research methods, participation, and development.* Toronto: Council for Adult Education.

Hannesson, R. 1991. *Socially beneficial fishing* (in Norwegian). Working paper no. 21. Bergen: Center for Research in Economics and Business Administration.

Hanssen-Bauer, J. 1991. Design or dialogue? A case to illustrate a multilevel strategy for work life development within a socioecological framework in Norway. Paper presented at International Work Conference, Action Research and the Future of Work, Leeuwenhorst, Netherlands.

Hanssen-Bauer, J., and S. O. Borgen. 1991. Network for learning, transformation, and productivity (in Norwegian). *Bedre Bedrift* 3: 24-33.

Hanssen-Bauer, J., and C. M. Snow. 1994. Responding to hypercompetition: The structure and processes of a regional learning network organization. In *Organization Science* 7(4): 413-27.

Hansson, A. 1994. *Arbetsplatsprogram vid Textilservice - N, Landstinge Hallands Tvätteri, 1991-1994,* Rapport 6, Halmstad University: Centre for Workinglife Research and Development

Harkavy, I. 1992. The university and the social sciences in the social order: An historical overview and 'where do we go from here?' *Virginia Social Science Journal* 27: 225.

Harkavy, I., and J. L. Puckett. 1991. The role of mediating structures in university and community revitalization: The university of Pennsylvania and West Philadelphia as a case study. *Journal of Research and Development in Education* 27: 225.

Harkavy, I., and J. L. Puckett. 1994. Lessons from Hull House for the contemporary urban university. *Social Service Review* 68 (3): 299–321.

Harrow, A., and D. Raffaelli. 1995. Self-action research: An institution reviews itself. Scottish Institute for Human Relations, Edinburgh. Unpublished manuscript.

Hayrynen, Y., and J. Hautamaki. 1976. *Manniskans bildbarhet och utbildningspolitiken* (in Swedish). Stockholm: Wahlstrom & Widstrand.

Heider, F. 1946. Attitudes and cognitive organizations. *Journal of Psychology* 21: 107-12.

Hellevik, O. 1982. *The sociological method* (in Norwegian). Oslo: University Press.

Henry, N. B., ed. 1953. *The fifty-second yearbook of the National Society of the Study of Education.* Pt. 2. Chicago: University of Chicago Press.

Herbst, P. G. 1971. Maps of knowledge and the design of educational organizations. In *Sociotechnical design.* London: Tavistock Publications.

Herbst, P. G., ed. 1971. *The process of democratization in working life.* Oslo: Universitetsforlaget.

Hirdman, Y. 1988. *Genussystemet reflexioner kring kvinnors sociala underordning,* in *Kvinnovetenskaplig tidskrift*: 3.

Höglund, S. 1991. The democratization of work organizations: Possibilities and problems (in Swedish). In *The conditions for work,* edited by I. B. Furuåker. Lund: Studentlitteratur.

Holmberg, C.. 1993. *Det kallas Kärlek,* Gothenberg: Anamma facklitteratur.

Holmer, J. 1993. Participant-oriented research and learning with research support (in Swedish). In *Participant-oriented research,* edited by J. Holmer and B. Starrin. Lund: Studentlitteratur.

Horney, K. 1937. *The neurotic personality of our time.* London: Routledge.

Horton, M., and P. Freire. 1990. *We make the road by walking.* Philadelphia: Temple University Press.

Jencks, C. C., and D. Riesman. 1968. *The academic revolution.* New York: Doubleday.

Johansen, R. 1978. Stress and socio-technical design: A new ship organization. In *Stress at work,* edited by C. L. Cooper and R. Payne. Chichester: Wiley.

Johnston, F. E., and R. J. Hallock. 1994. Physical growth, nutritional status, and dietary intake of African-American middle school students from Philadelphia. *American Journal of Human Biology* 6: 741–47.

Jonasdottir, A. 1991. *Love Power and Political Interst. Towards a Theory of Patriarchy in Contemporary Western Societies,* Göteborg Studies in Politics 25.

Josefson, I. 1991. *Kunskapens Former,* Stockholm: Carlsson Bokförlag.

Kalleberg, R. 1989. *The sociologist in society: On Vilhelm Aubert's sociology* (in Norwegian). Sociological yearbook 29. Oslo: Department of Sociology, University of Oslo.

Kalleberg, R. 1992. *Constructive social science* (in Norwegian). ISO report 24. Oslo: Department of Sociology, University of Oslo.

Kalleberg, R. 1993. Konstruktiv samhallsvetenskap (in Swedish). In *Participant-oriented research,* edited by J. Holmer and B. Starrin. Lund: Studentlitteratur.

Kanter, R. M. 1977. *Men and women of the corporation.* New York: Basic Books.

Karasek, R., and T. Theorell. 1990. *Healthy work: Stress, productivity, and the reconstruction of working life.* New York: Basic Books.

Katz, M. B. 1992. Chicago school reform as history. *Teachers College Record* 94(1): 56-72.

Keij, J. 1993. *Simply said: Lévinas* (in Swedish). Kampen: Kok Agora.

Kelly, G. A. 1955. *The psychology of personal constructs.* New York: Norton.

Kelly, G. A. 1970. A brief introduction to personal construct theory. In *Perspectives in personal construct theory,* edited by D. Bannister. San Diego: Academic Press.

Kelly, J. 1982. *Scientific management, job redesign, and work performance.* London: Academic Press.

Kerr, C. 1982. *The uses of the university.* Cambridge: Harvard University Press.

Kirby, S., and K. McKenna. 1989. *Experience, research, social change: Methods from the margins.* Toronto: Garamond Press.

Kirst, M. W. 1990. The crash of the first wave — recent state education reform in the United States: Looking backward and forward. In *Education reform: Making sense of it all,* edited by S. B. Bacharach. Boston: Allyn and Bacon.

Kuhn, T. 1962. *The Structure of Scientific Revolutions,* Chicago.

Kunneman, H. 1997. Een postmoderne hermeneutiek als wetenschapstheoretisch kader voor kwalitatief onderzoek (Postmodern hermeneutics as a scientific-theoretical frame of reference for qualitative research), in A. Smaling and E. Hijmans, eds. *Kwalitatief onderzoem em levensbeschouwing (Qualitative research and philosophy of life).* Amsterdam: Boom Publishing Company.

Kvande, E., and B. Rasmussen. 1991. *Women's new lives: Women in men's organizations* (in Norwegian). Oslo: Ad Notam.

Kvande, E., and B. Rasmussen. 1993. The organization as an arena for different expressions of femininity and masculinity (in Swedish). *Women's Science Journal* 2

Lagemann, E. C. 1989. *The politics of knowledge: The Carnegie Corporation, philanthropy, and public policy.* Middletown, Conn.: Wesleyan University Press.

Lauer, J. M., et al. 1991. *Four worlds of writing.* 3d ed. New York: Harper Collins.

Lazarsfeld, P. F. 1982. An episode in the history of social research: A memoir. In *The varied sociology of Paul F. Lazarsfeld,* edited by P. L. Kendall. New York: Columbia University Press.

Lazarsfeld, P. F., and J. G. Reitz. 1975. *An introduction to applied sociology.* New York: Elsevier.

Ledford, G., and S. Mohrman. 1993. Self-design for high involvement: A large-scale organizational change. *Human Relations* 46(2): 143-73.

Levin, M. 1993. Creating networks for rural economic development in Norway. *Human Relations* 46(2): 193-218.

Lévinas, E. 1991a. Otherwise than Being or Beyond Essence. translated by Alphonso Lingis. Dordrecht: Kluwer Academic Publishers.

Lévinas, E. 1991b. Totality and Infinity, an essay on exteriority. translated by Alphonso Lingis. Martinus Nijhoff: La Haye.

Lévinas, E. 1993. *Etik och Odndlighet: Samtal med Philippe Nemo.* Brutus.

Lewin, K. 1935. *A dynamic theory of personality: Selected papers.* New York: McGraw-Hill.

Lewin, K. 1943. Forces behind food habits and methods of change. *Bulletin of the National Research Council* 108: 35-65.

Lewin, K. 1947. Group decision and social change. In *Readings in social psychology,* 2d ed., edited by T. M. Newcomb and E. L. Hartley. New York: Holt.

Lewin, K. 1948. *Resolving social conflicts.* New York: Harper and Row.

Lewin, K. 1951. *Field theory in the social sciences.* New York: Harper and Row.

Lewin, K. 1969. Quasi-stationary social equilibria and the problem of permanent change. In *The planning of change,* edited by W. G. Bennis, K. D. Benne, and R. Chin. New York: Holt.

Lincoln, Y. S., and E. G. Guba. 1985. *Naturalistic inquiry.* Newbury Park, Calif.: Sage.

Lincoln, Y. S., and E. G. Guba. 1995. Pragmatizing communicative reason. In *Research in action,* edited by S. Toulmin and B. Gustavsen. Assen/Maastricht: van Gorcum.

Ljungberg van Beinum, I. 1991. *Effektiv dialog mellan kvinnor och män,* project description, Halmstad University: Centre for Working Life Research and Development.

Ljungberg van Beinum, I. 1994. *Effektiv dialog mellan män och kvinnor (Effective dialogue between men and women)* final project report, Halmstad University: Centre for Working Life Research and Development.

Maier, N.R.F., ed. 1946/1955. *Psychology in industry.* Boston: Houghton Mifflin.

Marrow, A. 1969. *The practical theorist.* New York: Basic Books.

Meland, H. P., *et al.,* eds. 1993. *North Norway and the coastal communities of the future* (in Norwegian). Oslo: Work Research Institute.

Meløe, J. 1992. Places (in Norwegian). University of Tromsø. Unpublished manuscript.

Metal Union Reports, 1978, 1980. Unpublished report.

Milgram, S. 1974. *Obedience to authority.* New York: Harper and Row.

Moscovici, S. 1968. *La psychoanalyse et son triage* (in French). Paris: PUF.

Munkejord, S. 1985. Policy for Norwegian fish-farming (in Norwegian). *Research and future* 2.

Naschold, F. 1993. Organization development: National programmes in the context of international competition. In *Constructing the new industrial society,* edited by F. Naschold et al. Assen/Maastricht: van Gorcum.

Naschold, F., *et al.* 1993. *Towards organizational renewal.* Assen/Maastricht: van Gorcum.

A new compact for learning. 1991. Albany: New York State Education Department.

Newcomb, T. M. 1953. An approach to the study of communicative acts. *Psychology Review* 60: 393-404.

Novek, E. M. 1993. Buried treasure: The theory and practice of communicative action in an urban high school newspaper. Paper presented to the Association for Education in Journalism and Mass Communication, Kansas City, Mo.

Organization and Leadership for Innovation. 1993. Research on organization and leadership for innovation. Report from a symposium at Halmstad University.

Pålshaugen, Ø. 1991. *As I said I did? Language as a means in action research and organizational development* (in Norwegian). Oslo: Novus.

Pålshaugen, Ø. 1992. Action research: A useful science? (in Norwegian). *Journal of Social Science* 33: 231-51.

Pålshaugen, Ø. 1995. A Norwegian Programme on Action Research for Participative Democracy" in Eikeland, O. and H. Finsrud, eds. Research in Action. *The Work Research Institute's Publication Series*, No. 1: 125-161.

Pålshaugen, Ø. 1996. "This is not the whole story . . ." In *Beyond theory*, edited by S. Toulmin and B. Gustavsen. Assen/Maastricht: van Gorcum.

Pasmore, W. 1988. *Designing effective organizations: The socio-technical systems perspective.* New York: Wiley.

Pasmore, W., and F. Friedlander. 1982. An action-research program for increasing employee involvement in problem-solving. *Administrative Science Quarterly* 27: 343-62.

Phillips, A. 1993. A male disorder. *Guardian*, Nov. 25.

Piore, M., J. S. Sabel, and F. Charles. 1984. *The second industrial divide: Possibilities for prosperity.* New York: Basic Books.

Popper, K. 1963. Conjectures and refutations: The growth of scientific knowledge. London: Routledge.

Porter, M. E. 1990. *The competitive advantage of nations.* London: Macmillan.

Produktivitetsdelegationen. 1991. *Forces for productivity and wealth* (in Swedish). Stockholm: Allmanna Forlaget.

Prokop, U. 1981. *Kvinnors Livssammanhang - Begränsade strategier och omåttliga önskningar,* Stockholm: Raben & Sjögren.

Qvale, T. U. 1989. A new milestone in the development of industrial democracy in Norway. In *International handbook of participation in organizations,* vol. 1, *Organizational democracy: Taking stock,* edited by C. J. Lammers and G. Széll. New York: Oxford University Press.

Qvale, T. U. 1991. Participation for productivity and change: A multilevel, cooperative strategy for improving organizational performance. Paper presented at conference, Workplace Australia, Melbourne.

Qvale, T. U. 1994. From the first to the fifth generation: The changing context and roles of worklife centres. A review of twenty-five years of action research programmes in Norway. Paper presented at meeting of the Academy of Management, Dallas.

Rankin, T. 1989. The development of new forms of work organization in Sweden. Ontario Quality of Working Life Centre, Ontario Ministry of Labour.

Reason, P. 1988. *Human inquiry in action.* London: Sage.

Reason, P., and J. Rowan, eds. 1981. *Human inquiry: A sourcebook of new paradigm research.* Chichester: Wiley.

Residents of Hull House. 1895/1980. *Hull-House maps and papers.* New York: Arno.

Ressner, U. 1987. *The hidden hierarchy: Democracy and equal opportunities.* England: Avebury/Gower House.

Ricoeur, P. 1990. *Soi-meme comme un autre* (in French). Paris: Seuil.

Ross, D. 1984. American social science and the idea of progress. In *The authority of experts,* edited by T. L. Haskell. Bloomington: Indiana University Press.

Ross, D. 1991. *The origins of American social science.* New York: Cambridge University Press.

Sahlins, M. 1972. *Stone Age economics.* Chicago: Aldine.

Sandberg, A., ed. 1981. *Research for change: On methods and conditions for action-oriented research in working life* (in Swedish). Stockholm: Swedish Center for Working Life.

Sanford, N. 1970. Whatever happened to action research? *Journal of Social Issues* 26(4): 3-23.

Sayer, A. 1992. *Method in social science.* 2d ed. London: Routledge.

Seierstad, S., *et al.* 1985. *Coastal societies on government support?* (in Norwegian). Oslo: University Press.

Selander, S. 1987. Reflection, action, and knowledge in educational research. In *Perspectives on action research,* edited by S. Selander. Stockholm: Institute of Education.

Shanin, T., ed. 1987. Peasants and peasant societies. London: Penguin.

Shils, E. 1988. The university, the city, and the world: Chicago and the University of Chicago. In *The university and the city: From medieval origins to the present,* edited by T. Bender. New York: Oxford University Press.

Shotter, J. 1993a. *Conversational realities.* London: Sage.

Shotter, J. 1993b. Cultural Politics of everyday life. Buckingham: Open University Press.

Sizer, T. R. 1984. *Horace's compromise: The dilemma of the American high school.* Boston: Houghton Mifflin.

Skjervheim, H. 1974. *Objectivism and the study of the human being* (in Norwegian). Oslo: Gyldendal.

Sklar, K. K. 1985. Hull House in the 1890s: A community of women reformers. *Signs: Journal of Women in Culture and Society* 10(4): 658-77.

Smaling, A. 1997. Argumentatie, coöperatie, en caritas in kwalitatief onderzoek (Argumentation, cooperation and charity), in A. Smaling and E. Hijmans, eds. *Kwalitatief onderzoek en levensbeschouwing (Qualitative research and philosophy of life).* Amsterdam: Boom Publishing Company.

Sørensen, B. A. 1982. Responsibility based rationality: On means-end thinking in women (in Norwegian). In *Women's sense of community,* edited by H. Holter. Oslo: Universitetsforlaget.

Sørensen, B. A. 1992a. *Evaluation of Norwegian working life research and action research* (in Norwegian). Oslo: Norwegian Council of Applied Social Science.

Sørensen, B. A. 1992b. Action research on and in working life (in Norwegian). *Journal of Social Science* 33(3): 213-30.

Spencer-Brown, G. 1969. *Laws of form.* London: Allen & Unwin.

Spjelkavik, Ø. 1990. Fish farmers' careers (in Norwegian). Ph.d. diss., Department of Sociology, University of Oslo.

Spjelkavik, Ø. 1992. *Fish farming and local community* (in Norwegian). Report 5. Oslo: Work Research Institute.

Spjelkavik, Ø. 1993. *Norwegian fish farming and West European integration* (in Norwegian). Report 1. Oslo: Work Research Institute.

Spjelkavik, Ø. 1994. Norwegian fish farming and the European Union (in Norwegian). In *Report on Nordland County.* Bodø: Nordland Nei til EU.

Spradley, J. P. 1979. *The ethnographic interview.* New York: Holt.

Stankiewicz, R. 1986. *Academics and entrepreneurs.* London: Frances Pinter.

Stavenga, G. J. 1991. *Science and liberation.* Amsterdam: Thesis Publishers.

Storper, M., and A. J. Scott, eds. 1992. *Pathways to industrialization and regional development.* London: Routledge.

Strauss, A. L., and J. Corbin. 1990. *Basics of qualitative research.* London: Sage.

Susman, G., and R. D. Evered. 1978. An assessment of the scientific merits of action research. *Administrative Science Quarterly* 23(4): 582-603.

Svala, C., and M. Andersson, eds. 1993. Network Halland: In search of development (in Swedish). Center for Working Life Development, Halmstad University. Research report.

Szanton, P. L. 1981. *Not well advised.* New York: Russell Sage Foundation and Ford Foundation.

Taylor, C. 1985. *Philosophy and the human sciences.* Philosophical Papers 2. Cambridge: Cambridge University Press.

Thomas, W. I., and Znaniecki, F. 1918. *The Polish peasant in Europe and America.* Chicago:

University of Chicago Press.

Thorner, D., et al., eds. 1986. *The theory of peasant economy.* Manchester: Manchester University Press.

Thorsrud, E. 1981. Policymaking as a learning process in working life. In *Man and working life,* edited by B. Gardell and G. Johansson. London: Wiley.

Thorsrud, E., and F. Emery. 1970. *Toward a new enterprise organization* (in Norwegian). Oslo: Tanum.

Totten, W. and F. Manley. 1969. *The Community School: Basic Concepts, Function, and Organization.* Galien, Michigan: Allied Education Council.

Toulmin, S. 1996a. Concluding methodological reflections. In *Beyond theory,* edited by S. Toulmin and B. Gustavsen. Amsterdam: John Benjamins.

Toulmin, S. 1996b. Is action research really research? in Concepts and Transformations. Vol I:1.

Toulmin, S., and B. Gustavsen, eds. 1996. *Beyond theory.* Amsterdam: John Benjamins.

Trist, E. 1953. *Some observations on the machine face as a socio-technical system.* London: Tavistock Publications.

Trist, E. 1976. A concept of organizational ecology. *Australian Journal of Management* 2(2): 161-75.

Trist, E. 1981. *The evolution of socio-technical systems.* Toronto: Ontario Quality of Working Life Centre.

Trist, E. 1983. Referent organizations and the development of the interorganizational domains. *Human Relations* 36(3): 247-68. ———. 1985. Intervention strategies for interorganizational domains. In *Human systems development: Perspectives on people and organizations,* edited by I. R. Tannenbaum et al. San Francisco: Jossey-Bass.

Trist, E. 1986. Quality of working life and community development: Some reflections on the Jamestown experience. *Journal of Applied Behavioral Science* 22(3): 223-37.

Trist, E., and K. W. Bamforth. 1951. Some social and psychological consequences of the longwall method of coal-getting. *Human Relations* 4(1): 3–38.

Trist, E., and H. Murray. 1990a. Introduction to volume II. In *The social engagement of social science,* vol. 2, *A Tavistock anthology,* edited by E. Trist and H. Murray. Philadelphia: University of Pennsylvania Press.

Trist, E., and H. Murray. 1990b. Historical overview: The foundation and development of the Tavistock Institute. In *The social engagement of social science,* vol. 2, *A Tavistock anthology,* edited by E. Trist and H. Murray. Philadelphia: University of Pennsylvania Press.

Trist, E., and H. Murray. 1990c. A new social psychiatry. In *The social engagement of social science,* vol. 2, *A Tavistock anthology,* edited by E. Trist and H. Murray. Philadelphia: University of Pennsylvania Press

Turner, S. P. 1991. The world of academic quantifiers: The Columbia University family and its connections. In *Social survey in historical perspective,* edited by M. Bulmer, K. Bales, and K. K. Sklar. New York: Cambridge University Press.

Tyack, D., and E. Hansot. 1983. *Managers of virtue: Public school leadership in America, 1820-1980.* New York: Basic Books.

Ve, H. 1989. *Gender difference in rationality - On the difference between technical limited rationality and responsible rationality,* in E. Gunnarsson. 1989. *Kvinnors Arbetsrationalitet och Kvalifikationer,* Stockholm: Arbetslivscentrum, Report No. 6 on the Quist Project.

Volosinov, V. N. 1973. *Marxism and the philosophy of language.* Cambridge: Harvard University Press.

Vygotsky, L. S. 1986. *Thought and language.* Cambridge: MIT Press.

Wadel, C. 1988. *The social scientific construction of reality* (in Norwegian). Flekkefjord: Seek A/S.

Waldén, L. 1989. *På kvinnors villkor efter mäns spelregler,* Pockettidningen R, Kvinnliga värden kan rädda världen, No. 4.

Waldén, L. 1990. *Genom symaskinens nålsöga,* Stockholm: Carlssons förlag.

Walton, M. 1986. *The Deming management method.* New York: Putnam.

Walton, R. E., and M. E. Gaffney. 1991. Research, action and participation: The merchant shipping case. In *Participative action research,* edited by W. Foote Whyte. Newbury Park, Calif.: Sage.

Ward, D. 1989. *Poverty, ethnicity, and the American city, 1840–1925.* Cambridge: Cambridge University Press.

Weber, M. 1947. *The theory of social and economic organization.* New York: Free Press.

Whyte, W. F., ed. 1991. *Participatory action research.* Newbury Park, Calif.: Sage.

Whyte, W. F., D. J. Greenwood, and P. Lazes. 1991. Participatory action research: Through practice to science in social research. In *Participatory action research,* edited by W. F. Whyte. Newbury Park, Calif.: Sage.

Whyte, W. F., and K. K. Whyte. 1984. *Learning from the field: A guide from experience.* Newbury Park, Calif.: Sage.

Whyte, W. F., and K. K. Whyte. 1991. *Making Mondragón: The growth and dynamics of the worker cooperative complex.* 2d ed. Ithaca, N.Y.: ILR Press.

Williams, R. L. 1991. *The origins of federal support for higher education: George W. Atherton and the land-grant college movement.* University Park: Pennsylvania State University Press.

Wilson, A.T.M., E. Trist, and A. Curle. 1990. Transitional communities and social reconstruction: The civil resettlement of British prisoners of war. In *The social engagement of social science,* vol. 2, *A Tavistock anthology,* edited by E. Trist and H. Murray. Philadelphia: University of Pennsylvania Press.

Winnicott, D. W. 1971. *Playing and reality.* Harmondsworth: Penguin Books.

Wormser, M. H. 1949. The Northtown self-survey: A case study. *Journal of Social Issues* 5(2): 5-20.

Yin, R. K. 1989. *Case study research: Design and methods.* London: Sage.

Subject Index

Name Index

In the series DIALOGUES ON WORK AND INNOVATION the following titles have been published thus far or are scheduled for publication:

1. NASCHOLD, Frieder and Casten VON OTTER: *Public Sector Transformation: Rethinking Markets and Hierarchies in Government.* 1996.
2. TOULMIN, Stephen and Björn GUSTAVSEN (eds): *Beyond Theory. Changing organizations through participation.* 1996.
3. GUSTAVSEN, Björn, Bernd HOFMAIER, Marianne EKMAN PHILIPS and Anders WIKMAN: *Concept-Driven Development and the Organization of the Process of Change. An evaluation of the Swedish Working Life Fund.* 1996.
4. MERRELYN, Emery: *Searching. The theory and practice of making cultural change.* n.y.p.
5. PÅLSHAUGEN, Øyvind, Björn GUSTAVSEN, Dag ØSTERBERG and John SHOTTER: *The End of Organization Theory? Language as a tool in action research and organizational development.* 1998.
6. GUSTAVSEN, Björn, Tom COLBJØRNSEN and Øyvind PÅLSHAUGEN (eds): *Development Coalitions in Working Life. The 'Enterprise Development 2000' Program in Norway.* 1998.
7. ENNALS, Richard and Björn GUSTAVSEN: *Work Organization and Europe as a Development Coalition.* 1999.
8. GREENWOOD, Davydd J. (ed.): *Action Research. From practice to writing in an international action research development program.* 1999.
9. VAN BEINUM, Hans (ed.): *Ideas and Practices in Action Research. An institutional journey.* n.y.p.